Praise for James B. Loc

AMERIC..
UNDERWATER AND SINKING

"[T]he new regulatory agency, led by friend and businessman Jim Lockhart, . . . concluded the GSEs had nowhere enough capital. . . . [T]he only way to prevent a disaster was to take Fannie and Freddie into government conservatorship. It was up to Hank [Paulson] and Jim."

> **—George W. Bush**, Former President and Author of *Decision Points*

"Jim Lockhart has held key posts in some of the government's most troubled agencies and remains clear-sighted about the challenges they face. Americans should be educated about the mounting problems he describes, and demand that their representatives enact necessary reforms."

> **—Charles Blahous**, Deputy Director of the White House National Economic Council, Public Trustee for Social Security and Medicare

"As with my Treasury team, so with my colleagues in government, Ben Bernanke, Tim Geithner, Sheila Bair, Chris Cox, John Dugan, Jim Lockhart. At times we differed on philosophy and strategy, but I never doubted their dedication to this country or their commitment to taking the bold actions necessary to save the system."

> **—Henry M. Paulson, Jr.**, Former US Secretary of the Treasury, Author of *On the Brink*

"Jim Lockhart is the rare public servant who grasps the broad sweep of national policy and the technical details required to make real change. Jim brought these skills and a wealth of private sector knowledge to the Bipartisan Policy Center where he led a diverse group to develop solutions to the financial insecurity facing millions of retired Americans. Jim's high regard among policy makers in both parties has made him an effective advocate for the BPC."

—**Jason Grumet**, President, Bipartisan Policy Center (BPC)

"This country faces a significant problem now that Fannie Mae and Freddie Mac are back under government control in a Democratic administration. Jim Lockhart's book will be invaluable to those concerned about the housing policies we will see from the Biden administration."

—**Peter J. Wallison**, Senior Fellow Emeritus, American Enterprise Institute

"Jim Lockhart has been there (underwater) and survived. Few persons today can speak with authority and knowledge of managing the shoals of critical government agencies and their continued need of repair. Even out of government, he continues to address reforms, most recently as co-chair with former senator Kent Conrad of the Bipartisan Policy Center's Commission on Retirement Security and Personal Savings."

—**G. William Hoagland**, SVP, Bipartisan Policy Center

"Through his tours of federal service, Jim Lockhart brings exceptional credentials and perspective to understanding the risks when government misprices insurance and to proposing changes that reduce taxpayer risk while improving economic outcomes."

—**Edward DeMarco**, President of the Housing Policy Council

"Jim Lockhart worked with his agencies to develop their pictures of success, the desired outcomes, and then worked with them to develop the realistically aggressive and affordable means to deliver them as planned and promised. The US government is prone to 'work at' being successful, but Jim and others like him have shown that federal agencies CAN be effective when the desired outcomes are clear and agency leaders work WITH their employees to accomplish them."

—**Clay Johnson**, Former Director of Presidential Personnel, and Former Deputy Director for Management at the Office of Management and Budget

America: Underwater and Sinking
Time to Surface with Lessons Learned
by James B. Lockhart III

© Copyright 2023 James B. Lockhart III

ISBN 978-1-64663-908-3

Published by

◄ köehlerbooks™

3705 Shore Drive
Virginia Beach, VA 23455
800-435-4811
www.koehlerbooks.com

AMERICA

UNDERWATER AND SINKING

TIME TO SURFACE WITH LESSONS LEARNED

JAMES B. LOCKHART III

VIRGINIA BEACH
CAPE CHARLES

To my wife, Cricket, our children, and grandchildren.
To my parents and grandparents
And to the millions who serve our country and
are needed to help America surface.

Table of Contents

INTRODUCTION

Why Underwater?

PRESIDENT GEORGE H. W. Bush once said, "There is nothing more fulfilling than to serve your country and your fellow citizens, and to do it well."

Like President Bush, my first government service was in the Navy, but not as heroic, and different—underwater, as an officer on a ballistic missile nuclear submarine. His 1989 remarks to the Senior Executive Service stuck with me when serving the country for him and Presidents George W. Bush and Barack Obama and working with five Treasury secretaries and many other cabinet secretaries. I was also nominated by a fourth president, Donald Trump, to be a trustee of Social Security and Medicare, but the Senate never held a vote.

Doing it well has always been the challenge. All my government jobs supported the "American Dream" of a secure retirement and homeownership, but the agencies were "underwater." They included the Pension Benefit Guaranty Corporation (PBGC), the Social Security Administration (SSA), the Office of Federal Housing Enterprises Oversight (OFHEO) overseeing Fannie Mae and Freddie Mac, and then the newly created Federal Housing Finance Agency (FHFA) overseeing Fannie, Freddie, and the Federal Home Loan Banks.

These government programs and the US government overall have serious, long known but *unfixed* problems. Why? Politics invariably gets in the way of most necessary fixes. Then, when the inevitable crisis occurs, the solution is to throw taxpayer money (actually, borrowed money to be paid by future generations) at the crisis to belatedly protect Americans. But as the Great Recession and COVID-19 have shown, lower-income Americans bear the brunt of the pain much too often.

For example, legislation to control the twin titans of the mortgage market was much too late to prevent them from becoming "the epicenter of the Global Financial Crisis."[1] As a result, the "Great Recession became devastating—more than eight million foreclosures, 8.8 million jobs lost, $7 trillion in home equity lost, and $11 trillion in stock equity——wiped out——with 24 other countries also experiencing their own banking crisis."

Many hundreds of billions of dollars were required to recover from that crisis. Unusually, most of it was paid back. Unfortunately, since then, unfunded trillions have been spent, piling up massive debts. Ben Franklin in *Poor Richard's Almanack* had a warning: "Beware of little expenses: a small leak will sink a great ship." Well, we have massive expenses, and the ship of state is sinking deeper underwater.

By sharing my experience facing the financial crisis, running agencies, working with dedicated public servants, dealing with Congress, and working with the Bipartisan Policy Center since 2014, I hope this book will help people understand that it is time to bury ultra-partisanship and this "winning at any cost" mentality. We must work together to provide cost-effective, long-lasting results for all Americans—present and future.

Following the inauguration of President Joe Biden on January 20, 2021, former presidents Clinton, Bush, and Obama spoke at the hallowed ground of Arlington National Cemetery and called for a renewed sense of bipartisanship. Obama urged Americans to "not just listen to folks we agree with but listen to folks we don't," adding, "There's no problem we can't solve when we work together."[2]

I spent my public service career trying to "do it well," under often trying circumstances. The lessons I have learned from my experiences are all here in this book, humbly offered to challenge our government to "do it better."

Working together, listening to all voices, opening our minds to the facts, and crafting bipartisan solutions is the way to solve America's problems and prevent the next crisis. We need to unite on a vision for America's future.

It is time to stop partisan bickering and "Surface!"

CHAPTER 1

Strength through Knowledge

"Some people have described [the federal government] as an insurance company with an army. The two things it does is insures people's health and retirement and runs the military. If the cost of healthcare and an aging society continues . . . that will be a huge fiscal burden."

—Bloomberg TV interview of Chairman Ben Bernanke by Tom Keene, May 3, 2017

MY FIRST GOVERNMENT job was in the Navy, literally underwater. I was the supply officer and an officer of the deck aboard the USS *George Washington Carver* (SSBN 656), a nuclear, ballistic missile submarine. This was during the MAD (Mutual Assured Destruction) era, when we had sixteen missiles targeted on the Soviet Union. I remember being awakened several times in the middle of the night with the alarm sounding "Battle Stations Missiles." As I rushed to the control room, I always hoped and assumed it was a drill and not the real thing.

The *Carver* was underwater for sixty days at a time, patrolling in the North Atlantic Ocean, only coming up to periscope depth once a day to get a satellite fix. After two months, the order "Surface, Surface, Surface!" was very welcome.

The submarine's motto was "Strength through Knowledge."

Inside a submarine, I learned my first lessons in managing risk and being prepared for all outcomes. That prepared me for my next four government positions, serving in agencies that were, metaphorically speaking, underwater. Those jobs centered on trying to lessen Bernanke's above mentioned "huge fiscal burden" by better managing the "insurance company," of which there are over 150.

My agencies were as follows:

1. The Pension Benefit Guaranty Corporation (PBGC), my first "underwater" government organization that was troubled and had never been audited. It rescued pension plans that could not pay promised benefits when their corporate sponsors went bankrupt.

2. The Social Security Administration's retirement program, which is underfunded for the long term; without reforms, benefits could be cut by 2035. Its Disability and Supplemental Security Income programs were designated high risk.

3. The Office of Federal Housing Enterprise Oversight (OFHEO), which, as the regulator of Fannie Mae and Freddie Mac, faced their accounting scandals and the mortgage crisis. They are referred to as government-sponsored enterprises (GSE), or just enterprises.

4. The Federal Housing Finance Agency (FHFA), which was created by the merger of OFHEO and the Federal Housing Finance Board, regulator of the twelve Federal Home Loan Banks. Thirty-eight days into its existence, the FHFA placed into conservatorships Fannie Mae and Freddie Mac, which were two of the top five US financial institutions.

Besides being a glutton for punishment, how did I get these jobs?

I am the son and grandson of successful corporate CEOs who prided themselves on making companies more efficient. The first J. B. Lockhart fixed companies for Howard Hughes. Pop-Pop, my mother's father, ran two Fortune 500 companies at the same time. As Republicans, they often talked to me about making the government more goal oriented, efficient, and fiscally responsive. Most of my career has also been as a businessman, in my case dealing with finance, insurance, investments, and pensions. As it was for my father and his father, serving as a naval officer was great training for my future career.

My family and education taught me the value of public service. Yes, I had the desire to make government programs more effective, but my political activities were limited to being treasurer of Republicans Abroad when we lived in London. It was the second President Bush who opened the door to my government jobs when he forwarded my resume to his father's Treasury and Labor Departments.

George and I bonded playing Andover JV football (he was the center, and I was the right guard) and stickball (he was the high commissioner, and I captained our dorm team). We survived our Spanish classes together, where he was called Señor Arbusto. We also were accepted and went to Yale together—surprisingly to some, as we were "late bloomers." I was a year ahead of him at Harvard Business School.

There was another take on why I got those government jobs. It occurred at an editorial board meeting with the *Wall Street Journal*, early in my tenure at OFHEO. To build my credibility, I described my career to the editorial page writers Paul Gigot and Brain Kearney. The first question Gigot asked was, "What did you do at school to make President Bush so mad at you that he gave you all these tough jobs? PBGC, Social Security, and

OFHEO?" I said it was a real "trifecta"! Jokingly, I mentioned that I had gone to three schools with him and so it would be hard to tell where I had made him mad.

Ironically, the question was well before the conservatorships of Fannie and Freddie. I then followed up, saying I liked challenges and that it was an honor to serve my country. The editors agreed that GSE reform was necessary, but their preferred solution was to close down Fannie and Freddie. As you will see, they wrote many anti-"Fan and Fred" editorials over the years.

One of my favorite quotes from Bush 43 is "It is compassionate to actively help our citizens in need. It is conservative to insist on accountability and results. And with this approach, we will make a real difference in people's lives."[3]

My brand of Republicanism steered clear of shouting. Instead, I preferred to keep a steady hand on the helm, serving the American people by confronting problems head-on, developing solutions, and working with all parties to implement them.

Although I am a lifelong Republican, partisanship was not in my mind when it came to dealing with these massively "underwater" insurance companies. Going back to the *Carver*'s motto, I was trying to gain and use knowledge to strengthen those programs, working with dedicated, knowledgeable government employees (never deep state) to better serve the American people in a compassionate and disciplined manner.

Many government insurance programs are worthwhile, but too often Congress has designed them with good intentions but conflicting goals. Then the responsible agency is not given the tools to make course changes. Government accounting too often hides the potential of future losses. The wishful thinking by Congress that everything will work out lasts much too long. Often, it takes a crisis to get remedial legislation. Too late!

It is my belief that successful government requires bipartisanship, which is not a sign of weakness or an absence of intellectual purity. It is just the opposite. It puts the American people first. I believe bipartisanship is the right way to create and update government programs to solve problems that the private sector alone cannot. Solving these problems is not just a question of throwing borrowed money at programs when a crisis hits. Our children and grandchildren will be burdened with that debt.

In 2020, the US government debt exceeded GDP for the first time since World War II. In thirty years, the Congressional Budget Office (CBO) projects that ratio to reach well over 200 percent, which is beyond third world numbers. The US government is sinking further and further underwater. To lessen the burden on future generations, we will need a smart, results-oriented, and bipartisan government.

In my last congressional hearing as FHFA director on June 3, 2009, I testified before the House Financial Services Committee: "My career has included work with several private-sector insurance companies and several government-backed insurance programs. My observation is that government insurance programs are high risk and invite the private sector to shift risk to the government. Among other issues, it is often difficult in a political environment to calculate or charge the actuarially fair price, resist pressure to broaden the mission, and prevent inadequately compensated increases in federal risk-bearing."

Successful insurance companies and military operations share common attributes, such as having clear missions, focusing on results, and chains of commands. Too often, government insurance companies have been created without a clear mission or a clear chain of command. Anticipating what bad things can happen and then taking actions to prevent them from happening is critical in the military and in insurance companies. The repeated drills on my submarine were designed to prevent those bad things from happening, which was a matter of life and death.

I used the motto of my submarine, "Strength through

Knowledge," in my speech when Elizabeth Dole, then secretary of labor, swore me in as executive director of the Pension Benefit Guaranty Corporation (PBGC) in 1989. Picking up the submarine theme, she warned me of depth charges. I used the motto several times again because it is such a strong message. And of course, it was so applicable to the career of George Washington Carver, who, according to Wikipedia, was "the most prominent black scientist of the early 20th century." But to me, the motto should be fundamental to everyone in government and beyond.

When I arrived at the PBGC, many pension plans were woefully underwater, meaning that they did not have the investments to meet their pension promises. And the PBGC was always underwater while I was there. Almost half the airlines (Pan Am, Eastern, TWA, and Continental) crashed. The steel industry melted down. Western Union was sending the wrong message. Unfortunately, all those bankruptcies were good training for the Global Financial Crisis (GFC).

The PBGC has an admirable mission of ensuring that workers and retirees of bankrupt companies with underfunded/ underwater pension plans receive adequate pensions. The problem was that the PBGC had a second, somewhat competing mission given by Congress: to promote the growth of defined benefit pension plans. To do so, Congress created an unsound insurance program with premiums much too low and with limited tools to push for higher pension funding. The PBGC had been un-auditable in its first fifteen years, but I insisted that it be audited. We got the job done. But it took well over a year after I left to secure some legislative reforms, however insufficient they were.

After the PBGC experience, you would think I'd have learned my lesson about government insurance programs. Maybe I spent too much time underwater; I answered Bush 43's call to become the principal deputy commissioner and chief operating officer of the Social Security Administration (SSA).

Social Security is the granddaddy of all government insurance programs, with annual expenditures of more than $1 trillion, providing retirement, survivor, and disability benefits. It also administers a taxpayer-funded Supplemental Security Income insurance program for lower-income disabled people and retirees. The SSA is the biggest government program in dollars spent, much bigger than the Defense Department.

Besides helping to run an agency with 65,000 employees and more than 1,200 offices, I volunteered to lead the reform effort to create a sound system to prevent the forecasted sea of red ink and painful benefit cuts.

My Bush-appointed Social Security boss refused to work on reforms. Touching the "third rail" of American politics was tough. AARP reneged on a promise to do balanced educational events on Social Security reform and then repeatedly broke promises not to call voluntary personal accounts "privatization," which they were not. Despite a massive campaign, we hit a congressional brick wall. That was another painful lesson on the hazards of political infighting and the challenges of countering misinformation.

Any sensible person would have gone back to civilian life at that point—"the real world," as my wife, Cricket, called it. The White House kept twisting my arm to become OFHEO director. When I succumbed in May 2006, Cricket thought I was crazy. Before I arrived, Fannie and Freddie were caught cooking their books. Therefore, my first job as regulator of these two behemoths with more than $5 trillion in mortgage assets was to get them to the point where they could file timely and accurate reports with the SEC. It took two years and more than 5,000 consultants, but they got the job done.

My second, concurrent and immediate challenge was to get legislation to rein in the systemic risk that Congress had created with Fannie and Freddie, most noticeably the ability to leverage themselves 100 to 1. Working toward getting that legislation,

I did many speeches, congressional hearings, and television appearances. Secretary Hank Paulson and his Treasury team pushed reform hard as well. Too late, reforms were passed by Congress in July 2008 and signed by President Bush on July 30.

By then, the housing market and the overall US financial system was melting down. In his book, *Stress Test*,[4] Tim Geithner had a metaphor that summer that is quite appropriate for this book. He wrote, "I had first heard from Goldman Sachs CEO Lloyd Blankfein: 'The rivets are coming off the submarine.'"

That is an antiquated analogy, as modern submarines are welded, but OFHEO's regulatory powers were also antiquated. Fannie and Freddie are not government insurance companies but something worse and more muddled. They are government-sponsored enterprises (GSEs). They were owned by shareholders, but they had government charters, which allowed them to sell their mortgage-backed securities and debt with an "implicit" government guarantee, resulting in low interest rates despite having extremely low capital requirements. They were very profitable until housing prices cracked. Then, they took on water quickly.

They also had muddled, contradictory missions and two separate regulators. OFHEO was charged with the safety of Fannie and Freddie, but Congress had not given the agency adequate powers or resources. The Department of Housing and Urban Development (HUD) was their "mission" regulator, which translated into pushing for the admirable goal of "affordable housing" for lower-income Americans. HUD and many members of Congress were much more interested in affordable housing than safety and soundness. As a result, HUD kept raising affordable housing goals to unrealistically high levels, which pushed Fannie and Freddie to take on much too much risk.

The tragedy was that the affordable home became unaffordable during the crisis. At the peak, 25 percent of all homeowners were underwater, as their houses became worth less than their mortgages. Too many homeowners lost their homes and net worth through foreclosures.

The Federal Reserve Board chairman, Ben Bernanke, and Treasury secretary, Hank Paulson, were my biggest heroes of the 2008 financial crisis. Flanked by Ben and Hank, as head of the FHFA I put the GSEs into conservatorship in September 2008. That meant that the FHFA was running those $5 trillion behemoths.

Paulson said later that the conservatorships went against everything Republicans stand for, but the "time-out" was necessary. It was the only way for the massive mortgage market to survive and protect homeowners. Failure might have caused another Great Depression. But the GSE rescue was not enough. It took Fed action and the $700 billion Troubled Asset Relief Program (TARP).

Bernanke was the chair of the TARP oversight board, where I served with Paulson and then his successor, Geithner; the SEC chairs; and the HUD secretaries.

There was a common Navy story I told in speeches in all these jobs. Unfortunately, it still rings true today about our "ship of state." It is not about submarines but about the largest nuclear aircraft carrier in the US fleet, which in my speeches I christened the USS *Franklin Delano Roosevelt*, as Roosevelt had created Social Security and Fannie Mae.

The story goes that it was a foggy night, and the radar was not working (both conditions are typical in Washington, DC). The captain of the USS *FDR* received a message to turn hard to the port—using port (left) rather than starboard (right) to be bipartisan.

Hearing the request, the admiral stormed to the bridge and sent a message: "Who do you think you are, telling a three-star admiral what to do?" A tentative answer came back: "I am a second-class Coast Guard petty officer, manning a lighthouse. If you don't change course, you will run aground."

Our nation needs to change course. Annual government deficits are in the trillions of dollars. Social Security has a $20.4 trillion present-value shortfall over the next seventy-five years and is selling Treasury bonds to pay benefits. Fourteen years later, with no end in sight, Fannie and Freddie are still relying on government backing to finance well over 50 percent of the US mortgage market. Even though the PBGC's guarantee is not backed by the US government, the multiemployer plans received an $86 billion government bailout from the 2021 American Rescue Plan Act.

Both parties seem to be more focused on "winning" than creating affordable, long-term solutions. President Biden's 2021 American Rescue Plan Act was much too expensive, as was President Trump's 2017 Tax Cuts and Jobs Act.

The important lesson to be learned is that strength and knowledge are inseparable.

Strength without knowledge can be dangerous and harmful for America. Unlike many countries, the United States has several layers of political appointees running most government departments and agencies. If they come in with experience and are willing to listen to the experienced career leaders, it can be a good combination. Most of the career government employees I worked with provided institutional memory and knowledge and were dedicated. If the political appointees do not work with the career employees, it can become dysfunctional. Sometimes, as during the Great Financial Crisis, there is a need for political appointees to think outside the box and bring Congress and career teams along.

Bernanke concluded the Bloomberg interview quoted at the beginning of this chapter by saying, "The crisis itself was a complicated phenomenon and it was essentially a big panic in the financial system. . . . Frankly the regulators and policy makers didn't see it coming or at least not enough. . . . [P]eople went through a lot."[5]

We need to see the next crisis coming and prevent it, or at least temper it. We did not do so with COVID-19. We need to prepare for the storms that surely will come, whether a fiscal debt crisis, asset bubbles, retirement crisis, housing crisis, failed infrastructure, educational shortcomings, income inequality, global warming, pandemics, or a military crisis.

Many preventive steps have been taken, but many more must be taken.

To me, finding solutions should not be about Republicans versus Democrats. We need to produce results for *all* Americans. Working together, as the three presidents said at Arlington, and opening our minds to the facts and costs is how to solve America's problems. That is what I did when co-chairing a Bipartisan Policy Center commission with former senator Kent Conrad (D-North Dakota). The nineteen commissioners were a mix of former politicians, corporate and union leaders, two former Social Security and Medicare trustees, academics, and other pension and think-tank experts. It was designed to have a balance of Democrats and Republicans.

Our report, entitled *Securing Our Financial Future*,[6] made recommendations on improving retirement for all. Agreeing on a balanced approach for Social Security, we created a sustainable, solvent plan for the next seventy-five years and beyond. Balance meant looking equally at benefits and revenues. We recommended increasing retirement benefits for lower-income workers while slowing the growth of benefits for the upper income. An increase in the taxable maximum level was coupled with a small, gradual increase in the overall payroll-tax rate.

Solutions such as the one we crafted should not stay on the shelf of a Washington think tank. It is time, well overdue, to figure out how to surface from this sea of red ink. To do that will take strength and knowledge to create bipartisanship and better government management.

The time to act is now.

We owe it to our children, grandchildren, and all future generations.

To graduate from Yale and to qualify for serving on submarines, one had to pass swimming tests. That was no problem for me, as my father, always the teacher, taught us four kids to swim at an early age. Those tests were easy, but there were many tougher ones to come. Let's dive into the water and help our government and its agencies swim to the surface.

CHAPTER 2

At the Ridge and Summit

"Underwater is scary."

—Grandson Nicky at age four

WATER WAS PART of my upbringing. When I was two, we moved to a new development called Riegel Ridge in western New Jersey. Our newly built house had the forerunner of the aboveground pool. It was a World War II Army surplus canvas water tank, about eight feet tall and twenty feet in diameter, held up by beautiful mahogany pillars. My father was always a bargain hunter, hence the water tank. He was also a teacher to his kids. For swimming, his authority was a famous Yale swimming coach, Robert Kiphuth. The first lesson was to float, labeled "dead man's float"—not a propitious beginning, but my three sisters and I started that way and became good swimmers.

I have many memories of that small community. My kindergarten teacher lived across the street. We had a great gang of neighborhood friends. My mother, who grew up with gardeners, took to mowing the lawn. She had a neighborhood kid take the governor off the lawnmower so she could mow faster. And then there was my father, mucking out the septic system quite regularly as the soil was all clay.

My father was a child of the Depression and therefore very frugal. Bargains were his thing. He grew up in Taunton, Massachusetts, as had his father. My father went to Yale on a scholarship and graduated in 1940. He played junior varsity football. His coach was a law school student and future president Jerry Ford. After Yale he wanted to go to business school. His father said he should go to a school in the Midwest to lose his Massachusetts accent. And so, he went to Northwestern and graduated a year later. He then volunteered for the Navy.

As a Navy lieutenant in World War II, he captained a very active minesweeper ship homeported in Trinidad; at one point it had swept more mines than any other minesweeper. He told me that as captain he had to lecture his crew about venereal diseases. As a person who loved to teach, he gave me the VD lecture several times. When his sister ship was being painted Arctic colors in preparation to being deployed there, he volunteered to go to the US Naval Academy in Annapolis to get the equivalent of a master's degree in meteorology. My mother always claimed she was a better weather forecaster.

My older sister, Joanie, was born there and baptized at the Naval Academy church. As she always has been the boss of us kids, I call her "the General," but maybe it should have been "admiral," given her Naval Academy beginnings. My father joined MacArthur's staff in the Philippines as the war was ending. I was born in White Plains, New York, because my mother was staying nearby with her parents in Hartsdale. I always considered myself an original baby boomer: counting back, I was conceived in San Francisco on VJ Day, just before my father went off to MacArthur's staff.

My next home was a trailer, which was practical as my father was a consultant after the war. One stop was in Louisville, Kentucky, where he was advising a meatpacking company. The story goes I liked to eat mud, which according to a doctor helped prevent me from getting sick. Another story was that one night my mother left me out in the baby carriage. I survived.

In New Jersey, my father supervised four paper mills for Riegel Paper Company, a Fortune 500 company. My mother's father, John Lawrence Riegel, was the chairman and CEO.

One of my favorite facts about my grandfather, which is so out of times with the present day, is that he never took stock options in the company. He had inherited Riegel Paper stock from aunts and thought it would be greedy to take more stock. He, like his father and grandfather, was concerned about the workers and provided housing for them.

Among many other firsts, Riegel Paper was the original inventor of the disposable diaper. It took a long time to catch on. A friend told me recently that the company demonstrated to a bunch of Wall Street analysts how good the disposable diaper was by flushing it down the toilet. The toilet overflowed.

Riegel Ridge had a company community center. I was a batboy in exchange for free ice cream, acted in several community plays, and participated in the annual Halloween costume show. My mother was always creative. I wore a real leopard skin brought back by my Lockhart grandfather from India, dressing as Tarzan one year. I felt sorry for my little sister Annie, who wore her underwear with stapled-on leaves, dressed as "Autumn."

The Ridge had one tennis court. My father, as creative as my mother, painted the balls yellow so that they could be easily seen. He should have patented that. Someone else picked up the idea as he discussed the yellow balls at a cocktail party. Much later he invented what he called plasti-tennis, which appears to be a pickle ball ancestor.

After my mother's funeral in 2014, it was nice to see that the Ridge still had an exhibit on Riegel Paper. My mother, my father, and Riegel relatives for almost 200 years are buried in Riegelsville, Pennsylvania. I was baptized at age three at the church there with Annie. One of my father's collateral duties was running the cemetery, so as kids we used to play there. Across the main street of Riegelsville from the church was the old Riegel Homestead, where our cousins lived. The land stretched from the Main Street to the Delaware River with the Delaware Canal in between. In those days they had cows, which I enjoyed seeing being milked. They also raised collies and gave us one, Rob Roy. Roy was a great dog. When he was a puppy, my cousin and I decided to see if Roy could swim. The three of us went out on the canal in a boat, which we capsized. Roy did make it ashore but hated water for the next fourteen years of his life.

On the Lockhart side, my father had an interesting relationship with his father, the first JBL. They were both called by our middle name, Bicknell, or "Bick" for short. To each other my grandfather was "Senior" and my father "Junior." Senior got sick after his first year at Yale. He dropped out and later joined the Navy as an officer. After the war he was an industrial engineer, but he was also playing professional basketball and being paid $100 per week. However, he decided basketball was interfering with his career, which paid something like $10 per week, so he dropped basketball. He was five foot nine and a great athlete. He was married in 1917, and my father was born in 1918, but Senior and his wife divorced in 1920. Junior was brought up by his grandparents and a maiden aunt, Aunt Bea, who was weakened by the Spanish flu.

My grandmother, Charlotte Bradford Babbitt, came from an old New England family of inventors, silversmiths, and a whaling ship captain. She wanted to be an actress and was in the Ziegfeld Follies. Her second husband managed the Schubert Theater in Boston. As both his parents married three times, my father was the only child of six parents.

In 1922 my Lockhart grandfather left to work for the Ludlow Jute Company in Calcutta, India, staying for thirteen years with a six-month home leave every three years. Eventually, with a new British wife from India, he returned to the US. He worked in a consulting company serving many clients, including Anheuser-Busch and the government during World War II.

In late 1948, as my father wrote: "Hughes Tool was one of JBL's very satisfied clients (he improved their profit picture by several million dollars) so JBL came to mind when they were looking for a general assistant for [Howard] Hughes."[7] After Hughes purchased TWA, JBL was offered the job of president of TWA, but he turned it down as he "felt it was wrong to bring in an efficiency expert to head up an airline because when they had a crash it would be too natural to say financial savings have been achieved at the expense of safety." The irony is that when I was at the PBGC, the whole airline came close to crashing. We temporarily saved it, which you will read later.

After turning down the TWA job, my grandfather wrote to my father, "Two days later I received a call from Noah Dietrich. He asked me if I was still interested in working for HH and I said yes . . . with the right amount of hesitancy." Senior's first assignment was in Hollywood to run the recently purchased RKO movie business that had 8,000 employees and forty-three labor unions. He wrote, "The place was a playhouse. Money was just something to spend. The company was millions in the red. Handling personnel was unusually difficult particularly dealing with the temperamental stars, directors, and producers."

After successfully turning around RKO by applying "business logic," he moved to Houston. As Senior wrote to Junior, Hughes "would have kept me in RKO if there had been no trouble anywhere else. Trouble having risen, that was my job. Naturally, I had to acknowledge that was basically our agreement." The job was to turn around Gulf Brewing Company, which he did. As my father wrote, "In one newspaper article he was reported as saying, 'Business troubleshooting is as fascinating as the tiger shooting' he has done in big-game hunts in India. 'Curing sick businesses is more fun than anything I know.'" I must have inherited dealing with troubled/underwater companies.

While Senior was nomadic, my other grandfather, John Lawrence Riegel, was not. His grandfather had started the predecessor of Riegel Paper Company in 1865. JLR's father took over running Riegel Paper, but he died when my grandfather was at MIT. Shortly after graduating in 1918, my grandfather began working for the company. By 1926 he was general manager and was made president in 1936 and then later chairman. In 1956 Riegel Paper joined the New York Stock Exchange. JLR's uncle, who was running what became Riegel Textile, died in 1941, and so JLR became its president.

In 1968 my grandfather wrote in a letter to his ten grandchildren when he was giving stock to us: "My grandfather, who was a worker, an investor, and a money maker in many fields, believed in giving his children and grandchildren property provided he thought the individual handled it wisely. . . . My father believed the same, but had less opportunity to show it as he was only 46 when he died. . . . My gifts to you are very much the gift and hard work of several generations not just a gift from me."

As Riegelsville is near Bethlehem, the Riegels were involved in the early days of Bethlehem Steel. Being conservative, they bought bonds instead of stock. For many years it was a wrong decision. When I was at the PBGC dealing with the LTV and Wheeling-Pitt bankruptcies, Bethlehem Steel was a survivor but went bankrupt later.

We called JLR "Pop-Pop." Pop-Pop's wife, my grandmother Maggie (Margaret Winslow Murchie), was from Calais, Maine, right on the Canadian border. She was very feisty and loving. Hers was a very old Maine family. We have a map hand-drawn on parchment by my great-great-great-grandmother, dated 1825. This ancestral mapmaker later married a man who became the first consul to Hawaii. He died there, and she brought back his body in a pickled barrel to be buried in Maine.

For many summers we went to the lake near Calais as my mother had when she was young. The cabin we stayed in on Lake Meddybemps had no neighbors, electricity, or running water, but it did have a two-seater outhouse. My father taught all four of us to paddle canoes, fish, and shoot pistols, rifles, and shotguns. With the shotguns we shot clay pigeons. Being ever frugal, my father threw the clays over the lake. We dove for the many missed ones and reused them.

Early in my grandparents' marriage, they splurged on a house on twenty-seven acres in Hartsdale, New York, reputedly built by McKim, Mead & White. We loved to visit. It had woods, a stream to explore, an apple orchard, sheep, Great Danes, a tennis court, and the first private paddle (platform) tennis court. It was "Hartsdale" to us. They loved it too, and Pop-Pop especially loved his gardens. They lived there until they passed away. My parents were married there in 1943 while my father was on a quick leave from the Navy.

Talking with Pop-Pop over the years was very instructive. He loved his family—his three children, ten grandchildren, and many great-grandchildren. Graci, our daughter, who to this day has a lot of personality, was baptized in his church and cried/screamed the whole time, breaking the minister's tradition of only happy babies. Pop-Pop did not seem to mind.

He loved our country and many times told me how to make it better. He had countless commonsensical ideas, and in many ways this book is about him. He was a Republican. Many years ago, he told me that we needed to increase the federal gas tax by fifty cents. He told me that he was disappointed that none of his grandchildren went into manufacturing; instead most of us went into finance. Hopefully, he would have been pleased that despite my finance background, I did try to make a difference in Washington, DC.

My father and my mother, Mary Ann, loved to travel. They traveled to over a hundred countries but especially loved Africa and New Guinea. They build a fantastic collection of artifacts from both, which were displayed wall to wall in their Orange, California, house and their last condo in Florida. They were also very active on nonprofit boards, including Big Brothers, Planned Parenthood in three states, the St. Paul Science Museum, and the Bowers Museum in California.

They met when my father took a road trip from Yale to Miss Porter's School, a "finishing school" in those days for young women in Farmington, Connecticut. Some of my mother's friends were lying about their ages. She told Bick that she was two years older than she was. He was very surprised to learn when they were married that she was only eighteen.

We moved from Riegel Ridge to Summit, New Jersey, when I was in the third grade. At that point we were four kids; my two younger sisters, Annie and Brenda, were born at the Ridge. One of my frugal father's favorite books was *Cheaper by the Dozen*; thank goodness we never reached that level of kids. He was also a prolific writer of family histories and biographies. Along the way he found a handful of Mayflower relatives, including William Bradford. He also wrote a couple of unpublished books. One was about accounting, and the other, for his grandchildren, was entitled *Be Rich, It is Your Choice*.[8]

He wrote: "Being rich is the condition of having more money than you need to satisfy your material needs. This can be accomplished in two ways. One can carefully work out practical needs and stretch available dollars to achieve the goal or it can be achieved by earning so many dollars that the status of riches can be obtained without careful work on the needs or on stretching dollars. The approach of this book is not to show you how to make more money. . . . The approach here is to show you how you can be rich on your present income." As an example, rather than spending money on an expensive atomic bomb shelter, he created one in a subbasement.

Getting back to the subject of water, he built a real pool in Summit. Of course, we did all the maintenance and painting of the pool. Once, he came home with ten swim trunks he'd gotten at a real bargain. They were for guests and me, and not very stylish. I went to the Summit public schools, and my sisters went to a girls' school, Kent Place. My youngest sister, Brenda, had pool parties with her classmates. One of her best friends, Cricket from Short Hills, was often there. More on her later.

Bick expected us to work around the house—painting, weeding, raking leaves, pruning, cleaning the pool, etc.—but we got paid for it. My mother was always in the thick of it, even though she had to give up lawnmowing when she got very severe arthritis in her mid-thirties. She was always a trooper and never complained, but by the end we used to call her the "Bionic Woman" as she had two artificial knees, two hips, two shoulders, and one elbow. She was our Cub Scout den mother. Having made it through Cub Scouts, I became a very active Boy Scout, going to Camp Watchung in the summer. By the age of thirteen, I was an Eagle Scout, proudly outdoing my father, who only ended at Star, two ranks lower. The summer of 1960, I went to the Jamboree in Colorado Springs. Ike was there.

But that was not my first sighting of President Eisenhower. My father was not much of a sports fan, but my mother encouraged me to be a Yankee fan. We listened to the World Series on the radio and on early television and then in person, and I saw Ike throw out the first pitch in the 1955 World Series at the Dodgers' Ebbets Field.

My father wanted us to learn about finance and the stock market, so he invented the "Stock Market Game" and trademarked it. At the start of the year, we were given a hypothetical $10,000. At the end of the year, we got a penny for each dollar we gained. One year, Annie was the big winner; she had bought Berkshire Hathaway because it was the most expensive stock. Too bad we all didn't do that going forward.

We moved to Summit because my father had been promoted to a new job at the Riegel Paper headquarters in New York City. He did very well and eventually became the CFO. Being an ambitious man, he wanted to be CEO, but his father-in-law, my grandfather, was not ready to retire. That frustrated my parents.

We recently found a letter from my mother in a desk that we inherited from my grandparents:

> Dear Daddy-
>
> Am glad Bick finally talked to you. It has lifted a weight from him & thus somewhat from me although I don't think the situation is mended. But you know you both want the same things from life—your family well brought up & happy & secure & safe & your company strong and well run. So anyway, I feel I've had a good business training & I think there's a real use for Bick in Riegel protecting the children's financial future. Love

Eventually, when a headhunter came calling, Dad decided to take a job running a company in St. Paul, Minnesota—Wood Conversion, which he later renamed Conwed Corporation. After that he led several other building products companies when he moved to Orange, California, due to my mother's bad arthritis. Later, my children loved to visit because their grandparents lived near Disneyland, Knott's Berry Farm, and the beach.

Unfortunately, when Pop-Pop retired, his chosen successor decided to dismantle Riegel Paper and sell off the pieces. Eventually Riegel Textile was sold as well. It is sad, but that is the way of destructive capitalism. None of the many companies I worked for over the years exist today. However, three of the government agencies are still with us.

CHAPTER 3

The End Depends on the Beginning

"Though goodness without knowledge is weak and feeble; yet knowledge without goodness is dangerous; in both united . . . lay the surest foundation of usefulness to mankind."

—The Constitution of Phillips Academy, in Andover, 1828

I NEVER THOUGHT of myself as the type, but I have collected many nicknames over the years. My mother called me Jimmie and Lamb Chop (not Pork Chop, the nickname of a Navy supply officer, which I later became). Her Riegelsville cousin, Alan Cook, an All-American football player at Lafayette, called me Tubby after his favorite teammate and maybe because of my belly. At Andover (Phillips Academy), which I started in ninth grade, I was Juice, Hart, and Gorilla.

Juice went with me to Yale, as so many of my Andover friends kept calling me Juice. Also, to some I was "Spider" Lockhart, after a New York Giant football player. "W" called me Juice in the White House. Jokingly, he told Karl Rove only he could call me that. Now my nickname has become enshrined: Cricket has our five grandchildren calling me Juice—not very dignified, but distinctive.

Andover was, in those days, an all-boys prep school, which was quite different than living with my three sisters. Bick encouraged me to go to Andover because almost half his Andover class had gone with him to Yale. In my day it was still a strong feeder school to Yale.

I made many friends in Andover, including one who created a real turning point in my life—George W. Bush, who came to Andover in the tenth grade. To Colonel Kemper, a West Point graduate who became headmaster in 1948, we were "men," not boys. There was limited nurturing. In *First Son George W. Bush and the Bush Family Destiny*,[9] the author, Bill Minutaglio, writes about Andover in our day: "Life at the school in the early 1960s was an ordered, structured world that allowed for little variance from Kemper's West Point edicts. Breakfast, chapel, or a school assembly were held early each morning, with demerits handed out to anyone who was even a few seconds late. [I only got one demerit. It was in my freshman year for chewing gum in chapel. Somehow a teacher in the back balcony saw my jaw moving.] School was in session through early afternoon; then there were sports and organized activities for two or three hours and finally late afternoon classes running to 6 PM."

The October 25, 1962, *Time* magazine cover showed Kemper with the headline "Excellence and Intensity in US Prep Schools." Interestingly, Minutaglio writes that in the article "Kemper said he had been struggling with how to maintain the academic diligence in Andover while struggling to 'teach them a sense of humanity and public service.'" Some of us in the Class of 1964 did well on the latter, if not always the former.

The academics were excellent but tough. Over the years we lost many classmates for academic reasons, including my first-year roommate and even Dick Wolf of *Law and Order* fame. The first couple of years, my grades were not too good. I was a great reader but not a good writer. My father made me write letters home once a week to improve my writing. He also started "accounts," which followed my sisters and me to college. The idea was that we could have all the spending money we asked for as long as we submitted accounts on how we spent the previous request. I am afraid there were a few more books and less Orange Crush soda expenses accounted for than actually happened.

I was bad at Latin, so after two years, I switched to Spanish. The teacher was another West Pointer. George was in the class. He was Señor Arbusto ("bush"); my name was tougher—Señor Cerrarvenado, which translates as "lock deer," as a hart is a type of deer; however, the *hart* in our name is actually shortened from *heart*: the heart of King Robert the Bruce. Before the king died, he asked for his heart to be taken on a Crusade. The first Lockhart did that and changed his name to celebrate that.

I'm afraid my teacher's translation mistake was minor compared to my many Spanish translation mistakes. I think George and I were also in a Spanish class together at Yale. To his credit, he stuck with it, and I didn't.

Sports were very important and required every afternoon. Andover had seven football teams for four grades. We never made varsity but started on the JV teams for three years, George as the center and I as a guard. I dislocated my elbow wrestling in the eleventh grade, and as result my only varsity letter came from managing the baseball team senior year. George was a pitcher. More informally, he was the stickball high commissioner, and I captained my dormitory's stickball team. Stickball was a welcome release from rigorous academics.

As Minutaglio writes: "In the pent-up environment of Andover, sarcasm became almost a common method of communication: 'The Andover atmosphere of sarcasm was sort of the language we spoke. When anybody did something good, the first comment was always something bad. Just to sort of even everything out. It was always . . . done in kidding. Certainly, George shared that with the rest of us,' said dormmate James Lockhart III."

In his book, *Decision Points*,[10] Bush 43 painted his Andover experience more succinctly: "The school was a serious academic challenge. Going to Andover was the hardest thing I did until I ran for president almost 40 years later."

Senior year spring break was a big deal. Many of my friends went to Bermuda, while I visited my parents, who had rented a house in Deerfield Beach, Florida. To get there I drove down with three friends—Jeff Garten (later a commerce under secretary and dean of the Yale School of Management), my roommate, Tom Seligson (an author and documentary filmmaker), and George. We took a detour to visit Barbara Bush's prep school, Ashley Hall, in Charleston, South Carolina, as George had never seen it. George spent a few nights with us before heading up to his grandparents in Hobe Sound. Despite the many articles that suggested I roomed with him at Andover or Yale, that was the only time.

Andover was an important enough school that the Yale dean of admissions came to interview students. His first question was "Are you one of the Yale Lockharts?" I was surprised and mumbled something like "I guess so." Given my marks up to that point, it would be very hard for me to get into Yale. However, I did have strong SATs and improving grades. Critically, I got one of the highest grades in the mandatory, senior-year American history course. It helped that my history teacher, Mr. Harrison, who was a distinguished Yale graduate and Andover baseball coach, wrote my recommendation. It was a very scary day when the Yale admissions letters arrived in the school post office. There was a crowd. My friends cheered when I got a fat envelope from Yale, and they did so for George as well.

The Andover seal of 1778, which was designed by Paul Revere, has two mottos that have stuck with me over the years. The first is "Non Sibi": "Not for oneself." That is an important life lesson. The second motto was "Finis Origine Pendet," meaning "The end depends on the beginning." That was certainly a good message for a school, but also for anyone starting a new endeavor. Andover toughened me up, and it was an excellent education.

Yale has an informal motto, "For God, for Country and for Yale." My sister Joanie's husband went to Yale and gave me a banner with that motto. I had it in my college room. The motto has stuck with me ever since.

My parents moved to Minnesota before my senior year at Andover. Minnesota would not have been my choice; getting off the plane for Christmas vacation, it was minus twenty degrees Fahrenheit. Summer was very nice, though. We had a small summer house on White Bear Lake. Of course, there were always chores to do.

One summer, my father's great idea was for me to paint the red asphalt roof shingles blue. Always safety conscious, he had me tie a rope around the chimney so I wouldn't fall off. My sisters often had friends from New Jersey to our lake house, including Brenda's friend Cricket. She was amused at seeing me on the roof but somewhat shocked when she had to join the family in moving rocks to create a better beach. With two brothers, she was not used to doing manual work. Cricket and Brenda would turtle our Sunfish sailboat, and I would have to rescue them.

I had other summer jobs, including working in a vinegar factory. One of the jobs was loading boxes filled with large bottles of vinegar onto trucks. Occasionally one of the bottles would break. Many a day I came back smelling of vinegar. I still hate that smell. Another summer, I traveled around the Midwest, selling encyclopedias. Besides Minnesota, we hit Wisconsin, the Upper Peninsula of Michigan, Iowa, South Dakota, and Nebraska. I cannot say I was a natural-born salesman, but I did manage to sell several sets.

Over thirty of my Andover classmates went to Yale, but I followed my father's advice to branch out and not room with any of them. I am not sure that was good advice, as all three roommates were very musical and I am not, I ended up truly branching out. I also met two friends who knew each other from

Oklahoma City, Russ Walker and Rob Beebe. For freshman spring break, we went to Nassau. We happily roomed together for the next three years.

We did party a lot at Yale with many of my Andover and other friends. As George put it in *Decision Points*, "My philosophy in college was the old cliché: work hard, play hard. I have upheld the former and excelled at the latter." Before football games we had a warm-up drink called "skip and go naked"—grain alcohol mixed with fruit juice and served in a garbage can. We often did road trips to girls' colleges (the last all-male class at Yale was 1968). My sister Joanie was at Connecticut College, and she was a good source of dates, as was my sister Annie when she was at Bennet Junior College my last two years at Yale. We also went into New York City occasionally to party.

A *New York Times* front-page article of June 19, 2000, recounts a trip: "Once while on the train to New York City from New Haven, he told a buddy, James Lockhart, that he had done a lot of partying in his freshman year but that he now wanted to buckle down. As Mr. Lockhart remembers the conversation, Mr. Bush said, very seriously: 'I want to do more. I want to make a mark here.'"

My father would not allow me to play lacrosse at Andover because I might lose my front teeth. Naturally, I took it up when I got to Yale. I started much too late to be good, but Russ Walker and I did get our freshman numerals. We sat on the varsity bench for one year, watching John Kerry and others play. My sophomore year, I joined Deke (DKE) fraternity, which was the jock/party house. That great building is now the Alumni House, as Yale repossessed it in the anti-fraternity years. George was the president our junior year.

Academics were tough, especially as I dumbly decided to take both physics and calculus freshman year. Yale was very competitive. One geology spot quiz provided a blank map of the

US and asked us to fill in the state names. Some students who did not do well complained that we were not told to prepare for the test.

Loving American history, I majored in American studies, which allowed me to take any courses related to America—history, art, religion, economics, and even forestry. My best grades, which tie back to the title of this book, were in a class nicknamed "wind and waves" (meteorology and oceanography). My senior thesis was on my father's and grandfather's birthplace, Taunton, Massachusetts. One of our ancestors there was the founder of the silver company Reed & Barton.

The summer before our senior year, Rob Beebe and I bought a Volkswagen bug at the Wolfsburg, Germany, factory. It was our first European experience. There were some fun highlights. Besides Germany, we traveled through Belgium, Holland, and Denmark, where we stayed at the castle of our fraternity brother Count Ditley Knuth-Winterfeldt. Nighttime featured ghosts, and for breakfast there was beer and chocolate. Many years later we returned to the castle for his seventieth birthday party, which was attended by the queen of Denmark.

After England, it was France for Bastille Day. Next was Spain, where we went to see a famous matador fight. We were late, and I somehow locked the car running with the keys inside. And it was still running when we got out. Rob decided in Switzerland that we needed to climb the Matterhorn. I didn't have mountain-climbing clothes. Halfway up, we were snowed off.

In Greece I crashed our car on a slippery road. Perhaps that foreshadowed my bad experience at WL Ross when we invested in a Greek bank, which did not turn out well. While the car was being fixed, we decided to take trains through Eastern Europe—Yugoslavia, Hungary, Czechoslovakia, and East Germany. Prague was my favorite. It was just before the Prague Spring, and everybody wanted to talk with Americans. The scariest part of our train trip was being stopped on the East German border and pulled off the train because we did not have the right visas. After several tense hours, the border guards allowed us to get back on the train. Many years later, Cricket and I visited Prague in a totally different style while visiting our friend Craig Stapleton, who was then the US ambassador, and his wife, Debbie.

The year we graduated from Yale, 1968, was a very tough one for America with the assassinations, Vietnam War protests, and riots. I was not anti-war and wanted to follow the family Navy tradition. I applied to Officer Candidate School (OCS). As part of the physical, there was a color-blind test. Being color-blind, I memorized the dot charts and passed. While waiting to get into OCS, I took a summer job at the First National Bank of Saint Paul, Minnesota (now part of US Bancorp).

The bank had an old-fashioned, personal banking floor, where all the officers were at desks arranged by seniority. On one wall was a picture of J. J. Hill, the railroad baron, and on the other was F. K. Weyerhaeuser, the timber baron. Working in the credit department and taking several banking courses turned out to be an excellent start to my later career.

CHAPTER 4

Really Underwater

"No one has done more to prevent conflict—no one has made a greater sacrifice for the cause for peace—than you, America's proud missile submarine family. You stand tall among our heroes of the Cold War."

–General Colin Powell, Speech, April 25, 1992

AFTER A YEAR of waiting, I finally got to Navy OCS in Newport, Rhode Island, in June 1969. It was very competitive. We were divided into sections named after the alphabet flags. Mine was Mike. We were graded on academics, drills, and sports, including water basketball, but we also had to make our beds squarely and clean bathrooms.

They gave a different color-blind test. I wanted to be a line officer because they are qualified to drive a ship; however, a line officer could not be color-blind as ships have red and green lights signifying port (left) and starboard (right). They gave me a full day of tests to prove I was color-blind. It was tense, and I failed, but they let me remain at OCS as a supply officer. After four months, we graduated and got our ensign commissions and our US Navy swords. Somehow, I was the top Supply Corps honor graduate.

Next stop was not underwater or even near water. Supply

Corps school was in Athens, Georgia, next to the University of Georgia. In the great tradition of the US Senate, some powerful Georgia senator decided it would be an excellent place for a Navy school. Graduating well from there, I got my first choice: submarines. Subs were the only ships (called "boats" in the Navy tradition) in which a supply officer could be an officer of the deck as ship lights do not matter underwater.

And so, it was next to New London for sub school and more training. The toughest part was supposed to be going into a 100-foot water tank and then surfacing. Somehow the water tank burned down, and so we never took the test.

Coincidently, Cricket had just transferred from Pine Manor to Connecticut College in New London. Our mothers conspired. I was told that I should ask Cricket out so that she would introduce me to her friends. Well, I kept asking her out, and her friends did not appear until later. She later confessed she'd had a crush on me for years.

I was assigned to the blue crew of the USS *George Washington Carver* (SSBN 656), which was homeported in Holy Loch, Scotland. The nuclear Polaris ballistic missile submarines had two crews of 160 or so each. The crew spent one month in Holy Loch fixing and resupplying the boat and then doing a trial run to ensure everything was okay for the patrol. The next two months were spent always underwater on patrol in the North Atlantic. The boats were very large, a third larger than a football field and thirty-three feet in diameter, which allowed for three decks. Even given the size, it was tough for some to be cooped up for two months. Coming back to Holy Loch, we were relieved by the gold crew and then flew back to New London/Groton for R&R and training for three months.

Our class of submarines was named for famous Americans. George Washington Carver, an African American agricultural scientist and inventor who'd taught at Tuskegee University, was an enlightened choice. But in those days the Navy was not politically correct, and because submarines were painted black, the boat was affectionally called the "Black Beauty." Carver had some great quotes, including "There is no shortcut to achievement. Life requires thorough preparation—veneer isn't worth anything."

As the supply officer, I had the two supply clerks in charge of spare parts. Obviously, spares were critical. We carried many redundancies. After one patrol I had to sign requisitions for almost 1,000 parts. Also reporting to me were four cooks and three stewards, who took care of the officers. Because we were a nuclear sub, we always had the top priority for food requisitions, including occasional lobster tails, but food was easy to complain about, and I did get complaints. There were some strange traditions; for example, we could not serve lamb as there had been bad lamb in World War II submarines. For meals, the captain sat at the head of the officers' wardroom table, and the supply officer (me) at the foot. I heard it when the food was not good.

The crew and the officers had six-hour watches, but the crew were on an eighteen-hour day. That meant they had twelve hours to eat, sleep, watch movies, and do other duties between their six-hour watches (luckily, I was not in charge of the movies, which got more complaints than the food). Officers were on twenty-four-hour days, which was much better.

The mission was simple but critical. We sailed slowly, normally at three knots, at a depth of 200 feet in the North Atlantic with our sixteen missiles always ready to fire on Russia. The nuclear deterrent threat was called mutual assured destruction (MAD). It worked throughout the long Cold War. Although I had a Top Secret-plus clearance, I was not allowed to be involved in the procedures to launch missiles. I only knew that if we did get a message to launch missiles, there was a safe with two keys that gave instructions, plus several other safeguards.

To accurately target missiles, we always had to know where we were. We came to periscope depth once a night to get a satellite fix. We also had to know when to launch the missiles. That meant we had to be in constant communications. To do so we trailed a very thick, mile-long wire that received ultra–low frequency signals from a station in Maine. The wire had another use: we were allowed to send and receive "family grams" a couple of times during patrol. My first to Cricket was for New Year's Eve 1971. I wrote, "I bet your resolution is to give up smoking, but you won't keep it." She decided it would become her New Year's resolution and has kept it all these years.

My first duty was to act as a planesman/helmsman. The stations are normally manned by enlisted sailors whose job is to steer and keep the boat at the ordered course and depth. My next step was to qualify as the diving officer supervising the two helmsman and the chief, who controls the depth by letting water in the tanks or blowing water out. Critically, when launching missiles, he had to "hover" the sub at a prescribed depth.

When off duty, learning all the boat systems was required to earn my "dolphins," the pin emblematic of having qualified in submarines. It was very intense, but it kept my mind off being underwater for sixty days. I even had to go into the reactor compartment, but only when it was shut down.

Back in Holy Loch, after qualifying during my first patrol, I had to undergo the barbaric tradition of "drinking my dolphins." That meant drinking a pitcher of almost straight alcohol to get to the bottom were the dolphin pin was. Luckily, there was a doctor on board. I did reach my goal of becoming an officer of the deck and having the "conn," which means controlling the boat.

To stay sharp, there were constant drills. The scariest was "Battle Stations Missiles." But there were more—leaks, fires, reactor shutdowns (scrams), and radioactive fluid spills. This was driven by a mentality of "practice makes perfect," inspired by the "father of the nuclear Navy," Admiral Rickover. The drills were real enough that we were never sure if they were just drills.

"Make your depth thirteen hundred feet!" commanded Captain Pray. I was the diving officer on the trials for my second patrol. As usual, as we sailed on the surface out of Holy Loch, we were being followed by a Russian "trawler" but lost it. The test depth for SSBN 656 was 1,300 feet, which means the submarine should not go below that level. Somewhere below that, she would implode. As I ordered the down bubble for the plainsman to go from 200 to 1,300 feet and for the chief to add water to the tanks, I was concerned and, pardon the pun on the captain's name, "praying" that she would stop at test depth. It was scary because we did not stop but leveled out shortly thereafter.

The cooks were a challenge. In Holy Loch, for my second patrol, the chief cook declared he was an alcoholic and could not go on patrol. It was too late to get another cook, so the first-class cook took over. Mid-patrol, his wife got very sick. For the first and only time during patrol, we surfaced so that he could be taken off by helicopter. We had a second-class cook in charge. The very good thing about the Navy is that there is so much training, practice, and discipline that the food was still okay. The captain did not complain too much.

Being in the North Atlantic, we crossed the Arctic Circle, and I joined the "Order of the Blue Nose." We also went under the ice briefly to test the boat's capabilities. After sixty days on our second patrol, we sailed across the North Atlantic back to New London for the *Carver* to get a new reactor. The North Atlantic in winter had well over thirty-foot waves, so it was a challenge to get our nightly satellite fix at periscope depth without cutting the communications cable. I never cut it. Even at our cruise depth of 200 feet, there was enough motion that some crewmembers got seasick.

We were scheduled to go into the Electric Boat Works

shipyard in Groton, Connecticut, for our overhaul. But first we had to sail to Charleston, South Carolina, to offload our missiles. That meant more time on the surface. On the surface, the officer of the deck is on the conning tower. When I had the duty, I always had a non-color-blind sailor, just in case, to help me with the red and green lights. On the way to Charleston, we sailed the boat into Annapolis so the Naval Academy midshipmen could tour her.

The next stop was Norfolk, Virginia, and Admiral Rickover. I had never met him. But all the officer "nukes" (line officers that qualified as nuclear engineers) had to interview with him to get into the nuclear Navy. The tales of those interviews were terrifying. Sometimes he would pop out of a closet and ask almost impossible questions. He was quoted as saying that they all had excellent resumes: "So what I'm trying to find out is how they will behave under pressure."[11] He believed "a person must compare himself intellectually and professionally and then use his powers to their fullest extent." Another quote was "I believe it is the duty of each of us to act as if the fate of the world depended on him."

Rickover was the man who made sure that the nuclear Navy was always funded by Congress. He was a master at that, and so he had many quotes about the government. As early as 1953, he said something that is very relevant, even if not followed, today: "It is incumbent on those in high places to make wise decisions, and it is reasonable and important that the public be correctly informed. It is consequently incumbent on all of us to state the facts as forthrightly as possible." Another one that reminds me of the many efforts I made in my later government career to get legislation passed is "Trying to make things work in the government is sometimes like trying to sew a button on a custard pie."

To promote the nuclear Navy, he brought several reporters on board with him. My role as supply officer was to fulfill his requirements, which entailed a four-page list of what he needed for what was only an eight-hour cruise. The list included new uniforms and special newspapers and magazines that were very hard to get in Norfolk. My favorite request was S.S. Pierce lemon drops. I did fail on that request, but luckily it was not mentioned.

The admiral was a stickler for detail, with the goal of ensuring the nuclear Navy was always safe. So it was drill, drill, drill. For the reporters, he "killed" the officer in charge of a nuclear reactor and then had an "accident." We passed the drill.

Before we took the *Carver* into the drydock, we had a dependents' cruise. My parents flew east, joining Cricket on board. We submerged in the Long Island Sound, and for a while I had the conn. I was on one periscope, and my father (the former minesweeper captain) was on the other. The Sound was very busy with small boats. My father, not realizing the magnification of the periscope, kept panicking that his son would hit one of the boats. I did not.

The year I spent in Electric Boat Works in Groton was quiet. As one of the few bachelors, I had many night watches, though Cricket and I managed to go to Yale football games. We got engaged. The captain, however, informed me that in the Navy tradition, I should have asked his permission before proposing! I did ask her parents.

In the shipyard, the Rickover safety mentality was always there. One day there was a small spill of radioactive water. The next day the engineering officer, a lieutenant commander and Annapolis graduate, was removed. The Navy was tough but a great learning experience. The lessons of discipline, learning the details of a powerful boat, training, unforgiving standards, a strong defense (MAD), and mission focus were all important. Strength through knowledge.

With the captain's permission, the mothers' "arranged marriage" happened in June 1972, right after Cricket graduated. Then, to further my knowledge, I got an "early out" to go to

Harvard Business School. After B School, I went to work for Gulf Oil in Pittsburgh. One of my first jobs was to understand the impact on Gulf's pension plans of ERISA (Employee Retirement Income Security Act), which was signed in September 1974. It was the start of my pension career.

Our son, JB, was born in Pittsburgh and became a lifelong Steeler fan. After three years, we were transferred to Gulf's Eastern Hemisphere headquarters in London. The work was great, visiting our European companies and on weekends touring England, Wales, and Scotland. JB went to Young England nursery school where one of his teachers was Miss (Lady and, later, Princess) Diana.

Next stop was Belgium where I was CFO for Gulf's Belgian, Luxembourg, and German operations. Graci was born in Brussels. When I moved back to Gulf Oil's headquarters in Pittsburgh, we sailed to America on the *Queen Elizabeth II*, which was a better crossing than the *Carver*. Cricket, unfortunately, had to stay in our cabin with a seasick Graci.

Pittsburgh was a little provincial after five years in Europe. I was an assistant treasurer. One of my last jobs was to help sell our European downstream (refining and gas stations) operations with which I had spent the last three years. It was time to leave.

In 1983 I accepted a job as treasurer of Alexander & Alexander Services, then the world's second largest insurance broker. It was not smooth sailing: a year before, they had acquired a London-based insurance broker run by a bunch of crooks.

CHAPTER 5

Setting Goals

"To be successful the Republican Party must have a memorable vision/goal. Reagan had it. Bush [41] did not. Clinton did and won the election."

—Op-ed in *Los Angeles Times* by J. B. Lockhart, Jr., Sunday, March 14, 1993

THAT QUOTE WAS harsh, and it ignored that the US was just getting out of a recession with over ten percent unemployment. However, it expressed my father's passion to push for a better America. My father also wrote a paper in 1990, which I forwarded to the Bush White House, entitled the "Goal for the USA—A Successful Society."[12] The start still rings true decades later: "Many people feel the USA is stumbling downhill. We read, see and hear our schools are failing, our youth is faltering, our industry is fumbling, our banking is foundering, and our government is fiscally and otherwise inept. I agree."

Being part of the "inept" government, I was initially reluctant to forward the thirty-eight-page paper to the White House. It was positively received by the policy staff, but President Bush did not like the ring of "Successful Society." He liked phrases like "America 2000."

My father said in the paper that for the country, "a desirable goal should be rooted in the past, but able to grow to the future." He suggested a rather long-winded unifying goal, which he summarized as "to help Everyone [present and future inhabitants of the USA] be successful by providing protection and advancement opportunities while carefully maximizing the resources of the country."

As he wrote, "This may sound Pollyanna-ish. It is not. The Goal is very self-serving for the individual and the country. It will make for individual happiness and national success as we become a 'Successful Society.'"

I agree that having unifying goals at the national, corporate, and government agency levels and personally are extremely important. Lewis Carroll's famous quote from the Cheshire Cat in *Alice in Wonderland* is "If you don't know where you are going, any road will take you there." Henry Kissinger rephrased it to "If you don't know where you are going, every road will get you nowhere." Too often, goals of government agencies, which are often specified by Congress, are muddled and contradictory rather than unifying and self-reinforcing. The result is the goals are not understood, not fully embraced, and therefore not used to focus appropriate actions.

To return to the "Successful Society," my father named and explained three subgoals, which are just as important today:

1. "'Maximizing Resources' means getting the maximum benefits from the use of our resources." Costs and benefits must be weighed and re-weighed to ensure successful results with the minimum expenditures. With the muddled goals too often in government, the opposite happens—bad results with maximum expenditures.

2. "'Protection' encompasses the whole structure of laws, courts, police, and prisons to protect Everyone

domestically, and the system of diplomats and military that does the job outside the country." He called the fulfillment of these goals "adequate." I am not sure that we can say that today.

3. "'Advancement' includes all forms of learning and training that help individuals be successful. . . . Goals of USA in its glory days included a strong standard of morality, ethics, and economics." He said schools are critical and should be augmented by technology, which is "awesome." He also focused on parenting. "The future of the country is the child today. Most of his [or her] character is formed by the parent. There are principles of good parenting that can be taught."

My father was a practical visionary but also very persistent. He kept pushing the Successful Society message to improve the USA. I sent a paper in July 1996 to Elizabeth Dole, my first boss as chair of the PBGC, as her husband, Bob Dole, was running for president. I helped edit the paper, but it was my father's practical primer on the US economy. His conclusion was as follows:

> Despite the complexity of the economy, it is very important to have a very clear goal that people can understand to guide economic policy. The goal acts as a discipline as well as helps to get the message out to the people and the press. It also inspires confidence which in turn stimulates economic growth. One such goal is to create a more Successful Society to give everyone a better opportunity to achieve success. To do that we need higher growth; lower, fairer taxes; higher savings; better utilization of resources; better education; and a smaller, more efficient government through delegislation [sic], privatization, entitlement reform and better management.

He focused on deficits, which "will have to be paid by future generations," and claimed, "Decreased spending is the right way to reduce the deficit"—not increased taxes. He wrote: "The Tax Code is a complex, ever-changing mess." He went on to say American savings are too low and, "from a social standpoint, savings also help people in their retirements. Pensions have historically been a major part of savings, but regulations and legislation to close 'loopholes' have discouraged pension formation and funding."

In the paper I sent to the Doles, he wrote (interestingly, given my involvement years later):

+ **ENTITLEMENTS**. To achieve simultaneous deficit and tax reductions, the issue of entitlements has to be tackled. Social Security, Medicare, and Medicaid make up the fastest growing component of government spending. The economics are obvious, but the politics are not. Controlling the growth of spending will require a consensus that people should be given economic incentives to lower their healthcare costs. The economics of Social Security are helped by higher growth rate and therefore higher payroll taxes. Just small changes in assumptions have very large impacts on the soundness of the system. One change that should be implemented gradually is to invest a small, but growing portion of the trust funds in equities. Over time the result will be a higher investor return, a sounder Social Security system will inspire more confidence[,] and more equity capital will help fund economic growth.

+ **PRIVATIZATION**. Another core element of economic growth policy should be privatization. There are many needed functions the government should perform, but it has also encroached on many areas that the private sector can do better including insurance, power production and delivery, healthcare, data collection and many others. For instance, now that we have fixed the PBGC it is a good candidate for privatization. Privatization helps stimulate investments and reduces the deficit through the proceeds and future taxes. It will take a concerted effort because many of these programs are intertwined with special interest groups. Also, in many cases such as the insurance programs, government accounting is misleading and hides the true economic picture. Moving these programs to the private sector will reduce the deficit over time, better utilize government resources and allow the government to concentrate on essential services.

He was rather optimistic on the PBGC because they had recently reported that they had a surplus for the first time in many years. However, the PBGC was only briefly above water. I also was overoptimistic and had written an op-ed calling for privatization, which became a dirty word during the Social Security reform debates. He was right on with his comments about government insurance companies' misleading accounting.

My father was a patriot with the strong passion and vision on how to make America better. Rereading these documents, I wish I had paid more attention to his writings and, of course, that the recipients had as well. It is extremely important to set clear, consistent goals and help unite people to support them. Congressional legislation approved by the president should be designed to fulfill the goals in an efficient, cost-effective manner.

Too often, government goals are high minded but muddled and shortsighted, ignoring real long-term costs and potential downsides. Reforms, if any, come too late.

CHAPTER 6

Welcome to the Underwater Pension Benefit Guaranty Corporation (PBGC)

"If you want to make enemies, try to change something. . . . To do things to-day exactly the way you did them yesterday saves thinking."

—President Woodrow Wilson, address to Salesmanship Congress in Detroit, July 10, 1916 (I used this in a 1992 speech)

"RENOVATIONS COMPLETED" WAS the title of a cartoon in *Pensions and Investments* showing my predecessor pounding in a sign in front of a PBGC house. If only! Like many government agencies, renovations never are completed.

At my swearing-in ceremony on July 11, 1989, a more realistic secretary of labor and PBGC chair, Elizabeth Dole, harkened back to my first stint of public service: "He was a deck officer on a nuclear submarine. . . . Now, Jim, your challenge is to make sure that you avoid depth charges, and that you set a course full speed ahead." A depth charge is an underwater bomb designed to cause enough of a shock to cause a submarine to sink. I did not realize at the time how true the warning would turn out to be. The depth charges grew to have names following the major bankruptcies of steel companies, many airlines, Western Union, and even an underwear company. But they never stopped me from going "full speed ahead."

The PBGC was created by Congress on Labor Day 1974 as part of the Employee Retirement Security Act (ERISA). A key inspiration for the legislation was the loss of all Studebaker workers' pension benefits when it closed its major car manufacturing plant in 1964. My first project at Gulf Oil had been to study the then proposed ERISA. As I said at the PBGC's fortieth anniversary: "I joined when PBGC was an unruly teenager turning fifteen. There were many who didn't think it would make it to forty. Noble purpose, but messy reality."

The PBGC does have noble, if somewhat contradictory, missions, one of which is ensuring that pensioners and workers get at least a major portion of their promised pensions if their employer goes bankrupt. The second mission was encouraging the growth of defined benefit plans, which were already starting to fade when I joined the PBGC in June 1989. Defined contribution plans—401(k)s—were taking over; they do not present the risks and costs to a corporate sponsor that a defined benefit plan does.

Unfortunately, like many government insurance agencies, the PBGC was set up by Congress, ignoring sound insurance principles by underpricing the insurance without the ability to do underwriting of the risks or to have strong enough claims in bankruptcy. The poster child at the time for a flawed government insurance program was the failed Federal Savings and Loan Insurance Corporation (FSLIC). I was criticized for comparing the PBGC to the FSLIC, although many others did as well. The PBGC's insurance premiums were originally a much-too-low $1 per person that did not reflect the potential risks, and the pension funding rules were much too weak.

We faced four major challenges, which became my goals:

1. Trying to encourage better funding of pension plans and prevent bankruptcies

2. Fixing the systems and accounting so the PBGC could be audited for the first time in its history

3. Dealing with major bankruptcies and maximizing recoveries for the terminated pensions

4. Getting Congress to enact reforms

That fourth legislative reform goal was needed in all my government agencies. It still is.

The PBGC's structure was and still is flawed, but one thing that certainly was not flawed was the dedicated PBGC team. They were very anxious to embrace change. They even put up with my constant handwritten "Jim-Grams" as I was late to email. They worked long hours, going up against lawyers, corporate executives, investment bankers, and actuaries who were paid many multiples of their pay. I thought our team was better in most cases, if not as polished. Disturbing to me, our employees were paid far less than the government banking agencies (the FDIC, OCC, and Fed).

I got permission from the Labor Department to do a study, which concluded that PBGC personnel should be paid similarly to the banking agencies. All hell broke loose as I was told in no uncertain terms that my team would not be paid more than Labor Department personnel and certainly not in 1992, an election year. Many years later, the PBGC did get approval for the higher pay scales.

Joining Secretary of Labor Elizabeth Dole and, from 1991 on, Lynn Martin on the board were the secretaries of Treasury, Nicolas Brady, and Commerce, Robert Mosbacher. When I arrived, the board had not met for almost ten years, primarily because of how messy our decisions were. I pushed hard, and we finally had an in-person board meeting at the Labor Department in December 1990. It was short, but at least it happened. We did have regular meetings with the secretaries' board representatives—their assistant or under secretaries.

On March 1, 1990, I described to the House Appropriations Committee subcommittee what the PBGC did:

> The PBGC was established under Title IV of the Employee Retirement Income Security Act of 1974 (ERISA) to insure private, defined benefit pension participants against the loss of benefits if their plan is terminated without adequate funding.
>
> The PBGC provides vital insurance protection to nearly 40 million active and retired American workers and about 100,000 private sector defined-benefit pension plans. This universe of plans has liabilities of about up $820 billion but assets of well over $1 trillion. However, PBGC has a $20–$30 billion exposure to underfunded pension plans. About half of this exposure is in just 50 companies in single-employer plans, mainly in the steel, auto and airline industries. Almost half the underfunding with these firms poses a very high risk.

At an April 5, 1990, Senate Finance Committee hearing I explained:

> Covered plans are required by law to pay a premium that is the PBGC's major source of revenue. We take very seriously the mission that Congress gave us when establishing the PBGC in 1974. We even put the mission on the cover of this year's annual report. It is . . .

+ To encourage the growth of the private pension system.

+ To ensure the timely payment of pensions.

+ To keep premiums at the lowest level consistent with carrying out our statutory obligation.

In order to prevent a large deficit, we have a strong loss prevention strategy which uses the legislative tools Congress has given us, most recently in 1986 and 1987. These tools are supplemented by regulation, litigation, and negotiations. The loss prevention strategy has three elements:

+ Encouraging sponsors to better fund their plans and avoiding uncompensated risks.

+ Discouraging companies from terminating underfunded plans through tough negotiation and litigation.

+ Minimizing losses, if there is a termination, by increasing recoveries.

In the president's fiscal year 1991 budget, OMB director Richard Darman discussed two topics that . . . bear directly upon PBGC: "hidden PACMAN" and "moral hazards." . . . "Hidden PACMAN" refers to federal liabilities [that] are not fully visible. Although this exposure represents less than 4 percent of the total liabilities, it is large in comparison to our annual premium income of $600 million.

A "moral hazard" occurs if the interests of the insured and insurance company are not aligned. An insured party

> may be willing to take a higher risk if he knows that the
> insurance company will pay. A moral hazard also exists
> when a government insurance company insures losses
> over which it has no regulatory authority. [ERISA had
> given the IRS authority to enforce funding and the Labor
> Department fiduciary enforcement.] A moral hazard
> should be balanced by controls or offsetting incentives.
> Otherwise, perverse incentives are created that may
> seriously increase our risk of losses.

One of the moral hazard problems was that if the rules were
stronger, no company would start a new defined benefit (DB)
pension. Well, new ones were not being formed anyway.

A September 10, 1992, *Wall Street Journal* editorial wrote:
"The present system is screwy. Management and labor are
exposed to unhealthy temptations, such as granting benefits they
can't afford and then trying to shuck the cost on to the insurance
fund. The same moral hazard infects their bankers, who
sometimes urge cash-strapped clients to blow off their pension
kitties and use the money to pay off private creditors instead.
Having a fat pension gap—basically a government-guaranteed
loan—just breeds corporate arrogance of the sort associated with
the phrase 'too big to fail.'"

That phrase was going to be famous many years later.

The PBGC insures single-employer and multiemployer
pension plans—union plans with many corporate sponsors. The
latter were less of an issue at that time as reform legislation had
been passed several years before and guaranteed benefits were
much lower than in single employer.

There are two major types of single-employer defined
benefit pension plans—final pay salaried and flat benefit union
plans. The year I joined the PBGC, salaried plans were about 76
percent of the total insured plans and were overfunded. Today,

overfunded plans are rare.

The flat benefit union plans (24 percent of the total) were the problem; their funding ratio was only 75 percent, persistently underwater. A GAO 1993 study cited in the *New York Times*[13] stated that "18 of 35 underfunded plans in the tire, automobile, airline and steel industries increased benefits by almost $2.2 billion in 1991." General Motors (a TARP bailee many years later) cited labor negotiation as the reason for their increased underfunding.

In contract negotiations with troubled companies unable to afford pay increases, their unions oftentimes requested pension benefit increases to show negotiating success to their members. After all, something was better than nothing, and pensions were "government guaranteed;" legally, there is no US government guarantee, but like many other government insurance programs, there was an assumed implicit government guarantee. The PBGC by law is funded by premiums paid by plan sponsors with a miniscule line of credit from the government.

Many members of Congress who followed government accounting looked at the annual positive cash flow from premiums, which helped reduce government deficits. The members ignored the underwater deficits for future benefit payments. Some people have called it a Ponzi scheme. *Fiscal Year 1992 PBGC Annual Report*, my last before I left in January 1993, showed a deficit of what I thought was an alarming $2.9 billion. It also reported $40 billion in pension underfunding. The underfunding dove further underwater over the years.

In theory, not guaranteeing all the full benefits of retirees was designed to eliminate some of the moral hazard of the program by making employees have a "deductible." A deductible is a feature in most auto and homeowners' policy as it helps incent people to reduce losses. The benefit haircut often affected early retirees more. The problem was they did not understand the potential to lose benefits, and their unions ignored it.

Sometimes the best way to overcome moral hazards is moral suasion. To counter this moral hazard of pension increases granted by troubled companies and encourage better funding, we published what became the infamous "Top Fifty"—or as some referred to it, the "Iffy Fifty"—list of underfunded single-employer plans. It was arranged by funding ratio, with lowest ratio on top. It also gave the amount underfunded. It was hated by the companies, their unions, pension organizations, and the National Association of Manufacturers. They all often told me so. Even the PBGC's advisory board, composed of union, corporate, and pension experts, hated it.

Controversy was not all bad: the list did get some action.

Not everybody was against the Top Fifty list. *Institutional Investor* magazine, in their twenty-fifth-anniversary issue of July 1992, had the list as one of the top 250 financial events over those twenty-five years, albeit at number 245.

As I said in the press release of the 1991 Top Fifty list on November 19, 1992, "As a government insurance company, PBGC is often compared to the Federal Savings and Loan Insurance Corporation disaster. PBGC has published this list . . . to help prevent a similar occurrence. The list helps workers, retirees, and creditors put more pressure on those companies to better fund their pension plans and treat pensions as real debt."

Many companies, such as Chrysler and General Motors (in dollar terms of underfunding, they were first and second largest in 1991), decided to make contributions above the legal requirement to get off or at least lower their position on the list. Chrysler did a $2 billion stock offering in 1993 and contributed $1.1 billion of the proceeds to their pension. I was quoted in an Allen Sloan column in the February 23, 1993, *Washington Post* as saying, "The use of proceeds was an amazing precedent; it was exactly the right thing to do." Unfortunately, many companies did not follow the precedent to make extra contributions. Many of those companies no longer exist.

The first year we put out the list, the Top Fifty underfunding for year-end 1989 was $14.2 billion, and just two years later it was $24.2 billion. It rose to $39.7 billion the next year and then fell to $13.5 billion. As I said in the 1992 press release, "PBGC could be a sound program were it not for these 50 companies. These plans represent less than 1% of the plans PBGC insures, but most of the significant exposure. If we ask the other 99% to pay for these problems through continued premium increases, they will drop out of this voluntary system, leaving the taxpayer holding the bag."

There were many dropouts, especially among small plans, as PBGC premiums soared. Companies dropped out by doing a standard termination, funding promised benefits with an annuity or lump-sum payment. In 1989 there were 100,000 PBGC-covered pension plans; now there are around 25,000. That reflects another insurance term: *adverse selection*. Healthy plans dropped out. Many of those that remained needed the PBGC insurance as they were underfunded.

Pressure built to do away with the Top Fifty list. As *Business Insurance* editorialized on September 1, 1997, "The top 50 list is not a perfect instrument. But it has accomplished—at least in some cases—the objective of improvement in plan funding. Perhaps if Top 50 lists had been started in 1980 instead of 1990, employees of companies that failed in the 1980s and early 1990s would have known of the extent of their companies' pension funding problems early on and would have put pressure on those companies to step up funding." Succumbing to pressure, a week after the editorial, the Clinton administration axed the Top Fifty list.

"Renovations" were definitely not completed. Before the PBGC had its Top Fifty list, the GAO had a list of high-risk government programs. We were put on the list. Being the full-speed-ahead guy, I invited this depth charge. The PBGC had never been audited. That was the GAO's responsibility, and they had tried in 1979 and 1980. The GAO's disclaimer[14] to the 1980 accounts was "Our examination disclosed material accounting and estimating problems, internal control weaknesses, and major uncertainties that significantly reduce the reliability of important account balances." After that, the GAO walked away. My predecessors decided to let sleeping dogs lie, which is not in my nature. The GAO's comptroller general, Chuck Bowsher, had given speeches comparing the PBGC to FSLIC. I called him and challenged him to come back and audit us.

A very ugly August 1, 1991, GAO report stated the PBGC's "estimated liability for guaranteed benefits was unauditable. . . . We caution users that the corporation's Sept. 1990 financial statements have limited reliability." We had started working on the problems much earlier. A key problem was that the premium processing system had not been working since August 1988. Companies were voluntarily paying premiums, but we did not know if they were accurate or even if all the insured companies were paying premiums. We got the antiquated system running in April 1990, but it needed to be replaced. We had also requested the creation of an inspector general. From an audit standpoint, the other key issues centered on the need to strengthen internal controls, specify the liabilities of the plans we had taken over, and estimate the potential liabilities from future terminations.

A *Pensions and Investments* editorial[15] entitled "Incredibly Inauditable" had a cartoon of a blind PBGC saying to a blind GAO, "After you." The GAO reply was "No, no, I insist . . . after you!!" There were many other ugly news stories, but with the help of outside consultants, new systems, and revised procedures, we got the job done. In a September 1993 letter to Congress, Comptroller General Bowsher wrote, "Because of the considerable progress the Corporation has made in improving internal controls, we were able, to opine on the Corporation's financial condition for the first time." (That only took eighteen years.)

The opinion stated: "The September 30, 1992, statements of financial condition were reliable in all material respects, except for the Multiemployer Fund's liability of $60 million." The 1992 accounts were on my watch. The PBGC also got off the high-risk list. Not untypically of the government, they did get back on that list years later.

When I arrived in mid-1989 at the PBGC, defined benefit plans were already considered dinosaurs. A big problem when we arrived was that companies with overfunded plans were being acquired in leveraged buyouts (LBO), oftentimes funded by high-yield/junk bonds plus the proceeds from terminating overfunded pension plans. To terminate a pension plan, a company would buy annuities for their pensioners and employees. The company would get the excess assets. The less the annuity cost, the more assets they got back.

The insurance company of choice was the AAA-rated Executive Life. Oftentimes, it had the lowest annuity price as their investment portfolio consisted mainly of high-yield/junk bonds. Sometimes the bonds were issued as part of the very same LBOs. Before the PBGC, when I was treasurer at the insurance broker Alexander & Alexander, we turned down a huge transaction with Executive Life because of credit concerns, despite their AAA.

Other companies with overfunded pension plans were also terminating plans to retrieve excess assets. There was Democratic congressional pressure to get the administration to take action to stop terminations. The new Bush 41 administration thought that eliminating the option would interfere with legitimate business decisions and cause companies to underfund their pension plans if they never had a chance to get back overfunding. Senate Democrats held up the nomination of the assistant Labor secretary for pensions, who had terminated a plan with his previous company. After six months, a compromise was reached, which allowed the assistant secretary to be confirmed.

In 1991, Executive Life did fail. Junk bond prices had been falling for a year with the slowdown in the economy. Annuitants were at risk of large cutbacks. The California state insurance regulator took over Executive Life to help the annuitants.

As the terminated pension plans no longer existed, the PBGC was not legally involved. However, Chairman Metzenbaum (D-OH) of the Senate Labor Committee said the PBGC should bail out the annuitants. We told him that we could not as it was not legal under our statue. He introduced legislation, which AARP supported, to make the PBGC pick up these potential losses. After much back-and-forth, he gave up. But this episode points out a big danger. After a government program is set up, there is always the risk of mission creep regardless of the cost.

Liabilities and premium collections were the big issues for the GAO in their audit. The investment side of the balance sheet was not an issue, but investments were very important to the PBGC's future. That was an area, given my experience, in which I felt comfortable.

Unlike other insurance companies, the PBGC historically has had fewer assets than liabilities, which are benefits payable to existing and future retirees in plans the PBGC has taken over. As the difference was a deficit, it was underwater. Normal insurance companies would not be allowed by their state regulator to operate with a deficit.

The insurance premiums the PBGC receives from the corporate pension sponsors are invested in Treasury securities because government accounting then treats the premiums received as a reduction in the federal deficit. The other assets in the portfolios are from terminated pension plans and recoveries from claims against the bankrupt sponsor. Over the years there has been a great deal of controversy on whether to invest these billions of dollars in stocks or bonds. It has been a yo-yo. The arguments are quite simple.

My predecessors and several successors favored equities because, though much more volatile, they tend to increase in value more than bonds over the long term. They viewed the PBGC as a pension plan, and as with many pension plans that are underwater, the theory was that taking on more risk should reduce the shortfall over time.

The second approach recognized that the PBGC was two businesses—first, a financial guarantee company insuring pension plans if a corporate sponsor goes bankrupt, and second, once a plan is taken, a fixed annuity–issuing insurance company. Fixed annuity–issuing companies rely primarily on bond investments.

To break the deadlock, we hired two advisors: Wilshire Associates and Goldman Sachs. Wilshire, the existing advisor with a pension client base, viewed the PBGC as a pension plan, not as an annuity insurance company. Goldman Sachs in the form of Fischer Black—co-creator of the Black Scholes option pricing model, which later won the Nobel Prize—disagreed.

Black's conclusion was that we should short the stock market. His reasoning was the PBGC had massive equity-based contingent liabilities, which were exposures to the potential bankruptcy of companies and, if there was a bankruptcy, to their underfunded pension plans heavily invested in equities. It was happening. The theory was right, but I just could not see myself testifying in Congress that we would short the US stock market.

In the end we decided to reduce the equities exposure dramatically from 48 percent in 1989 to 17 percent by 1993 and increase the bond exposure. As we did not have enough assets to cover the exposure of the book liabilities, we got creative. With the help of the Treasury Department, we converted our regular Treasury bonds to zero-coupon Treasury bonds, to match the dollar duration of the liabilities. As Treasury bond rates fell over the next several years, not only were the zero-coupon bonds a very good hedge, but they also outperformed the stock market.

Goldman Sachs, then a private partnership, decided not to bill us for their advice as they did not want to be exposed to all the disclosure requirements of a government contractor. Government contracting can be messy. Trying to influence the selection process is a criminal offense. As a result, even though I was probably more experienced at selecting investment managers than anyone at the PBGC, I elected to stay away from the selection process.

The bond-versus-equity debate renewed with the arrival of every new executive director. The yo-yo continued. Equities were pushed back up, reaching 39 percent before the "dot-com" crash. That was very unfortunate timing. Over the years there were several disruptive changes in investment strategy, all of which had to be approved by the board of directors. The first PBGC director for Bush 43, Steve Kandarian (later the chairman and CEO of MetLife), went back to a bond strategy, but his successors swung back again to more equities. In April 2019, the PBGC again reverted to a bond, liability-driven investment strategy. Hopefully, it will be the last change. But as the history of the PBGC has shown, with executive director turnover, recessions, equity market crashes, and bond market gyrations, nothing is certain.

CHAPTER 7

The PBGC Is Frightening: Bail Outs, Bankruptcies, and Reforms

"The question is: Will we fix it [PBGC] or will we bury our heads in the sand? . . . My concern is that this is the same old dodge that was used before when we were forced to bail out the railroad unemployment system, the farm credit system, the bank insurance system, and yes, the savings and loan system."

—Chairman Jake Pickle of House Ways and Means Subcommittee on Oversight hearing on February 4, 1993

THROUGHOUT MY TENURE at the PBGC, concern grew about the eventual need for bailouts given the growing corporate bankruptcies with massive, underfunded pension plans. A *Business Insurance* February 10, 1992, editorial entitled "Preventing a debacle" had a cartoon of an hourglass. The top half was a conventional hourglass with sand labeled *PBGC DEBT*. The bottom half was the Capitol Dome with that sand pouring out of the bottom.

Although the PBGC was a small government agency in terms of people, it was overseen by four congressional committees: House Ways and Means, Senate Finance, and the House and Senate Labor committees. Despite having so many members overseeing us, it was my sense that less than a handful really understood the program. One who did understand the PBGC well was the House Ways and Means subcommittee chairman, Jake Pickle (D-TX). In 1991, referring to the PBGC's present and future liabilities, he called the PBGC "frightening." Many members of Congress left much up to their staffs, some of whom were very knowledgeable. But other staffers, especially on the Labor committees, were too political.

Carl Icahn made a very big mistake. In 1988 he took the airline TWA private by buying more than 90 percent of TWA shares and unsuccessfully tried to fix the airline. In 1992 TWA filed for bankruptcy. Its pension plan was underfunded by almost $1 billion. TWA did not have the money to fund it. As Carl was over 80 percent owner, he and all his "assets" were part of the control group. He was on the hook for the TWA pension plan if the PBGC terminated the plan. He would have had to pay all that shortfall. He was not happy with his advisors, who had overlooked the control group exposure when he took it private.

And he was very unhappy with the PBGC when we would not let him off the hook. He was not as rich back then (he claimed $900 million net worth at the time) as he is today. The pension claim could have wiped him out.

He launched into action, calling and meeting with the three secretaries on the PBGC board: Labor, Treasury, and Commerce. It was 1992, a presidential election year, but the secretaries held in there. It became a game of chicken. To force Carl to fund the pension plan, we would have needed to terminate the pension, which would have potentially cut back benefits of 15,000 pensioners and cause 25,000 employees to lose their jobs, many of whom lived in Missouri. The fight dragged on past the election. The recession, which was hitting so many of the companies the PBGC was dealing with, helped dragged Bush down.

Icahn kept lobbing in calls. It was not the first time we had dealt with him: he was a major creditor in the Western Union 1991 bankruptcy. He had been fighting with another major corporate raider, Bennett LeBow, who was the major shareholder in Western Union's parent, New Valley. Icahn wanted the PBGC to join forces with him to have the PBGC terminate and take responsibility for Western Union's $400 million underfunded pension. We did not.

On Thanksgiving Day, Icahn rose to a whole new level. He called me and spent well over four hours on the phone as I was trying to celebrate with my family at my in-laws' house—an incredible performance by him, as it was almost impossible to get a word in edgewise. He had no case to stand on, but he kept telling me how he could turn around the airline and fund the pension with more aggressive investments. Icahn was a master at being able to talk/bully his way into making money.

He did not care that he interrupted our Thanksgiving dinner. Cricket and her mother were not happy, wondering why I was upstairs on the phone for so long. Cricket's 98-year grandmother, who lived to be 105, was more forgiving. My turkey was cold, and I missed my favorite team's, the New York Giants, televised game with the Dallas Cowboys. Not bad as they lost. I also missed quality time with my son, JB, who was back from Andover for Thanksgiving.

TWA was the last major bankruptcy we faced while I was at the PBGC. In the airline industry alone, we had faced the demise of Eastern Airlines (underfunded by $700 million) and Pan Am (underfunded by $900 million). Continental filed for bankruptcy to try to avoid responsibility for Eastern Airlines' pension underfunding, as Continental had acquired Eastern. Trump acquired the Eastern Shuttle, which did not work well. Others were teetering.

One thing Carl did not know was that I had a connection to TWA. No, it was not award miles, which I had to surrender under government rules as it was thought miles might prejudice my judgment. Rather, as mentioned earlier, my grandfather had turned down Howard Hughes's offer to run TWA because he felt that as a cost cutter, he would be blamed if a plane crashed.

TWA crashed anyway, but not on my watch. With the end of the Bush 41 administration looming, the will of the PBGC board diminished at the thought of putting 25,000 people out of work. There was heavy pressure from the Missouri and Kansas senators and representatives on the PBGC's board chair, Secretary Martin. The pilots' and stewardess' unions applied pressure as well. Even the hawkish Treasury Department, spearheaded by Under Secretary Jay Powell (later the Federal Reserve chairman), wanted a compromise. Despite the dovish board, we stayed tough and kept negotiating for Icahn to give the pension more money.

In the end, we worked out a very complicated deal to protect the pensions and get TWA out of bankruptcy. Icahn agreed to put $240 million into TWA pensions over time, lend TWA $200 million to keep it flying, and better manage the pension investments. In return, he got some airline tickets to sell. The pension also got a $300 million note from TWA, secured by their international routes and anything that had any value, including the wrenches in the Kansas City maintenance facility. The plans were frozen. The three board cabinet secretaries happily concurred in December with our settlement. Icahn said TWA was "obviously the worst investment decision I ever made."[16] He also said, "All sides made substantial compromises," and I was quoted, "Everybody blinked at the same time."[17]

My PBGC team was unhappy with the decision to do a deal with Icahn because they thought we could get more out of him. To her credit, our general counsel, Carol Flowe, wrote a February 15, 1993, letter to *Business Insurance*, strongly defending the deal. As always, the team had fought very hard to protect the pensions and their pensioners. It was one of my toughest decisions. We might potentially have been able to seize most of Icahn's assets after many years of litigation, but in the meantime, we would have shut down TWA, causing massive job losses. Earlier, we'd had no choices with Pan Am and Eastern Airlines. The airlines were bleeding money, and their pensions were too far underwater. But we had a choice with TWA.

As Pickle said to me in a February 1993 House hearing:

> When you reach the stage of continuing an operation or a plan going under, it is a very difficult question for the PBGC or Congress to say whether we should let it go under and put 25,000 workers out of their jobs or should we try to cut the best deal we can. PBGC cut the best deal it could. I don't know whether you were right or wrong. . . . What happened to TWA could happen to any company in the future. . . . That ought not to happen.

TWA lasted for another nine years before it filed for bankruptcy for the third time and was taken over by American Airlines. And yes, the still grossly underfunded (by $700 million) pension plan was terminated and taken over by the PBGC.

TWA was my last PBGC bankruptcy, but my first occurred before I arrived. In July 1986, what was then the largest bankruptcy in US history had occurred, LTV. It was one of the original conglomerates, including steel, aerospace, Wilson sporting goods, Hummer cars, meatpacking, and other pieces. The PBGC terminated their three pension plans with over $2 billion in underfunding. Two were union plans, and the other was a management plan, which became underfunded as the retirees opted to take lump sums when they saw LTV was in trouble. After learning more about LTV's financial position in September 1987, the PBGC found that LTV could afford the pensions. The driving impetus was that LTV had created "follow-on" plans. They created new pensions when combined with the PBGC's guaranteed benefits, fully restoring the benefits. To us that meant they could afford the original plans.

The bankrupt LTV refused the PBGC's pension restoration order, saying the decision was "arbitrary and capricious." A district court agreed with LTV, but the PBGC's general counsel, Carol Flowe, adamantly disagreed and asked my permission to appeal to the Supreme Court. I gave permission. The PBGC has what is called "independent litigating authority," which means we could go to the court directly without going through the Justice Department. One of my favorite memories was hearing Carol argue the LTV restoration case (*PBGC vs. The LTV Corp. et al*) in the Supreme Court in February 1990. Cricket and I were seated in the front with our two children, JB (age thirteen) and Graci (age seven).

It was a great civic lesson. Even better, it was announced in June that the PBGC had won and the plans were restored. It was headline news in many papers. Looking back at them, the *Financial Times* of June 19, 1990, stands out; its two top headlines that day were "US court orders LTV to honor pension contributions," and a future omen, "Trump in last-ditch attempt to save stricken empire." At least as far as we knew, he did not have underfunded pension plans.

We still needed to get the LTV plans funded through tough multiparty negotiations with various creditor groups, equity holders, management, and unions. A bankruptcy judge slashed the pensions claims by using an unbelievably high discount rate. We threatened to sue again to force funding. Wilbur Ross, representing LTV's creditor committee, said: "We hope to get them [PBGC] back to the bargaining table."[18]

We eventually cut a deal in late 1991 to fund the pension with significant up-front cash, plus annual payments, and then, when they emerged from bankruptcy in 1993, an additional $700 million from asset sales, $100 million in LTV stock, and $787 million in cash. We also created a contingent value right that gave the PBGC some upside, which did work out when LTV did a public offering a few years later. Ross told me he liked our creativity.

When hard times hit again for the steel industry, LTV declared bankruptcy in December 2000. Its pensions were terminated by the PBGC in 2002 with underfunding of $2.2 billion. Wilbur Ross's new private equity firm bought LTV out of bankruptcy. He combined LTV with another failed steel company, Bethlehem Steel, whose massively underfunded pension plans of $4.3 billion were terminated by the PBGC. The rescues worked, with the help of steel tariffs imposed by President George W. Bush in 2002, which helped raise domestic steel prices. The combined companies turned out to be a great investment for Ross's funds. Bush, years later, told me he did not know Ross and that he regretted the tariffs. Ironically, as Trump's commerce secretary, Wilbur served on the PBGC board.

To help us with our negotiations, we got creative. We established an Early Warning Group in 1991, composed of people with strong financial talent whose job was to engage troubled companies with underfunded plans and create solutions before the plans were on our doorstep. The group prevented several pension terminations and helped to reduce losses when the pensions were terminated. The group got a "good government" award from Harvard Kennedy School and is still very successfully functioning today.

Another battle was with Chrysler. They had been through bankruptcy earlier with a government bailout, but by 1990 they were having difficulties again. The CFO, Steve Miller, who later saved many troubled companies, came to tell us that Chrysler was going to sell over 20 percent of their shares in Chrysler Financial. That would have removed one of Chrysler's best assets from the control group. When we said no, they got very angry. After weeks, things calmed down. We ended up agreeing to the sale, but only if they would pay $1 billion into the pension plan. They decided not to do that, and pensions stayed well underwater.

Fast forward to late 2008, the newly approved Troubled Asset Relief Program (TARP) provided a loan to Chrysler which was effectively converted to another bankruptcy bailout in 2009. In the world of government, things that go around come around. I was then on the TARP oversight board. The good news was that when Chrysler was acquired by Fiat, the pensions covering 250,000 workers and retirees remained ongoing.

Most of these heavyweight negotiations occurred in our boardroom. I had pictures there of steel mills, airplanes, and other assets of bankrupt companies whose pensions we had terminated. There was also a chart in the boardroom; as described by *Institutional Investor*:[19] "James Lockhart has hung a chart displaying two scenarios of PBGC funding over the next decade. The optimistic forecast slopes gently upward from the current billion-plus deficit to a $1.5 billion surplus by the end of the decade. The pessimistic one resembles a run for expert skiers, with the finish line at an $8 billion deficit." The pictures and the chart were a not-so-subtle warning to the negotiators on the other side.

In most bankruptcies, the PBGC tended to be the largest claimant, representing the claims of the underfunded pension plans, but there would be many other groups—management, equity investors, secured and unsecured creditors, unions, and even the IRS, all with their own sets of advisors. Our team was composed of our very strong in-house lawyers, actuaries, and early warning negotiating team, sometimes supplemented by investment bankers. The bankers were expensive, and so were the external lawyers.

There were so many bankruptcies with so many lawyers billing the bankrupt estates that we ended up assigning two of our lawyers the full-time job of reviewing the lawyers' billable hours. They caught overbilling in many cases. My favorite finding was a senior law firm partner who billed over twenty-four hours in a day. He claimed he was on a plane flying west. Lawyers and other professionals did very well from the bankruptcies; but far too many hardworking retirees and workers had their benefits cut.

During my three and half years at the PBGC, I gave over fifty speeches to any group that would listen and testified on the PBGC in Congress seventeen times plus three more after I left. As one of the PBGC's three missions was to promote defined benefit (DB) pension plans, many of my earlier speeches were slanted to promoting DB plans more than reforms.

As mentioned earlier, the PBGC had conflicting missions. The dilemma was that the best way to protect benefits was to strengthen the pension funding rules and increase premiums, which would discourage new DB plan formations and encourage terminations of well-funded plans. Even more perversely, a corporate pension contribution is scored in government accounting as a "tax expenditure." That means if legislation increases pension contributions, corporations pay less taxes. The resulting higher corporate deductions for the next ten years are scored as increasing the deficit.

Years later, Congress gave troubled airlines an ability to delay funding their pensions, which was positively scored for reducing the deficit. In the American Rescue Act of 2021, pension funding rules were delayed, helping pay for the cost of the plan. Very shortsighted.

While trying to stay positive about defined benefit plans, my speeches soon turned to promoting reform and pointing out the problems. It was a tightrope I had to walk in my subsequent government job as well. We did not want to scare people, but we wanted to get Congress to act. The key reforms I called for in the single-employer program were higher priorities for pensions in bankruptcy, realistic government accounting that showed that the PBGC was underwater, stronger pension funding rules, and limited guarantees for new benefit increases in underfunded pension plans.

In a 1992 speech to the AFL-CIO Pension-Net Conference, I expressed our dilemma by using an analogy to one of my hobbies—gardening: "While there are many roses in the defined benefit world, there are also many weeds. The roses are the well-funded plans, those that make the overall system healthy. . . . Another rose is the multiemployer program [with] a surplus approaching $200 million. The single-employer program is plagued with weeds."

Perhaps going a little too far with the rose theme, I then said: "There are those who persist in looking at PBGC through rose-colored glasses. . . [as] currently we have a positive cash flow . . . to pay benefits. But that says nothing about the future. I am convinced that these are the same rose-colored glasses through which many people viewed the late, but not lamented, Federal Savings and Loan Insurance Corporation."

The day before my AFL-CIO speech, President G. H. W. Bush's budget was released, calling again for PBGC reform, and so I said: "The Bush administration believes . . . it is time to stop the band aid approach to repairs and confront the structural problems of the insurance program once and for all."

One could and should replace "insurance program" in the above sentence with almost every government insurance program. Some commentators said I was crying wolf. Others questioned why I was "doing a good impression of Jeremiah, brandishing his staff and rod all over Washington, threatening steep rises in premium payments and prophesying the collapse of yet another federal safety net?"[20]

In 1992, a presidential election year, a somewhat convoluted audience question about Social Security and the "Pension Guaranty Fund," suggesting it would be bankrupt in 2026, came up in the University of Richmond debate on October 15, 1992, among President Bush, Governor Clinton, and Ross Perot. Bush misspoke by saying there was a government guarantee for the PBGC, Perot sounded off, not answering the question, and Clinton said, "I don't know as much about it," and then compared it to the "guarantee on the S & Ls."[21]

There are so many government programs that it's unsurprising that, as an unkind *Pensions & Investments*[22] headline put it, "President Bush draws a blank on PBGC legislation." The article more kindly wrote, "In a gentle reminder, the PBGC said 'the Bush administration has introduced legislation in 1991 and 1992 to reform the program to increase pension funding, limit guarantee growth and increase recoveries on PBGC claims in bankruptcies.' Without the reform, 'PBGC will have a crisis well before 2026.'" It was a tough election year for Bush with two opponents. Cricket worked on the campaign at the DC headquarters' executive floor, assisting a former Veterans Administration secretary.

A recession had started in July 1990. It was one of the reasons so many plans were terminated during my PBGC tenure, aggravating the poorly designed insurance program. The recession was a key reason President Bush lost in November 1992. The administration was not very upbeat as unemployment kept rising, a so-called "jobless recovery." We later learned that the recession ended in March 1991.

In total, eighteen PBGC reform bills were introduced in 1992. Nothing happened.

At a Senate Judiciary Committee hearing on July 24, 1991, the PBGC's weak claims on behalf of beneficiaries in bankruptcy was the topic. I testified: "PBGC's history is the history of large bankruptcies. Eastern, LTV, Wheeling-Pittsburgh, Kaiser Steel and Allis-Chalmers are costing us and therefore our premium payers well over $1.5 billion. It is important to understand that PBGC is now the largest creditor by far in many of the bankruptcies involving corporate sponsors of defined benefit pension plans."

Later, in one of my last PBGC speeches to the American Society of Pension Actuaries in October 1992, I said (as I could not stay away from roses): "We had hoped by now that we would be in the Rose Garden for a bill signing ceremony. . . . Apparently, the 102nd Congress took some advice from Mark Twain: 'Never put off until tomorrow what you can do the day after tomorrow.'" I kept pushing for reform legislation even after I left the PBGC, testifying to the 103rd Congress. My approach in testimony was always to try to be as informative as possible. At times that could be difficult because many members did not know the details of the program and their follow-up questions could be confusing. That meant sometimes I politely tried to answer the question the member meant to ask.

Chairman Pickle's opening statement in that February 4, 1993, hearing, which I quoted at the beginning of this chapter, began:

> We are holding these hearings because of financial instability of the PBGC and the resulting liabilities which may be borne by workers and the American taxpayers. PBGC had a deficit of $2.7 billion by the end of 1992 . . . If that is not enough cause for worry, the total level of pension underfunding for which the federal government is potentially liable has now reached the $51 billion, up from $30 billion only two years ago. . . .
>
> The question is: Will we fix it or do we bury our heads in the sand? I do not know what the Congress will do. . . . They know that in the end the federal government will be forced to stand behind these otherwise empty promises. They are not troubled that American workers who have no pensions and no health benefits may be forced to pay

higher taxes to bail out some of the largest companies in the country. They say, "Don't worry."

Those of us who care about addressing these issues are accused of "frightening the elderly and scaring the workers." I personally reject those charges. . . . I believe allowing the minority of companies to seriously underfund pension plans is bad pension policy, bad industrial policy, bad tax policy, and bad social policy. It ought to be stopped immediately.

Before my turn to testify, a retiree from a plan that had been terminated by the PBGC was asked to testify. Retirees were always tough to hear. He concluded: "I had the American dream. . . . Now I have lost my entire savings. I have lost most of my pension, and all of this affected my health."

In my remarks, I strongly supported Chairman Pickle's insightful comments, testifying:

> The financial problems in this single-employer program are a consequence of fundamental weaknesses in insurance principles supporting the program, similar to the weaknesses of the now defunct Federal Savings and Loan Insurance Corporation. The "moral hazards" of inadequate minimum funding rules, liberal guarantees, low premiums for underfunded plans, and the probability of low recoveries from employers in bankruptcies still encourage financially weak companies to underfund their pension plans. Companies in financial difficulty view pension increases as cheap compensation, and their workers agree to these empty promises because of our pension insurance.
>
> In summary, PBGC needs legislative change. . . . To echo the sentiments of PBGC's former chairman,

Secretary Lynn Martin, and numerous editorials, "The
time to act is now before another crisis occurs."

Congress did act, but almost two years later, with the signing
in December 1994 of the Retirement Protection Act. It was a
stronger "band aid" as it did increase funding requirements and
premiums and require more information for retirees and the
PBGC. Over the years, the PBGC muddled along. Other reforms
happened, with the premiums being raised from the original $1
per participant premium to $80 and up to $591 for a severely
underfunded plan.

The most recent PBGC reform was in 2006. It touched not
only the single-employer program but also the multiemployer
program. However, that multiemployer reform was too strong
to be successfully implemented. My 1992 multiemployer "rose"
became the "crisis" with a massively underwater $63.7 billion
deficit threatening the pension benefits of millions of workers.
The good news is the single-family program—due to belated
congressional reforms, a strong economy, and strong stock and
bond market—reported a small $30.9 billion surplus in 2021.

Despite no government guarantees, the recent American
Rescue Plan of 2021 bailed out the union multiemployer plans
with $86 billion in funding, producing $0.5 billion in surplus. As
no significant reforms were required, the future is problematic.

Like all Bush appointees without a term, I was out of a job on
January 20, 1993. My boss, Secretary Martin, made us political
appointees apply for unemployment benefit in front of news
media, which was somewhat embarrassing. But I soon joined
Smith Barney as a managing director in their insurance company
and private equity advisory groups. I left several years later to join
National Reinsurance as senior vice president of finance. A year
later, it was acquired. I then helped found a risk-management
advisory and software firm serving major financial institutions

with an old friend, Gene Shanks, the former president of Bankers Trust.

As I had been helping George W. Bush's campaign part-time, the next stop in my voyage was Social Security.

CHAPTER 8

Setting Sail: Social Security and Our Presidents

"To reach a port, we must sail, not tie at anchor sail, not drift."

—President Franklin Delano Roosevelt, Fireside Chat, April 14, 1938

SOCIAL SECURITY IS truly the foundation of the American dream. One my favorite spots at Social Security's Baltimore headquarters was the 65th Anniversary Garden, which had presidential quotes. The FDR opening quote is from when he signed the Social Security Act on August 14, 1935:

> We can never insure one-hundred percent of the population against one-hundred percent of the hazards and vicissitudes of life. But we have tried to frame a law which will give some measure of protection to the average citizen and to his family against the loss of a job and against poverty-ridden old age. This law, too, represents a cornerstone in a structure which is being built, but is by no means complete. . . . It is . . . a law that will take care of human needs and at the same time provide for the United States an economic structure of vastly greater soundness.

FDR was not a favorite of my family growing up, but Cricket's family had an unusual tie to him. Her mother and aunt went to Todhunter School for Girls in New York City, whose co-owner was Eleanor Roosevelt. She also taught current affairs and history there. Cricket's mother told the story of how Eleanor once caught her going down a flight of stairs that was restricted to faculty. They awkwardly tried to pass one another. As the story goes, Mrs. Roosevelt accidentally tripped Cricket's mother, causing Cricket's mother to fall down the stairs. She loved to tell the story. Despite that, she and her older sister got to do weekends in the White House during their senior years, including tea in the Rose Garden. Maybe Eleanor had some memory of the stair incident after all: Cricket's aunt got to sleep in the Lincoln Bedroom, but Cricket's mother did not.

A later FDR quote was "We shall make the most orderly progress if we look upon social security as a development toward a goal rather than a finished product. We shall make the most lasting progress if we recognize that social security can furnish only a base upon which each one of our citizens may build his individual security through his own individual efforts."[23]

A feistier FDR quote is "We put those payroll contributions there so as to give the contributors a legal, moral, and political right to collect their pensions. . . . With those taxes in there, no damn politician can ever scrap my Social Security program."[24]

President John F. Kennedy built upon FDR's change message: "The Social Security program plays an important part in providing for families, children, and older persons in times of stress. But it cannot remain static. Changes in our population, in our working habits, and their standard of living require constant revision."[25] I used the JFK quote in my speeches when I was calling for Social Security reform.

A 1977 fix lowered the over-indexed inflation benefits for those born after 1916. There was a phase-in of the lower COLA for those born between 1917 and 1921, creating "notch babies," including my father, born in 1918. Despite my many explanations of the "notch babies" to my fiscally conservative father, he always felt cheated as all those born before 1917 got higher benefits.

Financially, my father's generation did very well from Social Security. The truth is his grandchildren (and even his children) will be "cheated" if we do not fix Social Security, as their benefits will be cut.

President Ronald Reagan faced a crisis in Social Security. "Social Security hit bottom in 1982," according to a book by Paul Light.[26] The old-age trust fund had to borrow from the disability trust fund, but even then, "Social Security would run out of money on the third day of July 1983." Light's book is about "how two aging political opponents, President Ronald Reagan and House Speaker Thomas P. ('Tip') O'Neill . . . [created] a legislative miracle. . . . Without the $170 billion package of tax increases and benefit cuts [including slowly raising the retirement age], millions of checks would have been delayed." That was the sixteenth Social Security reform since its 1935 creation—and the last.

President Clinton wanted to reform Social Security and proposed personal accounts that would be known as USA (Universal Savings Accounts), but the campaign ended abruptly when scandal hit.

It was then President George W. Bush's turn for reform.

CHAPTER 9

You're Toast: Touching the Third Rail of Social Security

"For as long as I can remember, Social Security has been the third rail of American politics. Grab hold of it, and you're toast. In 2005, I did more than touch the third rail. I hugged it. I did so for one reason: it is unfair to make a generation of young people pay into a system that is going broke."

–George W. Bush, *Decision Points*, 2010

CRICKET AND I were invited to Camp David the weekend of September 11, 2004. It was during President Bush's tough reelection campaign but also the third anniversary of the 9/11 terrorist attacks. He did not campaign that weekend out of respect for the solemn anniversary. My son, JB, sometimes referred to as "Juice Junior" by the president, had been walking right by the World Trade Center when the first plane hit. Some debris hit a woman walking nearby. He helped get her to safety. He then went to his office at Lehman Brothers inside the World Financial Center. After the second plane hit, thinking his building might be next, he left to walk uptown. As he turned around, he saw the first tower fall, parts of which hit Lehman's office. To this day, he does not like to talk about it.

On the first anniversary of 9/11, we attended the memorial service at St. John's Episcopal Church across Lafayette Square from the White House with President and Laura Bush. I had to fly back and forth from an International Social Security Conference in Vancouver, Canada; but it was important to be there. The church service of "Prayer and Remembrance" was moving. President and Laura Bush and Vice President and Lynn Cheney lit candles. The final hymn was "America the Beautiful." The service was a touching remembrance of a horrendous day.

On Friday evening before the Camp David weekend, I flew home from DC to Connecticut so that Cricket and I could drive down together. In one of the most embarrassing situations in my life, we hit traffic due to an accident on Highway 81 and were late for Saturday lunch. We called ahead, and they graciously waited for us. Luckily, Bush had been biking and they did not have to wait too long.

The lunch of Tex-Mex food and banana cream pie was excellent. The guests included the newly designated secretary of state, Condoleezza Rice; Chief of Staff Andy Card; an old friend, Clay Johnson, who was Bush's first head of Presidential Personnel and then became the deputy director for management at the OMB; Clay's successor at Presidential Personnel, Dina Powell, and her husband; and the Bushes' decorator, Ken Glassman. We were excited to be invited, but Social Security was on POTUS's mind. He was campaigning again on Social Security reform.

At the start of his first term, he had established a high-powered commission, co-chaired by Richard Parsons and Senator Patrick Moynihan. The key and controversial recommendation in their December 2001 report was voluntary personal Social Security accounts, which could be invested in stocks and bonds. We had been working at supporting their recommendations, but it was tough sledding. Our efforts were not helped by my boss, Jo Anne Barnhart, with her resistance to reform, especially personal accounts. She knew President Bush was strongly pushing for reform, and though not believing in it, she had campaigned hard to get the commissioner job.

President Bush announced at the Camp David lunch that he was moving forward on Social Security reform and asked about Jo Anne. I said she was not interested in reform, as she considered herself an "operator."

Bush: "She doesn't have a longer-term vision."

Me: "No, she is more interested in disability. She thinks reform is bad politics."

Bush: "That is my job. Is she working against it [reform]?"

Me: "No, not really."

Andy Card confirmed my statement. And according to Clay Johnson, Andy had a meeting with Jo Anne after the election in December 2004 just to be sure. He told her Bush was going to push Social Security reform and wanted it to be out front. She said she would do so.

It became obvious that I was mistaken in telling the president she was not working against reform. She would not authorize the Social Security staff, who were anxious to address the reform issue, to do a public education campaign. Many of them thought it was the biggest problem the Social Security Administration (SSA) faced.

Despite our embarrassing late arrival, it was a great weekend. We had a golf cart with a license plate with my name and title and stayed at "Birch" cottage. In the afternoon, we had a hilarious chipping contest onto a putting green. The teams were Clay, Andy, and me versus Bush and Rick. Bush's dog, Barney, was the star, as he kept stopping the balls. The president kept telling Barney to only stop our team's balls, with limited success. Our team won the first match but graciously lost the second so that it ended in a tie.

Bush had told stories about Barney to a bunch of his Yale

friends during a January 2004 campaign trip to Greenwich. Apparently, Barney was territorial. He bit the tail of a bomb-sniffing German shepherd and wouldn't let go because the dog had "scented" the backyard. He also told how he acquired Barney. Christie Todd Whitman brought him to her interview for the EPA job. She offered to give Barney to Bush, but George said he had to check with Laura, who agreed to keep him. Whitman gave Barney to Bush with a surprise bill for $1,000.

"That is why she is so rich," he said to us.

In that meeting of Yale friends, the cost of Social Security reform personal accounts came up. He told the group, "Juice is in charge."

I wrote a letter to him on February 3, 2004, thanking him:

> As I mentioned, my view is that we cannot afford not to strengthen Social Security. Reform would be an excellent investment. It is only because of the funny way the US government keeps its books that makes reform look expensive [an issue, by the way, I remember fighting at PBGC during "Bush 41"]. . . . Personal account plans can replace a major portion, or in some cases, all the promised benefits at a much lower cost than the $10.5 trillion, or even the $3.5 trillion unfunded obligation of today's unreformed program. The "cost" of personal accounts, which will be spread over 20 to 30 years, produces a very high rate of return on investment because it eliminates the unfunded obligation, increases economic growth and personal savings, and creates an ownership society.

Obviously, I did not clear this letter with Barnhart; she would never have let me say it publicly.

After golf, we went off for skeet shooting while Condi and Bush watched college football (Notre Dame versus Michigan; she is a big Notre Dame fan). Luckily, I hit several clay pigeons, but Cricket and Dina missed every time. After a nice dinner, Andy wanted to go to the rec center for bowling, which we did.

Camp David is a Navy base with Navy officers, a chaplain, and stewards. Sunday morning, we walked the perimeter of the grounds with Laura as POTUS whizzed around on a mountain bike, followed by Secret Service agents on bikes and in SUVs, trying to keep up. As he sped by, he would occasionally wave, much to Laura's displeasure. Scary!

We then attended church with the Navy chaplain. It was a baptism, which was quite nice on a 9/11 weekend.

Who could have guessed in high school that the president to pray for would be our classmate George W. Bush? Andover always had required Sunday chapel, but one could go to the Episcopal church, which George and I did. Perhaps that was because there were Abbot Academy girls there?

We had a quick lunch, as the Bushes had to go to the Russian embassy to offer condolences over a school massacre in Russia. Social Security reform was still on POTUS's mind as he prepared to leave on the Marine One helicopter.

"Juice," he said, "do you think we can get Social Security reform?" Ever the optimist, I said, "Yes, Mr. President."

I believed that we could get it done; Republicans and Democrats were saying changes had to be made. President Bush came out of that weekend fighting for Social Security reform, starting Monday in a bus tour through southwest Michigan.

As the Associated Press reported, "President Bush chided Senator John Kerry and fellow Democrats on Monday for asserting that Republicans will undermine Social Security. . . . Bush said, 'You'll hear the same rhetoric you hear every campaign, believe me—"They're going to take away Social Security checks." It's the most tired, pathetic way to campaign for the presidency.'"[27]

A cartoon on September 10 in the *Akron Business Journal*

by Chip Bok had the two candidates bickering away while a giant Social Security bomb was ticking away.

Social Security reform was a key element of President Bush's "Ownership Society": "If you own something, you have a vital stake in the future of our country. The more ownership there is in America, the more vitality there is in America, and the more people have a vital stake in the future of this country."

President Bush's Ownership Society had a much more upbeat message than my *Underwater* title. His message unifies my government agency jobs. A White House fact sheet[28] that contained the above quote was released on August 9, 2004, leading up to November election, and said: "American families should have choices and [the] access they need to affordable healthcare and homeownership; Americans should have the option of managing their own retirement."

Under "Expanding Homeownership," he called for more affordable housing, down payment assistance, and financial education, as "homeownership is the cornerstone of America's vibrant communities and benefits individual families by building stability and long-term financial security."

The fact sheet pushed for strengthening Social Security and expanding ownership of retirement assets, emphasizing 401(k)s and IRAs. On Social Security it said:

> President Bush is committed to ensuring that Social Security benefits are protected for all seniors and allowing younger workers the option of investing in safe personal retirement accounts. Americans can also help secure their own future by saving . . . voluntary personal accounts for younger workers that would allow them to build a nest egg for retirement that they would own and control and could pass on to their families. The president's vision for Social Security includes a permanently strengthened

Social Security system, without changing benefits for those now in or near retirement, and without raising payroll taxes on workers.

My guarded optimism that Commissioner Barnhart would make a major effort to promote Social Security reform was based on earlier 2003 actions. President Bush received a letter dated January 23, 2003, from six Democratic members[29] of the House Ways and Means Committee. They asked for a bipartisan congressional working group, saying, "We are committed to strengthening Social Security for future generations of Americans." They also wrote, "We must take action now to solidify the program."

The letter ended with "Generic discussions of redirecting payroll taxes into individual accounts without accompanying specifics does little to inform the debate or inform the American people. It is our sincere hope that you will work with leaders from both parties to define common ground on such a critical issue. We look forward to . . . working with you on behalf of all those who rely upon Social Security as the bedrock of their economic security."

The letter was referred by the White House to Social Security for a "five-day reply." The commissioner's reply, however, was over two months late. There were several internal back-and-forths. An earlier draft by the Congressional Affairs group was nixed by the commissioner. She wrote, "NO!" I assume the offending language stated that the president believed in six principles, the last of which was "Modernization must include individually controlled, voluntary personal retirement accounts, which will augment the Social Security safety net. These principles increase retirement security by facilitating creation of wealth for all participants by transferring Social Security from a government IOU into personal property and real assets that workers will own and be able to pass along to their children."

However, she did acknowledge in the final response to the

congressmen's letter that the "just-released 2003 trustees report continue to show that Social Security is unsustainable. . . . The sooner we address the problem, the less abrupt changes will have to be." She also echoed the need for a bipartisan effort.

How wrong I was about Commissioner Barnhart surfaced only two months after my response to the president at Camp David. Her intransigence was already getting noticed by the press. On November 29, 2004, the *Washington Prowler* quoted a former White House staffer: "You have senior people in the SSA who do not want any form of private investment in the plan. They will not be working with us . . . . He [Bush] needs a few more fighters."

To be a fighter was my job, along with a few other Social Security political appointees.

Barnhart basically tried to disarm the Social Security Administration. By early 2005, she was getting pressure to pledge that Social Security would not support specific reforms, especially personal accounts. On January 24, 2005, I emailed Barry Jackson, deputy assistant to the president, that Social Security was putting out a statement to our tele-service representatives "because of a Move-On.org email that urges people to call our 800# and complain about using employees to promote reform."

Barnhart released the statement:

> There has been a lot of misinformation lately and I am glad to have this opportunity to set the record straight. I have never, nor will I ever, ask or direct Social Security employees to promote or advance any specific proposal for Social Security reform. Our job at Social Security is to provide services and benefits and to educate the American people about the programs and finances of Social Security. The role the Social Security Administration plays in educating the public, as well as the messages we are using, have not changed in the past decade.[30]

She repeated that message in a February 4, 2005, letter to Democratic leader Nancy Pelosi. Her statement, however, was not true. The Clinton administration's Social Security commissioner, Kenneth Apfel, established an "Ambassador Program" in which "all 65,000 employees were trained in basic solvency features of Social Security." For "1,500 field office managers and public affairs specialists," there were week-long training programs at the University of South Carolina.[31]

Barnhart told her team in January 2005 that only the 16 political appointees (most of whom were her old friends) out of the 65,000 employees could talk about Social Security solvency. Showing her resistance to reform, she also told her staff proudly that Senator Frist (R-TN) said that we were not doing enough on reform.

What I later learned from her two key aides was that as part of her confirmation process, Chairman Max Baucus (D-MT) of Senate Finance asked her to sign a letter not to support specific reforms. It may have been broader. I asked for a copy of the letter, but I was told that it was lost. To my knowledge, she never told the White House that she signed the letter.

The drumbeat continued. Citizens for Responsibility and Ethics in Washington pushed a *New York Times* article on February 24, 2005, titled "Democrats Criticize Social Security Official." It stated that I had appeared with four Republicans— Senator Santorum (PA), Majority Leader Tom DeLay (TX), and Representatives Rob Portman (OH) and Jim Kolbe (AZ)—at events "devised to promote personal retirement accounts."

Sen. Lautenberg (D-NJ) was quoted: "The administration is running one of the most sophisticated grassroots lobbying efforts in history, and they are using federal employees and taxpayers' money to do it."

Sen. Schumer (D-NY) added: "It is absolutely inappropriate for officials from the Social Security Administration to hit the hustings in support of the president's plan."

My response was that I was helping to "educate the American public about the need for reform in Social Security and that it should be sooner rather than later. . . . Personal accounts are one of the alternatives that definitely have to be considered. . . . We're trying to be nonpartisan about this. We're trying to lay out the facts."

On February 25, the American Federation of Government Employees (AFGE) released a press statement saying that it was "inexcusable" and "scandalous" that "Lockhart is using his position with the Social Security Administration, traveling around the country, to promote privatizing Social Security."

Barnhart gave no support to my activities. AFGE had 28,000 employees at Social Security. The irony is that she refused to meet with AFGE on work-related activities. So they had reached out to me as chief operating officer, and I met with them.

The drumbeat grew louder to try to back the SSA down from supporting the need for reform. A February 28 letter from the minority members of the House Committee on Government Affairs was titled "New Report Details the Politicization of the Social Security Administration under President Bush." The minority members claimed that changes in a SSA document to better reflect the future of Social Security were "political cover for President Bush" and "shameless politicization." The first change they cited was the "The Future of Social Security" booklet, which used to begin "Will Social Security be there for you? Absolutely," and now begins "Social Security must change."

That change did not seem shameless to me; Republican and Democratic trustees had for many years pointed to the need for change.

A January 2005 letter from seven senators[32] to Comptroller General Walker asked him to rule if the SSA was violating grassroots lobbying rules. The GAO general counsel's answer was no. He also wrote: "Federal agencies and departments have a legitimate need to communicate with the public, as well as with Congress, regarding their policies and activities. . . . This includes executive branch officials expressing their views regarding the merits or deficiencies of existing or proposed legislation, even when their objective may be to persuade the public to support the agency's position—so long as the public is not urged to contact members of Congress."

Something called MASS.live complained about my events with the four Republican members, saying the "Bush administration has put privatization at the top of his domestic agenda." Of course, personal accounts were not privatization. They were only a voluntary part of the existing and continuing Social Security program. My favorite quote was "Lockhart works for the Social Security Administration, not for the Bush administration."

Is there a fourth branch of government?

That the SSA was independent of the administration was Barnhart's view as well. She kept trying to rein me in. On a draft op-ed I wrote, mentioning the benefits of voluntary personal accounts, she wrote: "This is an ad for personal accounts— remember—educating, not proselyting."

In subsequent drafts, she would not let me say that President Bush was against tax increases. In a May 17, 2005, House Ways and Means Committee Subcommittee on Social Security, she carefully did not get into any specifics on reform.

The next day, *Pensions & Benefits Daily* reported, "Barnhart did not take an advocacy position for President Bush's proposal to let workers divert a portion of their payroll tax contributions into individual investment accounts. But she told the panel, 'The program today, absent any changes, is not risk free.'"

I wrote a note about that hearing: "[She] sat next to Larry Love [acting deputy commissioner for policy and her long-term gofer]. He was at the hearing because he is JAB's [Barnhart] good luck charm. Went to every one she has had over 20 years, except one last year when he was in Europe. He told me she brought a picture of him to that hearing."

Barnhart became more cautious over time. One of the four *S*s of our strategic plan was "SOLVENCY, To achieve sustainable SOLVENCY AND ENSURE Social Security programs meet the needs of current and future generations." By 2005, she had dropped one of the performance indicators for measuring the public's knowledge of Social Security, including long-range financing, as she was afraid the Democrats would attack her if the plan mentioned personal accounts.

She declared that we had completed a third indicator: "Provide support to the Administration and Congress in developing legislative proposals and implementing reforms to achieve sustainable solvency for Social Security." How we completed the last part I will never know.

Her six-year term was up in January 2007. Not surprisingly, the Bush administration did not nominate her for a second term. An article in *Government Executive* on March 1, 2007, entitled "Bye-Bye Barnhart," called Social Security reform President Bush's "major domestic initiative":

> He pushed for private accounts, among other changes, which failed to gain traction in Congress but certainly succeeded in igniting controversy. But Barnhart—who is no stranger to the political world, with stints in the office of Sen. William Roth, R-Del, and as minority staff director for the then-Senate Government Affairs Committee—opted out of the hullabaloo surrounding Bush's bid to overhaul Social Security.
>
> "It's an independent agency," Barnhart says. "The whole idea of creating the independent agency was to take the politics out of Social Security."

My response is how could the head of the largest government

agency not push for creating a solvent, sustainable program? Her lack of support, especially not utilizing the large, countrywide public affairs group that was greatly expanded and trained by the Clinton team, was a big detriment to reform. But even as she was taking a pass in February 2005, some reform editorials were positive, even though the events were controversial.

For instance, after town halls with Representative Portman at Xavier College and the Sharonville Community Center, the *Cincinnati Enquirer* of February 27, 2005, called for gathering more information on Social Security. On the same day, *The Washington Post* had an article entitled "An Opening on Social Security."

As for President Bush's question about achieving Social Security reform as we were leaving Camp David, I was biased. Unlike Barnhart, I was a believer in voluntary personal accounts.

During his first campaign, I was advising his policy team and did an op-ed on Sunday, October 8, 2000, in *Greenwich Time* and *Stamford Advocate*. I wrote: "Governor Bush's plan does it right. He would move both assets and liabilities to private accounts for younger workers while fully protecting the promises to the older workers and retirees. It is time to apply private sector innovation to Social Security." After I was nominated to be the deputy commissioner of Social Security on July 18, 2001, I said in an August 11 article for *Greenwich Time*: "Certainly, I'm in favor of private accounts. . . . Educating Americans about Social Security is the key to successfully revamping the system."

My confirmation hearing was on November 15, 2001, with six others. There had been a backup of nominations after 9/11. Barnhart's hearing had occurred the week before 9/11, and she was sworn in only a week before my hearing. My testimony picked up on my PBGC theme about the need for renovations. I highlighted Barnhart's "4-S" strategy: solvency, service, stewardship, and staff. I wrote on every page of my testimony a fifth *S*, "slow," as I was afraid that I would read it too quickly. With so many nominees, there were no questions about personal accounts, just the disability claims backlog and Social Security number (SSN) abuse because of 9/11 hijackers.

However, Senators Baucus (D-MT) and Rockefeller (D-WV) did send follow-up questions relating to personal accounts. Baucus asked why, as executive director of the PBGC, I promoted defined benefit plans using two of my quotes, and then concluded that defined contribution individual accounts would be a good substitute for the defined benefit Social Security.

My response was "A mix of both defined benefit and contribution plans are better than either alone. Likewise, moving to private accounts for a portion of one's Social Security benefit may give a better balance, diversification, and a chance for higher benefits. A lot will depend on how the private accounts are structured and invested. . . . I am looking forward to reading the alternatives from the president's commission and working with Congress to achieve bipartisan reforms."

The group of us were approved by the Senate Finance Committee on December 18, 2001, with the expectation of a full Senate vote before Christmas recess. It did not happen. Senator Biden (D-DE) put a hold on all nominees; after 9/11, he first wanted better security on Amtrak because he commuted from Wilmington. He was later nicknamed "Amtrak Joe."

I heard that he was releasing some holds, and as Barnhart was from Delaware, I asked her to call Biden to expedite my confirmation. She did not do it. It was an early indication that she was not happy with a "Bushie" being imposed on "her" agency.

The Senate confirmed me on January 25, 2002, but Barnhart did not allow a ceremonial swearing-in for me. In fact, I was not sworn in until March. Before I arrived, she did away with the "office of DCOSS" (deputy commissioner of Social Security) to lessen the normal powers of the deputy commissioner and staff support.

CHAPTER 10

Can We Reform Social Security?

"I am encouraged by the unprecedented level of bipartisan interest in Social Security modernization. Many comprehensive proposals have been put forward to strengthen Social Security . . . showing that if we give workers the opportunity to invest a portion of their wages in personal accounts, Social Security will be able to offer higher benefits than [might] otherwise be the case. . . . I hope that Members of Congress will join with the Social Security Administration and other interested parties in a national dialogue about how best to strengthen and protect Social Security. . . for today's and future retirees."

–Statement by President Bush on 2003 report of the Social Security trustees, March 17, 2003

BEFORE ISSUING THE above statement, the president had a meeting with the government trustees and his economic team in the Roosevelt Room in the White House. At the table on his side were Josh Bolten (OMB), Labor secretary Elaine Chao, Treasury secretary John Snow, POTUS, SSA commissioner Jo Anne Barnhart, HHS secretary Tommy Thompson, and Chief of Staff Andy Card. On the other side was Ari Fleischer (press), David Hobbs (Congressional Affairs), Karl Rove (policy), Steve

Friedman (NEC chair), Keith Hennessey (NEC), Chuck Blahous (NEC), and Scooter Libby (VP staff). I was seated in a row behind the table with three others, facing the president.

Bush looked at me and said, "Hello, Juice." Only Jo Anne Barnhart knew to whom he was talking. He then asked Jo Anne how I was doing. She said she'd agreed not to use my nickname. Bush said, "I can."

At one point he asked an unscripted question on how we could afford personal accounts given the deficit. No one answered. He had been occasionally winking at me but now looked at me directly when no one answered the question. I tentatively raised a finger. He called on "Jimmy," explaining to the group that we were old college friends. I stumbled a little but got a coherent message out. Blahous, who had been the staff head of Bush's Social Security Commission, later emailed that I answered well.

Always a naysayer, Barnhart took Bush's question to mean that he was not in favor of voluntary personal accounts. In a memo to her after she complained that I had said something positive about personal accounts, I wrote:

> Personal accounts were the keystone of his reform principles. The statement that he put out about the March meeting strongly supported personal accounts. The dialogue we had at the meeting was not against personal accounts, but how to fund them.
>
> Yes, we have been asked to educate and join a national dialogue about "how best to strengthen and protect Social Security."
>
> Hopefully, we can continue to work out a message so that we can use the media effectively. They will no doubt probe as to what SSA's position is on personal accounts. I think it would be news if we did not support the president's position.

Although I did draft a media plan as part of our detailed solvency education plan, it was not implemented. Her strategy was to avoid the media.

There was no doubt that AARP was the 900-pound gorilla when it came to retirement. They had not been supportive of PBGC reforms. Therefore, working with AARP became one of my most important goals in 2003. The White House had also begun conversations. I started at a dinner discussion with Jim Parkel, president of AARP, in February. We had also started conversations separately with John Baroody of the NAM (National Association of Manufacturers) about doing joint events with AARP and the SSA.

On March 18, AARP's CEO Bill Novelli put out a statement reacting to the 2003 trustees report and calling for reform: "Social Security and Medicare remain strong. Social Security benefits are assured until 2042. But the solvency projections are not nearly good enough. Congress and the administration should begin planning modernization and improvements now, while both Social Security and Medicare are assured stable funding. The sooner we begin the process, the more moderate and affordable the impact of those changes will be."

Working with the White House team of Jackson, Hennessey, and Blahous, we thought the statement was a reasonable start. But it was always a balancing act: a week later, AARP's board put out a more negative statement.

Throughout the spring and summer, we had discussions with John Rother and Chris Hansen of AARP. We worked hard with them and the White House to agree on a set of Social Security facts and principles, which we finally did. After much discussion, AARP agreed to have the NAM join with the two of us. The "SSA, AARP and NAM Agreement on Social Security Facts, Retirement Savings and Reform Principles" (2003) included the following section:

Approaches to Furthering Solvency

Changes must be made to move towards sustaining Social Security's solvency for future generations.

Possible options include reducing benefits or increasing revenue through such measures as increasing payroll taxes, transferring funds from general revenues and/or improving the rate of return.

The sooner action is taken, the more modest the changes and the more time people have to adjust their retirement plans.

"Improving the rate of return" was an attempt to bridge Bush's proposed personal accounts, which AARP was against, and AARP's proposal to invest trust funds directly into the market, which the administration opposed. We agreed that they would not use the word *privatization* and instead use *voluntary personal accounts*. They stuck to that agreement for a while by saying that they were against "carve-out" personal accounts but okay with "add-on" accounts. Carve-outs were from Social Security payroll taxes, while add-ons were from additional contributions like an IRA. The promise not to use the word *privatization* did not last. Privatization became their big accusation.

The three organizations also agreed on a plan for bipartisan town halls. The idea was to have a Republican and Democrat senator and/or representative participate together in a Social Security educational event "to help spark national interest on Social Security's future and set the stage for achieving a bipartisan solution."[33]

By October we were starting to go public with our plans. Hansen, Baroody, and I made a presentation to Senate Finance staff. On the twenty-eighth we met with Minnesota senators Norm Coleman (R) and Mark Dayton (D). The latter had been a Yale hockey goalie and a good friend of many of my friends. The senators agreed to a December 8, 2003, event in Minnesota, which was then postponed until January.

But AARP got cold feet, and not because they did not want to go to Minnesota in the winter. The Associated Press and the *Washington Post* came out with articles about the proposed events that made the AARP nervous.

Late in November, AARP had endorsed President Bush's Medicare Part D legislation, which was signed into law on December 8, 2003. Congressional Democrats were mad at AARP for siding with the administration. An Associated Press[34] article said that "seniors have been ripping up or burning their cards and flooding the group with complaints in what has been characterized as the largest revolt in its ranks in decades." The article also said AARP was pulling the plug on our partnership to do the forums. A quote was that AARP did not want to "be connected to groups with partisan agendas." (Unlike AARP?) I was told by Chris Hansen that "AARP can't be seen to be working with the administration" again after Medicare Part D. The next day, AARP put out a press release confirming that they had decided not to engage in these co-sponsored dialogues but would do Social Security educational events by themselves. Both Novelli and Rother did say it was unfortunate as they enjoyed working with us.

During 2003 and 2004, I continued to push Social Security reform. I testified at the Senate Aging Committee in July 2003 and May 2004. I could not resist a Navy quote in a Senate Aging Committee July 28 hearing: "The world isn't interested in the storms that you encounter, but whether or not you brought in the ship." I added, "My son's and future generations will care primarily that we have been able to attack and strengthen the Social Security program so it can remain a safe harbor for them and their children."

For the May 2004 testimony before the Senate Aging Committee, as was standard, my written testimony was cleared by the White House. I took my oral testimony from the written, but Barnhart drastically cut it, including deleting the following passages: "In Canada the trust fund has directly purchased stocks. . . . About thirty countries have established some form of personal accounts. . . . In the United States, we have a great example of an efficient simple, government-sponsored personal account system, the federal government's Thrift Saving Plan." And, of course, she deleted "As President Bush said in his State of the Union address 'younger workers should have the opportunity to build a nest egg by saving part of their Social Security taxes in their personal account.'"

In a January 2004 House Ways and Means hearing in Boca Raton, Florida, I said: "Personal accounts for younger generations could help most workers receive much higher total retirement benefits than are presently payable. The accounts, which allow more personal choice and control, would be inheritable in many of these proposals. They also raise the private savings rate. . . . Absent changes, schedule benefits under the current program would have to be reduced 27 percent by 2042."

I continued that a "counter argument is that the required 'seed' financing from general revenue that many personal account proposals require is not affordable. If we do not reform Social Security, as I have noted, $10.5 trillion in present-value dollars would be needed to enable the current program to pay schedule benefits indefinitely. By setting aside money today in personal accounts, the expected cost to the taxpayer of paying schedule benefits could be considerably reduced."

I also gave speeches throughout the country. At one in Florida in 2003 at a high-net-worth retirement facility, I made the point that no one over fifty-five years old would have their benefits changed and those voluntary personal accounts would help their children and grandchildren. An elderly woman spoke up, saying, "I wouldn't trust my son to make investments." That quote stuck with me as a sign that more financial education was needed. I did town halls with Senator Craig throughout Idaho and town halls in Texas with Representatives Sam Johnson and Pete Sessions.

One of the many speeches I gave in 2004 was to the AARP October convention. I said I was against tax increases as they have been increased nineteen times since Social Security was founded. I said: "The late Senator Daniel Patrick Moynihan, who chaired President Bush's Social Security Commission and was widely known as 'Mr. Social Security'—championed personal accounts within Social Security." The speech was politely received.

A key part of our educational efforts in talking about Social Security reform was to lay out many of the reform alternatives to show their impact on Social Security's solvency and the benefit impact on individuals. Andrew Biggs, a senior political appointee member of the Social Security policy group, built an interactive policy simulator that I used extensively in my presentations throughout the country. The younger generations loved it. The audience could choose among tax, benefits, and/or investment changes, and in several of the categories they could fill in the blanks with different amounts.

Under "Taxes" the choices were as follows:

✦ Increase payroll taxes by ___% of wages

✦ Enroll all newly hired state and local workers [in Social Security]

✦ Increase maximum taxable wages from $90,000 to $155,000 [for the younger crowd that was always a popular choice]

Under "Benefits":

✦ Gradually raise full retirement age to 70

✦ Index initial OASDI benefits to Prices Progressive Longevity [this choice took some explaining]

Under "Investments":

✦ Invest ___ % of payroll taxes (wages) in personal accounts

✦ Invest additional ___ % of wages in personal accounts (like a 401(k))

✦ Invest ___ % of Trust Fund in equities

The participants then could choose whether they expected to be a low, medium, or high earner and input their birth year. Those fifty-five and above saw no changes in their benefits. Younger ones got three outputs:

✦ Payable benefits, which meant the benefits they would receive once the trust fund was depleted

✦ Scheduled benefits are those promised under the current formula

✦ The benefits under their selections from the simulator

A typical proposal included increasing the tax maximum, progressive indexing of benefits, 1.2 percent of payroll taxes in personal accounts, and an add-on personal account of 1.6 percent. The seventy-five-year shortfall (at the time) of $4.1 trillion was reduced to $0.1 trillion, and trust fund exhaustion was pushed back from 2042 to the mid-2050s. For low-income individuals, benefits were significantly higher than payable benefits and even scheduled benefits.

My optimism about reform was renewed by a January 6, 2005, meeting with Novelli and Rother as AARP made Social Security reform their top legislative reform priority for 2005. In a follow-up letter to Novelli on January 13, referring to his recent press conference, I wrote that I liked that he was calling for "reform sooner than later"; "You also praise President Bush for putting 'Social Security reform high on his agenda' and said your 'goal, like his, is long-term solvency and fiscal soundness.'" In his book *Good Business*,[35] Novelli said for some reason AARP was surprised by Bush's push for Social Security reform. In my letter I also said that their ad calling personal accounts "gambling" was not helpful. I always thought that the gambling argument was strange since AARP, through a joint venture, sold mutual funds to the elderly.

The optimism was short lived. In response, Novelli sent me a speech which he had given. It rearranged AARP's top priority: "And so we are strongly opposed to individual accounts taken out of Social Security. Opposing this approach—if it goes forward—is our top priority in 2005." Novelli's new boss had worked at Social Security and was very against reform. In a full-page ad AARP wrote:[36]

> IF YOU have a problem with the sink, YOU DON'T tear down the entire house. Let's not turn Social Security into Social Insecurity. Yes, the program is in need of reform, which can be done with a few minor changes, but is not in need of radical overhaul. Creating private accounts to take money out of Social Security is an extreme measure that will hurt all generations and could add up to $2 trillion in more debt. Let's not stick our kids with the bill. Call your legislators.

The $2 trillion number was misleading; the goal of the proposed reform was to encourage individuals to volunteer for and fund personal accounts from payroll taxes. It would have been paid for many times over as the massive projected shortfall was reduced in a sustainable solvent system. We are now "sticking our kids with the bill."

One of AARP's "moderate changes" included investing Social Security assets in the stock market. They forgot to mention that if FICA taxes were not invested in treasury bonds and instead in other assets as AARP was proposing, they would be scored as "trillions in more debt."

I did do several events with AARP in 2005. With my congressman Chris Shays (R-CT), I did town halls in April in Connecticut. One was with the new president of AARP, Marie Smith. It was a very large crowd. Shays became intimidated and backed off Social Security reform. Cricket, who was in attendance, was enraged by his performance. Novelli wrote in his book that Smith was happy with the results.

In an event sponsored by AARP at Lake of the Woods, Virginia, in May 2005, there was a different outcome. The audience was composed of many federal retirees who were in the federal 401(k)-equivalent Thrift Savings Plan. The low-cost personal accounts were modeled on them. Much to AARP's chagrin, the audience was in favor of personal accounts.

Apropos of our long, unfruitful discussions with AARP, a cartoon[37] has W and the AARP in a rowboat labeled SOCIAL SECURITY REFORM. They each have an oar but are pulling in different directions. W says, "By the time we get anywhere, I'll be on Social Security." That was much too optimistic!

Those AARP events were part of the administration's 2005 education blitz. Treasury secretary Snow set up the Social Security Information Center to track events. From March 3 to May 1, 2005, the administration set out to do "60 Stops in 60

Days." As Secretary Snow wrote in his "60 Stops in 60 Days Recap": "Dozens [actually 31] of administration officials—from the president and vice president to assistant secretaries and assistants to the president—crisscrossed the nation to participate in 166 events in 40 states." In total we did sixty-one town halls with thirty members of Congress.

The town halls were mainly with Republicans, but I did two with Democrats. My favorite, which was built on the scrapped AARP model, was an AFL-CIO Social Security town hall in Michigan with Representatives John Dingell (D) and Joe Schwartz (R). Behind Congressman Dingell was a picture of FDR signing the Social Security Act with Dingell's father looking on. Dingell called private accounts "dangerous," and Schwartz said they were like a "Christmas tree ornament" as they were not the main part of reform.[38]

March 24, 2005, was Radio Day, the day after the trustees' annual report. There were 199 interviews covering all fifty states. As the one who did the most interviews, I reported: "My virtual trip covered 23 local radio stations from Maine to Hawaii and Minnesota to Mississippi as well as nationally broadcast Bloomberg news. In total, I spoke with stations in 22 states—all without leaving the office. Tele-travel does have the advantages, but nothing compares to good old-fashioned town halls that allow me to address the concerns and questions of citizens face-to-face. So, tomorrow I am off to snowy Billings, Montana for a listening session hosted by Senator Burns and Representative Ryberg."

Of course, there are always critics. Chairman Henry Waxman (D-CA) of the House Committee on Oversight and Government Reform asked the GAO to do a review of the administration's Social Security reform events and their costs, covering the first six months of 2005. For some reason the GAO's reply letter was not sent until August 10, 2007.

The GAO reported 228 events, of which Social Security did

the most with 73; Barnhart did a token 4; my senior advisor, Mike Korbey, did a yeoman's job with 20; and I did 47, by far more than any other participant. I kept up with the speeches, editorial boards, and radio interviews right until I left Social Security in May 2006.

In a handwritten note for a 2005 speech, I wrote:

> Over the last months I have been traveling around the country visiting Social Security offices [over 100 offices] and have been helping to educate the American people about the serious problems it faces for future generations. Oftentimes the audiences quickly hone [sic] in on investments, but I believe in what Ben Franklin said, "The best investment is an investment in knowledge." More and more I hear the elderly, the young and the middle aged and Republicans, Democrats and Independents agree that the problem is serious and growing every day. Yes, there is controversy about how to fix it, but that is healthy.
>
> There is one reaction that continues to perplex me. The very vocal group of generally elderly people oppose reforms. . . . Some appear to have very similar talking points. Some have suggested that they were sent into the town halls by AARP or some other group. But I know . . . that the president's and most members of Congress cardinal principle is the promise that benefits of retirees and those age 55 are safe and secure. I remember one of my first conversations with now retired President of AARP, Parkel, that we agreed in our educating efforts it was, especially important, not to scare the elderly.

At an October 4, 2005, Rose Garden press conference announcing a Supreme Court justice nomination, President Bush admitted, "I've advocated the need for people to come together to address the Social Security issue. . . . There seems to be a diminished appetite in the short term, but I'm going to remind people that there is a long-term issue that we must solve, not only for the sake of the budget, but, more importantly, for the sake of younger workers."

AARP's anti–personal account message overwhelmed their supposed strategy of "moderate changes," as I told Novelli in a January 2006 meeting.

A Millard Fillmore cartoon summed up the AARP approach.[39] A little girl is in bed screaming, "MOMMY!! There's an AARP ad under my bed!!" Then from under the bed, the balloon reads, "Big Bad Social Security Reform is gonna eat you UP!!!" Too often in Washington people say that they are in favor of reform, but then they dig in too deeply to reach compromises for the necessary reforms. The result is ever-increasing problems. We keep kicking the can down the road to the next generation. Both sides push too hard. The "third rail" continues to be untouchable. Politicians are afraid to do President Kennedy's "constant revision."

In 2004, the projected trust fund exhaustion date when benefits were going to be cut was in 2042—thirty-eight years away. Eighteen years later, the 2022 trustees' forecast is for exhaustion in 2034, so we are only twelve years away from when benefits will be reduced by 25 percent. The old assumptions turned out to be too optimistic. Obviously, over a seventy-five-year forecast, small changes do make a difference, but as the exhaustion date gets nearer and nearer, the needed changes become much larger.

Terms like *insolvent* and *bankrupt* were thrown out often about Social Security and are still used by advocates for reform. Some people say that may be going too far, but the Social Security program is definitely underwater. Since 2010, costs have exceeded income. In 2021, total costs were $1.145 billion, while total income was $1.088 billion. For the first time, the SSA had to redeem

Treasury bonds in the trust fund to cover the shortfall.

Looking back in the PowerPoint I used in 2004, I presented a graph that used two present-value numbers—the shortfall over the seventy-five-year forecast, which was $3.5 trillion, and the shortfall over the infinite horizon (forever) of $10.5 trillion. The deterioration since then has been massive. The forecast in the 2022 trustees' report is that the seventy-five-year present-value forecast shortfall is $20.4 trillion. The infinite horizon present-value shortfall is $61.8 trillion. Both are six times the 2004 shortfall. I used to say a stitch in time could save nine. It turns out it could save tens of trillions.

The 2021 trustees report was over four months late and buried in late August, and the 2022 one was several months late. There was no sense of urgency from the Biden trustees (secretaries of treasury, HHS, and labor, and the acting Social Security commissioner). That is not surprising as the two public trustee positions have been vacant for over seven years. I was nominated in 2018 and again in 2019 to be the Republican trustee, but the Republican-controlled Senate was not happy with Trump's Democratic nominee. Nothing happened.

The 2022 trustees repeated the phrase that has appeared for many decades: "The Trustees recommend that lawmakers address the projected trust fund shortfalls in a timely manner." That phrase has become mere lip service.

Social Security should not be a third rail. There are trade-offs that can and should be made. We need to protect the lower-income retirees while doing better for all participants whose benefits will be forcefully reduced when the trust fund is depleted. We used to say benefit cuts would not hit the baby boomers, but now it will hit even the oldest boomers like myself and former presidents Clinton, Bush, and Trump. Some say Social Security solvency was a mathematical exercise. Yes, there is math, but Social Security is all about people, as it touches almost all Americans.

In 2014, I agreed to co-chair with former senator Kent Conrad (D-ND), who was a great partner, a nineteen-member Bipartisan Policy Center Commission on Retirement Security and Personal Savings, split between Democrats and Republicans. It included policy experts, politicians, and corporate and pension leaders. As we progressed over two and a half years, a consensus arose around using a 50/50 tax and benefit constraint to create a solvent Social Security. It was too late and controversial to do anything on the investment side.

As we wrote,[40] "The good news is that shoring up Social Security is feasible. But taking the needed actions requires political leadership—and sooner rather than later. The cost of fixing the program grows as corrective action is delayed. A package of reforms that balances changes to scheduled benefits, which cannot be funded by current dedicated taxes, with changes to revenues would renew the promise of Social Security and reassure Americans that the program will remain strong for decades to come."

The report contained many other proposals on increasing savings and 401(k)s, some of which have been passed by Congress (SECURE Act of 2019), and proposals on financial literacy and accessing housing wealth in retirement. There were thirteen specific and balanced Social Security recommendations. On the benefit side, the recommendations created a basic minimum benefit for the lower-earning beneficiaries and increased survivors' benefits. For the better off, they slowed down the growth of benefits by making the system more progressive, slowly raised the retirement age, and used a more accurate inflation rate for benefit increases.

On the tax side, the recommendations included gradually increasing the maximum taxable earnings level, increasing the payroll tax by 1 percent over a ten-year period (0.1 percent per year, half paid by employees and half by employers), and increasing the income tax on Social Security benefits for the highest-income beneficiaries.

The Social Security chief actuary, Steve Goss, scored the package of recommendations as "sustainable solvent system," which means Social Security would be solvent through the seventy-five-year period and beyond. The report was well received by the think-tank world, and we had a hearing at the Senate Aging Committee. Still, too many administrations and members of Congress are afraid to touch the third rail.

My question to them is how can they ignore Social Security reform? As the trustees wrote, Social Security played "a critical role in the lives of 66 million beneficiaries and 182 million workers and their families during 2022."

CHAPTER 11

Managing Government Programs for Better Results

"We are not here to mark time, but to make progress to achieve results and to leave a record of excellence."

–President George W. Bush, October 15, 2001

TOO OFTEN POLITICAL appointees are much more interested in policy, politics, and media than in managing their agencies. Policy and remedial legislation are very important, but results also depend on strong management. Unfortunately, often management is not at the top of the list for political appointees. That is exacerbated by poorly designed programs and revolving top leadership.

Realizing the need for better government management, in 2001 the Bush administration established the President's Management Agenda (PMA) and the President's Management Council (PMC), of which I became an executive committee member. A presidential memo from July 11, 2001, entitled "Implementing Government Reform" laid out three objectives:

✦   Citizen-centered—not bureaucracy centered;

✦   Results-oriented—not process oriented; and

✦   Market-based—actively promoting, not stifling innovation
    and competition.

The memo required the departments and agencies to
establish chief operating officers (COO). They were expected to
be deputy secretaries or their agency equivalents. Their duties
included implementing the president's and agencies' missions
and goals; "assisting agency heads in promoting government
reform, developing strategic plans and measuring results";
overall organizational management to improve performance; and
overseeing the five areas of the President's Management Agenda:

✦   Budget and Performance Integration

✦   E-Government

✦   Financial Performance

✦   Competitive Sourcing

✦   Human Capital

When I arrived, Barnhart's plan was to not designate a
COO. She had not wanted a deputy commissioner, according
to her chief of staff, as she'd had trouble with her deputy in her
last government job as HHS's assistant secretary for children
and families. She had done away with the office of the deputy
commissioner of Social Security, thereby in her mind removing
any power from me. Her job description for the deputy
commissioner was to be her "alter ego," which I guess meant to
only do what she told me to do. With White House pressure, she
did designate me COO.

Social Security has a confusing titling structure, starting

with the fact that it is not a commission, and then most of the department heads were also called deputy commissioners. As the only Senate-confirmed deputy and with the rank of a cabinet deputy secretary, my predecessors and successors added the word *principal* before *deputy commissioner*. She would not allow that.

Barnhart's efforts to demean the deputy commissioner's job was a recurring theme. In July 2003, an Atlanta human resource lawsuit requested to depose me. The SSA's reply was that I did not have to because I did not "have managerial responsibility over any of the various components of the Agency." (That is rather strange for a COO and not true.)

The SSA did have management challenges, as I pointed out in a January 2005 presentation to the National Academy of Public Administration (NAPA), entitled "Getting to Green." I cited in 2004 that the SSA serviced 111 million Americans:

✦   65,000 employees plus 15,000 state employees (making initial disability determinations)

✦   1,500 field offices

✦   36 teleservices centers

✦   28 international offices

The management challenges I mentioned included targeted 2 percent annual productivity growth; large backlogs, especially in the paper intensive disability process; protecting Social Security numbers from identity theft; large erroneous payments; pending baby boomer workloads; Medicare Part D implementation; and solvency education and reform.

One would have thought that with all those challenges, Barnhart would welcome experienced help, but she did not from me. She distrusted anyone she had not known for years. After several tries and postponed meetings, in the fall of 2002 we agreed on the list of "DCOSS Areas of Interest" which I had given to her. It included the President's Management Agenda; solvency; direct reports to me of policy, chief information officer, and strategy (not "Stratergy," as the sign read on Bush's Camp David desk); involvement with finance; and a whole series of key outside relationships and management challenges.

Over time she slowly ignored this agreement and sometimes me. By April 2004, after she had postponed several meetings with me, I wrote her a note enclosing the list: "Despite the successes over the last two years, my role seems to be diminishing. There are restrictions on who I can contact . . . [and] the continuing problem of not getting invited to meetings and lack of any clear authority, had diminished my effectiveness . . . [and] Social Security's effectiveness."

I also wrote: "An important part of my duties should be to ensure that you get more complete and timely information to make informed decisions on solvency and stewardship issues. As an example, the recent SSN [Social Security number] replacement card meeting that highlighted the $26 cost for charging for a replacement card would have been much more useful if they had looked at a more efficient mechanism for charging, as I had requested."

Replacement cards were a major workload (many thousands of man years) and clogged up field offices even though cards are not supposed to be used for identity purposes. To cut down on requests, charging for replacement was put forward. The problem was that she and the deputy commissioner of finance refused to have credit card machines in the offices, and cash would have been a nightmare. Along the same lines, she was against pushing recipients to get their monthly payments by direct deposit. I worked with the Treasury and the Fed on implementing a direct deposit initiative, but she refused to have the SSA join in the marketing campaign.

I concluded my note hopefully: "Both of us are here to make a difference. SSA has had some great results in many areas over the last two and a half years. However, there is still a strong *status quo* element at SSA. With your leadership and support of my role, I believe that over the next two and half years we can fundamentally improve Social Security for future generations."

One of those early successes was Supplemental Security Income (SSI). Since 1997 it had been on the GAO's high-risk list of government programs. With our earlier successes of getting the PBGC off the list, I thought it was worth a try. But I kept being told it was too complicated: SSI had medical, earnings, work, and income tests that needed to be monitored. As I had known the GAO's comptroller general, David Walker, since the Bush 41 days, I arranged a meeting with him, Barnhart, and myself. She was wary of the GAO and other government organizations such as the OMB.

At the meeting we committed to put together a corrective action plan (CAP). Seven million people received SSI benefits with the average payment being less than $400 a month. We pulled together an interdisciplinary task force that met regularly. As my senior advisor, Korbey, told me, it was a novel experience for some participants. The twenty-eight-page SSI CAP was published in June 2002. It included a "root cause" analysis, a long list of action items and projected dates, and a monthly performance indicators report. On the strength of the CAP, we got off the high-risk list in January 2003 but kept up the intense regular meetings to monitor and report on progress.

The PMA was another major success for the SSA. The agencies were graded green, yellow, and red on two categories, status and progress, hence the title of my NAPA speech, "Getting to Green." The very rigorous goal setting and reporting of "results" were implemented by the OMB deputy director for management, Clay Johnson. He is a no-nonsense, tell-it-like-it-is guy, even to old friends. In *Decision Points*, Bush describes a 2006 meeting with Johnson telling him that the White House organization chart was "a tangled mess, with lines of authority crossing and blurred." And according to several people, the structure "started with cluster and ended with four more letters."

Johnson's team were tough graders, but the SSA did well. We started out with three yellows in status (human capital, financial management, and e-government) and two reds, in competitive sourcing and budget/performance integration. The SSA team was against competitive sourcing, which was outsourcing government functions to the private sector if they could do it better and cheaper. By 2003, financial management's status had been upgraded to green, and we were all green in progress.

Johnson had a PMC meeting with Bush on August 9, 2004. Given our PMA results, I was one of the five at the head table. Quietly Bush said, "Hi, Juice." He may have had other things on his mind given the coming election, but he made a strong statement about the importance of management, concluding by saying that was why we were there. He did call Johnson "brilliant." Johnson mentioned in his presentation to Bush the SSA's PMA successes and his coming to our Baltimore headquarters for our "Getting to Green" ceremonies. Everybody at SSA loved those events.

By the end of the first quarter of 2005, we were green in all but competitive sourcing, which was yellow as the SSA expressed "significant concerns in using [independent] contractors in their secure facilities." The SSA has Social Security numbers (SSN) and wage information, which are very confidential, but sometimes our paranoia went too far. For instance, the commissioner decided not to have a second backup data center in Detroit because there were too many Middle Eastern people there.

The SSA's successes also included the CEAR (Certificate of Excellence in Accountability Report) award for our annual performance and accountability report from the Association of

Government Accounts. The SSA has received the award many years in a row. I might add proudly that the Federal Housing Finance Agency has gotten the CEAR award every year since the FHFA was created in 2008.

There were other presidential priorities, which I took the lead on and testified to Congress about. Barnhart was happy for me to do the messy ones. These priorities included SSN protection and identity theft, immigration, working with the Homeland Security Department on the system to verify legal workers (E-Verify), and improper payments. I represented the agency on the "Save for the Future" campaign, financial literacy, the Hurricane Katrina task force, and Ending Homelessness groups. I also worked with the White House team on Medicare Part D (drug) legislation and its implementation.

Barnhart's passion was not solvency, but she did love to have her picture taken with long lines of employees and later sign the pictures. Funnily, I don't have one. Her true passion was disability reform, which she thought was going to take Democratic support. She did not want to offend them by pushing solvency reform.

Disability was put on the GAO's high-risk list when SSI was taken off. Disability is a very important but tough program. To qualify for Social Security disability, one must be unable to work for mental or physical reasons for at least twelve months. A key problem is when the economy downturns and unemployment rises, disability applications soar, often encouraged by lawyers who specialize in disability. The qualification process is complex and very time consuming—sometimes taking several years. Then, once one goes on disability, it is very hard to get the recipients off, even if their health has recovered and they could get a job.

Given my SSI experience, I spent time learning the disability process, meeting with state disability determination offices, field offices, processing centers, hearing offices, and administrative law judges. I even went to the Kansas City salt caves where some of the disability files were kept. One case had files that were over five feet long. Barnhart did not want my help. After watching disability processing team members toggle back and forward on one monitor through the electronic records, I recommended dual computer screens. Her answer was no. After prodding from the SSA's regional directors, she reluctantly agreed.

Barnhart set up a task force to work on disability reform, excluding me. She brought in experienced managers from the field, including one who happened to be Bush's chief of staff's cousin. Barnhart hired Booz Allen Hamilton to do a study, and they in turn hired her partner in her old consulting firm. Despite my prodding, she never produced a disability corrective action plan, which had been the key to getting SSI off the high-risk list. The task force did produce a flowchart that was well over fifteen feet long, which she proudly displayed at congressional hearings. As I said, disability was extremely complex, and to this day it still needs reform.

As deputy commissioner, I was the secretary of the Social Security Board of Trustees. I was very involved in the trustees' annual report, a seventy-five-year forecast run by Social Security's actuaries. The report is reliant on many economic and demographic assumptions. Steve Goss, Social Security's longtime and strong-willed chief actuary, and Barnhart were resistant to changes, but over the years of working with the public trustees and staff of other government trustees, we were able to make some significant changes, including dampening some of the too-optimistic assumptions.

One chart that bothered me showed three lines of potential trust-fund-exhaustion/benefit-reduction dates. There was the base case projection date, a pessimistic one showing exhaustion several years earlier, and an optimistic one that showed no problems. The latter was built on a whole set of internally inconsistent assumptions. We forced a stochastic (probabilistic) analysis, which showed that even at the ninety-ninth percentile level, there was an exhaustion date. With the Treasury's pushing, we also put in the infinite horizon measure.

As agreed, the policy group reported to me. Its acting head when I arrived was Paul Van de Water. In the small-world department, he was in my Summit, New Jersey, Cub Scout den of which my mother was the den mother. We hired two excellent PhD economists: Andrew Biggs, who had worked on the 2001 Social Security Commission and was later involved in Bush's solvency events, and Ed DeMarco from the Treasury, who later became my deputy at OFHEO/FHFA.

We also hired a new deputy commissioner of policy, Paul Hewitt. Barnhart took that opportunity to try to get me out of the policy loop. She told Hewitt that he reported to her and not me. He rudely refused to meet with me; he scheduled meetings with outsiders, whom I knew, without telling me; and he complained if I brought a policy person to a meeting. He tried to reorganize, with Barnhart's approval, the policy shop to drastically cut back Biggs's solvency team.

Paul Hewitt did work on Jo Anne's reform plan, which involved add-on accounts funded by the government for those under forty years old. It went nowhere. I warned Barnhart that Paul was freelancing, but she refused to rein him in.

In mid-2004 he put together his proposed reform, called early retirement accounts. His idea was to raise the early retirement age from sixty-two to sixty-eight and the normal retirement age to seventy-two. Add-on early retirement accounts would fund the period until one was eligible to retire. As I told Barnhart, the plan could be perceived as anti–lower income and Black people, who tended to live shorter lives and therefore would have less time on Social Security. Somehow, what her chief of staff called her "paranoia" did not kick in.

Paul gave an unauthorized interview to a friend, which was

published in *Fortune* magazine in October 2004, just a couple of weeks before the election. Kerry's vice presidential candidate, John Edwards, picked up on Hewitt's plan quickly. An Associated Press[41] article of October 23 titled "Edwards Vows Not to Touch Retirement Age" quoted him asking during a rally, "How many factory and mill workers[,] . . . nurses, elementary school teachers, taxicab drivers would now have to work more?" The article went on to say, "Although Bush was not named in the [*Fortune*] report, Edwards pinned the news on the president and claimed Bush is hiding the truth of what would happen in his second term." Edwards was quoted as saying, "There's one person we all wouldn't mind sending into early retirement, and his name is George W. Bush." Bush rightly denied that it was his plan.

Hewitt was fired the week after the election. I expected Paul Van de Water to be named acting again. Although we did not always agree on policy, he was very steady, extremely knowledgeable, and reliable. Without consulting me, Barnhart named her counselor and "good luck charm," Larry Love, to be the acting deputy commissioner of policy. He admitted that he knew nothing about Social Security solvency. Paul Van de Water retired several months later.

Barnhart had a pattern of driving away good people loyal to me. At one point she even took away my secretary, which forced my speech writer to do that work. Barnhart denied and then delayed a bonus for my driver, Jimmie Brand, who was very loyal to me. Afraid he would be mistreated or fired after I left, I had him transferred to OFHEO with me. He was due a bonus before he left. I agreed to have OFHEO reimburse the SSA for the bonus payment he was due, but Jimmie never got his bonus. She was not penny-pinching on her two drivers. Somehow her math was two drivers were cheaper than the occasional overtime for Jimmie.

One of my early assignments was to be Social Security's representative to the International Social Security Association

(ISSA) in Geneva, Switzerland. As the SSA had the world's largest system by far and the ISSA's secretary-general was an American, we had an important role to play. The ISSA was working on a big initiative on adequacy of benefits, migrant workers, and health insurance. In early meetings, it became clear that they did not have the resources to undertake such an ambitious initiative, which I pointed out. Larry Dye replaced me in a subsequent meeting, but being a good-government type, I followed up on what happened at that meeting. In a March 2003 letter to the ISSA's secretary-general, I expressed the concern that the assumed funding of the initiative was based on uncollectible receivables, which should have been written off.

Writing about the upcoming ISSA triennial meeting in China, I ended the letter, "We need to get this behind us soon to set the stage for Beijing. I recently heard from the US ambassador, who is an old friend and is looking forward to our visit." Barnhart took me off the ISSA team. She and her friends went to China and the other international meetings without me.

A key aspect of management is managing upward. Certainly, with my early Navy training, I very much respected the chain of command. I tried, but it was tough as she was so against a Bush interloper in "her independent" agency. My relationships above her were very good, including the OMB, NEC, Treasury, and the president. To her that was a black mark. She was not a proponent of Bush's vision of a leader as "someone who brings people together."

We had a very tough relationship given her "paranoia" and unwillingness to listen to new ideas. She tended to work from ten to four and took off many Fridays, complaining of a bad back. Her chief of staff told me that she often ranted about me and that she was a micromanager who could not delegate.

It became clear early on that she was not a Bush team player, as she not only was against Social Security reform but also pushed back on the PMA and other Bush agenda items, which she did not think were good politics. Presidential Personnel team and Johnson, who had selected her when he was running Presidential Personnel, became concerned. However, she had a six-year term and could only be fired for cause (malfeasance or neglect of duty), which could be very messy. That does encourage one to feel entitled.

I was told she was asked to resign in January 2005. In April 2005, after she had a lunch with Chief of Staff Card, Clay Johnson told me that Card said we could not fire her. Johnson said yes, we can. Nothing happened.

At the annual 2005 Christmas friends and family White House dinner, President Bush asked me if "we had pulled the plug" on her. I said no. Card did meet twice with her later in December. I gave him a list of issues. He told me that the meeting did not go well and that we could not remove her for malfeasance. It is a tough test, but I thought a case could be made for cause. However, by that time Social Security reform was dormant and Presidential Personnel was offering me other jobs.

As this chapter is about better government management, I will end it on a more positive note by citing my "Top Ten Results Lessons" about government management from my 2005 NAPA presentation:

1. Provide senior management leadership, commitment, and involvement.

2. Develop a sense of urgency.

3. Encourage open communications.

4. Enable and train committed managers and teams.

5. Promote openness to change and improvement.

6. Identify, illuminate, and fund priorities in an integrated, long-term plan.

7. Set ambitious but reachable goals.

8. Assign responsibilities and deadlines.

9. Track performance regularly.

10. Recognize performance.

CHAPTER 12

Fannie and Freddie—Systemic Risk?

"Just the belief of investors in the implicit government backing up the GSEs does not by itself create problems of safety and soundness for the GSEs, but it does create systemic risk for the US financial system as the GSEs become very large."

—Fed chairman Alan Greenspan speech on government-sponsored enterprises to the Conference on Housing, Mortgage Finance, and the Macroeconomy, Federal Reserve Bank of Atlanta, May 19, 2005

THE IMPLICIT GUARANTEE Greenspan cited in the above speech meant that Fannie Mae and Freddie Mac could become off-the-books government insurance companies, potentially leading to systemic risk for the US economy. They had serious safety and soundness problems because of their flawed regulatory structure. Greenspan and many others referred to Fannie and Freddie as GSEs. OFHEO preferred to call them enterprises to differentiate them from other government-sponsored enterprises.

OFHEO was established in 1992 with the mission "to promote housing and a strong national housing finance system by ensuring the safety and soundness of Fannie Mae and Freddie Mac." The enterprises were congressionally chartered, publicly owned companies listed on the New York Stock Exchange, and "were created to provide a secondary mortgage market to support affordable housing and to provide stability and liquidity to the secondary mortgage market."[42]

The enterprises are monoline (only mortgages) financial guarantee companies with very large portfolios composed primarily of mortgages and mortgage-backed securities (MBS). Fannie Mae (Federal National Mortgage Association) was founded in 1938 as a government agency. It was "privatized" in 1968 to get its debt off the US balance sheet. Freddie Mac (Federal Home Loan Mortgage Corporation) was founded in 1970 by the government and originally owned by the Federal Home Loan Banks, which are also GSEs, to act as a Fannie Mae competitor.

The enterprises buy single-family mortgages up to the "conforming loan limit" ($417,000 in 2006) and multifamily mortgages from banks and other mortgage originators. In their major business, they package these mortgages into MBS backed by their guarantees. The mortgages are serviced by the originator or specialized mortgage servicers, which collect monthly payments, issue reports, usually hold escrows for tax and insurance premiums, and forward these payments on. If the mortgage is troubled, the servicer works with the buyers to modify the mortgage. If unsuccessful, they foreclose. If a mortgage has a higher than 80 percent loan-to-value, the loans are required to have mortgage insurance, provided by specialized mortgage insurance companies.

In February 2003, OFHEO produced a study for Congress entitled "Systemic Risk: Fannie Mae, Freddie Mac and the Role of OFHEO." The paper defines systemic risk as the possibility that a systemic event will occur that creates "a financial crisis that causes a substantial reduction in aggregate economic activity."

The paper envisions some possible scenarios for Fannie and Freddie. In the worst scenario, one enterprise's large losses cause a "contagious illiquidity" throughout the US and global markets.

Prophetically, it says, "If the government does not prevent a financial crisis, the potential decline in aggregate economic activity may be very large." Definitely underwater and sinking.

The report calls for some legislative changes to prevent the systemic event, but the message is muted by a statement in the first paragraph, which says, "The risk of either company causing a systemic disruption is highly unlikely under the comprehensive safety and soundness regulation of the Office of Federal Housing Enterprise Oversight (OFHEO)." That statement was much too optimistic, which I found out when I was parachuted into OFHEO as the acting director in late April 2006.

As Social Security reform efforts ran aground, in the summer of 2005 the White House pushed me to run OFHEO. Cricket was encouraging me to come home, but I like challenges. I was living during the week in an apartment on Capitol Hill, my "hovel on the hill." I would fly home most weekends. As the government did not pay for the flights, it meant I was always searching for the cheapest one—LaGuardia, White Plains, JFK, and Islip. By her count, Cricket made over 700 trips to airports, dropping me off early Monday and picking me up late Friday.

Before I took OFHEO job, I had been reading for several months about Fannie and Freddie, their risks, and the regulator's weak, statutorily constrained powers. The PBGC was good training. I talked with and read many articles by Peter Wallison of the American Enterprise Institute (AEI). He also called them systemic risks.

In Greenspan's speech quoted above, he said GSE systemic risk "can be effectively handled by limiting their investment portfolios." He also said that "the GSEs need a regulator with authority on par with that of banking regulators, with a free hand to set appropriate capital standards, with a clear and credible process sanctioned by Congress for placing a GSE in receivership." The implicit guarantee allowed them to borrow cheaply and thereby create outsize profits on their portfolio investments. As the GSEs' capital requirements were so low, that was an easy way to increase their shareholder returns for their shareholders. Greenspan said that as a result, their return on equity was 30 percent versus 15 percent for banks. Reflecting the common wisdom at the time, he continued, "Mortgage securitizations, unlike the GSE portfolio holdings, does not create substantial systemic risk." He added, "Huge, highly leveraged GSEs subject to significant interest-rate risk are not conducive to the long-term financial stability that a nation of homeowners requires."

Their large portfolios invest in their own MBS, the other enterprises' MBS, whole loans (including serious delinquent loans bought out of their guaranteed MBS), and most problematically, private-label mortgage-backed securities (PLS). The PLS were issued by banks with no guarantees but were divided up into credit buckets called tranches. The enterprises were only buying the highest-rated AAA tranches.

OFHEO was an independent agency within the Department of Housing and Urban Development (HUD). One of the many regulatory problems was that OFHEO was the safety and soundness regulator, but HUD was the mission regulator. That meant HUD could specify what types of mortgages Fannie and Freddie could buy. It also imposed affordable housing goals on the enterprises, pushing the goals ever higher and thereby increasing their risks. By 2008 the low/moderate housing goal was 56 percent of all mortgages they purchased. OFHEO was not involved in setting the affordable housing goals.

The capital charge by law was only forty-five basis points (less than half a percent) for their guaranteed MBS. The portfolios had a capital requirement of 2.5 percent. Their MBS were off-balance sheet even though they were fully guaranteed by the enterprises. The FASB later changed the accounting to require the MBS to be on the balance sheet. The accounting treatment did tend to confuse. For instance, a report by Freddie Mac on systemic risk prepared for OFHEO, which ignored their guaranteed MBS, showed a 4.46 percent capital level at year-end 2005, based on $806 billion in assets. A more accurate measure would have included their guaranteed MBS of $974 billion, giving a 2 percent capital ratio. That ratio was well less than half of any of the big banks at the time. Despite that, Freddie Mac wrote in their 2005 annual report, "To put it simply, Freddie Mac's financial strength is beyond question." Fannie was the older and bigger sibling with year-end 2005 assets of $850 billion and $1.57 trillion in net MBS outstanding, giving a ratio of 1.6 percent.

As Mark Calabria, who was a Senate staffer during this period and the director of the FHFA from 2019 to 2021, said in a September 2013 Cato speech, "Fannie and Freddie had the very unusual capital determined by statute rather than regulation, as is the case with the federal depositories." He also noted that the 1992 act that established those rules included risk-based capital standards, which "were even lower and never a binding constraint." As he said in retrospect five years after the crisis, "Both Fannie and Freddie were guaranteed to fail due to extremely high levels of leverage which Congress believed that they should operate."

Systemic risk and regulatory reform were key issues, but the immediate issue when I was parachuted in was a pending report on Fannie Mae's accounting scandal and negotiating a settlement agreement. The investigation of Fannie Mae was prompted by the January 2003 disclosure by Freddie Mac that they were going to have to restate their 2002, 2001, and possibly 2000 earnings. The errors were found because Freddie had to change auditors when their original one, Arthur Andersen, failed because of the Enron scandal.

A law firm, Baker Botts, was hired to review the situation and concluded there been numerous accounting violations to smooth earnings. In layman's terms, "Steady Freddie" was using "cookie jar" accounting to show growing, nonvolatile earnings that Wall Street loved. In December 2003, OFHEO entered into a consent agreement with Freddie Mac that included a $125 million fine and required a 30 percent increase in their capital requirements. That meant that the forty-five basis points for MBS became sixty basis points and 2.5 percent for the portfolios became 3.25 percent.

It became clear to OFHEO that Fannie Mae was manipulating earnings as well. On July 2003, OFHEO director Armando Falcon testified to the Senate Banking, Housing and Urban Affairs Committee that OFHEO was going to conduct a special examination. Leading up to the final report, there were interim reports. Fannie Mae agreed in September 2004 to a 30 percent capital surcharge, significant organizational and accounting changes, and separation of the CEO and chairman position. Late in 2004, the SEC required Fannie to restate earnings.

OFHEO draft report was well over 300 pages. It was startling even though I had seen many troubled and mismanaged companies in my career. Gulf Oil had made payments to politicians. The report on those payments helped lead to the passage of the Foreign Corrupt Practices Act. Shortly before I arrived at Alexander & Alexander, they had acquired a large UK insurance broker, which resulted in an UK Serious Fraud Office case and potential criminal charges for inadequate disclosure. We had a former SEC chairman, Rod Hills, on our board who helped settle the case successfully. Many of the PBGC's problem companies had been mismanaged.

As a Senate-confirmed person, I could be named acting director immediately, but I kept my Social Security position for another month. I gave a scheduled Social Security speech in May, showing my two government Blackberry phones as proof I had two jobs. The commissioner was not sad to see me go.

OFHEO was another tricky personnel situation. Falcon had left in May 2005, and his deputy, Stephen Blumenthal, became acting director. The general counsel, Alfred Pollard, became the acting deputy director. As general counsel, Pollard turned out to be very helpful. Blumenthal had a real hatred of Fannie Mae's executive team and some members of Congress and their staff who had supported Fannie. It may have been justified, but we agreed in July that it was best for him to leave OFHEO.

The White House wanted him replaced as acting because he had given a speech in Hong Kong in which he endorsed the House's 2005 GSE reform legislation, which the administration had opposed as being too weak. The Senate Banking Committee passed a stronger bill that would shrink the GSEs' portfolios.

In a January 2006 letter to Senator John Sununu (R-NH), Greenspan wrote that the Senate bill "provides this much needed anchor [portfolio limits]," but the House bill "neither takes the steps needed to create an effective GSE regulator nor addresses the systemic risks posed by Fannie's and Freddie's investment portfolios."

I read the draft special examination report and set up daily meetings with the staff. The report needed editing. Blumenthal also gave me a first draft of the GIR (government and industry relations) section. It was explosive. He pointed fingers at many Fannie executives, members of Congress, staffers, and other government employees. The first paragraph read as follows:

> Fannie Mae's efforts to circumscribe, constrain, circumvent and undercut OFHEO were a matter of corporate policy, implemented by every office in the company but most particularly legal and government relations. Employee performance was evaluated by their success in these efforts and the techniques used principally included a campaign of disparaging the efforts of the agency, attacking the competence, integrity and motivation of officers of the agency, [and] limiting

agency budget and appropriations through the legislative process. . . . Fannie Mae undertook a concerted effort to limit and obstruct the investigation by working with the legislators and their staff to generate repeated IG investigations to divert agency resources and attention away from the special exam.

I have a handwritten note—*TONE?*—next to that paragraph. I'm not sure whether I meant the report's tone was too strong or whether we should mention the corrosive "tone at the top," which was a major theme of the report. The next section in the Blumenthal GIR draft was "Almost from the creation of its regulator, OFHEO, in 1992, Fannie Mae took the position the regulator had little authority over the company, a position bolstered by the numerous FM officers who played a role in writing the legislation that became law. . . . Government and Industry Relations team worked to ensure that the agency remains small, underfunded and understaffed."

We did tone down the GIR section because it was so inflammatory and might have caused an unnecessary backlash, especially as it named many people who were not pertinent to the accounting scandal. In the final 340-page report, the GIR section was still strong: "Fannie Mae's Government and Industry Relations Department had a special relationship of cooperation and support with select congressional staff. In the spring and again in the fall of 2004, enterprise lobbyists, with the knowledge and support of senior management, used their long-standing relationship with congressional staff to attempt to interfere with OFHEO's special examination."

We mentioned four HUD IG (inspector general) investigations, saying for the fourth investigation the IG received an April 2004 congressional request to investigate. OFHEO had found a draft of the congressional request later on Fannie

Mae's computer system that was nearly identical to the request letter, but it was dated almost two weeks earlier. That implied that Fannie wrote the original draft for Congress. The IG report was designed to discredit OFHEO team for leaking information. Somehow, Fannie got the confidential report published on a congressional website for one hour so it could be disseminated. The special examination report states, "Thus, Fannie Mae succeeded in creating a large volume of negative publicity about OFHEO examination report, in an effort to distract attention from its multi-billion-dollar accounting errors."

After finalizing the report,[43] we held a press conference on May 23, 2006. The report laid out a whole series of "unsafe and unsound practices" committed or tolerated by Fannie Mae's senior management, internal auditor, risk manager, external auditor, and board of directors. A sign of the corporate culture was a November 2004 memo from Chief Operating Officer Daniel Mudd, who later became the CEO, to the then CEO, Franklin Raines: "The old political reality was that we always won, we took no prisoners, and we faced little organized political opposition. . . . We used to, by virtue of our peculiarity, be able to write, or have written, rules that work for us."

We started the "Misapplication of GAAP (Generally Accepted Accounting Principles), Weak Financial Controls, and Inappropriate Earnings Management" section as follows: "The extreme predictability of the financial results reported by Fannie Mae from 1998 through 2003, and the ability to hit EPS (earnings per share) targets precisely each quarter, were illusions deliberately and systematically created by senior management." They misapplied accounting principles, under-hedged their interest-rate risk, and used "cookie jar reserves, certain Real Estate Mortgage Investment Conduit (REMIC) transactions . . . fed by investment bankers . . . to achieve annual EPS targets and maximize bonuses for senior management." The earnings manipulation was to impress Wall Street by showing that Fannie was a high-growth and low-risk company. As to bonuses, "In 1999, Mr. Raines set a goal to double Fannie Mae's EPS within five years from $3.23 in 1998 to $6.46 in 2003." During that period, he earned over $90 million, $61 million of which was in the last three years, as he got better working the system.

We wrote, "Most inappropriately, Mr. Rajappa, senior vice president for operations risk and head of Fannie Mae's Office of Auditing, corporate financial watchdog, gave a speech to his internal auditors, which encapsulated the tone at the top and corporate culture of Fannie Mae under Mr. Raines's stewardship:

> By now every one of you must have 6.46 branded in your brains. You must be able to say it in your sleep, you must be able to recite it forwards and backwards, you must have a raging fire in your belly that burns away all doubts, you must live, breathe and dream 6.46, you must be obsessed on 6.46. . . . After all, thanks to Frank, we all have a lot of money riding on it. . . .
>
> We must do this with a fiery determination—not on some days, not on most days, but day in and day out; give it your best, not 50%, not 75%, not 100%, but 150%. *Remember, Frank has given us an opportunity to earn not just our salaries, benefits, raises, ESPP, but substantially over and above if we make 6.46.* So, it is our <u>moral obligation</u> to give well above our 100% and if we do this, we would have made a tangible contribution to Frank's goals. [Emphasis added, underscore in the original]

In the May 23 OFHEO press release, I was quoted as follows:

> The image of Fannie Mae as one of the lowest-risk and best in class institutions was a façade. Our examination

found an environment where the ends justified the means. Senior management manipulated accounting; reaped maximum, undeserved bonuses; and prevented the rest of the world from knowing. They co-opted their internal auditors. They stonewalled OFHEO.

Fannie Mae's executives were precisely managing earnings to the one-hundredth of a penny to maximize their bonuses while neglecting investments in systems, internal controls and risk management. The combination of earnings manipulation, mismanagement and unconstrained growth resulted in an estimated $10.6 billion of losses, well over a billion dollars in expenses to fix the problems, and ill-gotten bonuses in the hundreds of millions of dollars. . . . As a government-sponsored enterprise, Fannie Mae has a unique position among American corporations and an extremely important mission. It is also the second largest borrower in the world, only behind the US government. As such, Fannie Mae has a special mandate and position of public trust. The previous management team violated that trust and did serious harm to Fannie Mae.

I said in the press conference they were "a hundredth of a penny wise, and tens of billions of dollars foolish." Our chief accountant, Wanda DeLeo, ended her presentation saying, "Management did not insure a proper internal control environment, and both internal and external audit failed in their oversight role."

SEC chairman Chris Cox spoke after our team at the press conference. Cox said, "Today both of our agencies are jointly announcing the settlement of accounting fraud charges against Fannie Mae. The settlement includes payment of a civil monetary payment of $400 million." He said that the announcement was "especially bitter" as "Fannie Mae is the largest private borrower in the world . . . and it is a major player in the derivatives market."

Simultaneously with finalizing the report, I was negotiating a consent order with CEO Mudd. The order was built upon the previous agreements but added many more restrictions, OFHEO-approval requirements, timelines, and much stronger controls covering topics ranging from governance, board, capital plans, and internal controls to accounting and compensation.

After tough negotiations with Mudd, a former Marine and GE executive, I added the following clause: "Fannie Mae shall not increase its 'mortgage portfolio' assets as shown in the minimum capital report to OFHEO for December 31, 2005." There was also a list of eighty-one actions required to have this portfolio limit lifted, including a clean audit opinion specifying that their internal controls complied with the Sarbanes-Oxley Act.

My Senate confirmation hearing was scheduled for June 8. I was asked to testify at a June 6, 2006, hearing to a House Financial Services Committee's subcommittee on the Fannie Mae settlement. White House Legislative Affairs advised me not to do a hearing two days before my confirmation hearing in case I said something controversial. However, I did accept the invitation. I reviewed the key points in the examination, including the recommendations at the end of the report, which were incorporated in the consent agreement. I also said several recommendations were directed at OFHEO: "We recommended that we continue to strengthen and expand our regulatory infrastructure and regular examination programs, and also importantly that we continue to support legislation to provide the powers essential to meeting our mission of ensuring safe and sound operations at Fannie Mae and Freddie Mac."

To a question about legislation I answered, "There is very significant systemic risk here . . . a giant exposure to the world economy."

The confirmation hearing included three others who played a significant role in the Great Financial Crisis: Sheila Bair, FDIC chair nominee; Kathleen Casey, SEC member nominee; and Don Kohn, Fed vice chairman nominee. The chairman of the committee was Senator Richard Shelby, and ranking member was Senator Paul Sarbanes. As I had a second hearing scheduled on the fifteenth with the committee, the confirmation hearing was not too tough. However, Senator Sarbanes told me, "I have this concern about the independence of the regulator," citing that I had done Social Security forums promoting partial privatization and had been a friend of the president since high school and college. I replied that I understood independent agencies as OFHEO was my third.

I started by introducing Cricket. I then said it was my fourth opportunity for government service. I cited my old standby of the USS *George Washington Carver*'s motto, "Strength through Knowledge." I added, "A secure retirement and homeownership are key components of the American dream. In many ways, trying to make those dreams come true has been the missions and goals of all three agencies for which I worked. The three share a need for strengthening."

The witnesses during the five-hour Senate hearing on the fifteenth were Chairman Chris Cox, Fannie Mae chair Stephen Ashley, CEO Mudd, and me. Senator Shelby and other Republican senators were tough on the Fannie team. Senator Charles Hagel (R-NE), in his opening remarks, while "banging his hand on the dais," said, "What we're dealing with is an astounding, an astounding failure of management and board responsibility, driven, clearly by self-interest and greed."[44]

After the tough opening remarks from the senators, Mudd said, "I have heard your comments today, and I have heard many more in private. The days of arrogant, defiant, 'my way' Fannie Mae had to end. We have begun to build a Fannie Mae that listens better, welcomes accountability, works with our regulators and with Congress, and serves the market by putting our mission to serve housing first."

He then listed all the remedial actions he had taken since being named CEO in December 2004, including hiring 1,000 employees and 2,500 contractors. They had already invested over $800 million to solve their problems, primarily new systems. I said in answer to a question, "These companies were so poorly run that it's going to take many years to fix."

My written testimony's conclusion was "If the agency had sufficient budget authority to enhance its staff, more robust legal authority . . . and other powers similar to those of other financial regulators including receivership, flexible capital standards, new product and growth controls and more streamlined enforcement authorities, then there is a strong possibility OFHEO could have prevented the many unsafe and unsound practices cited in our report."

Mudd also said, "We continue to support legislation to create a strong, well-funded regulator." However, that message did not get through to his team, especially to his lobbyists.

Senate Democrats, who still had not signed on to the Republican GSE reform bill because they thought it was too restrictive on the portfolios, were easier on the Fannie team and tougher on me. One asked whether the GSEs were a systemic risk. I said yes, adding that they were "more highly leveraged than any other financial institution" with $1.5 trillion in debt, $1.3 trillion in derivatives, and $2.6 trillion in guarantees, all supported by only $75 billion in capital.

Senator Chris Dodd (D-CT), my senator, called it a "very, very big sloppy mess." Senator Charles Schumer (D-NY) said he was disappointed with Fannie, but then politically added, "This week we have seen a full-frontal assault on Fannie Mae and indirectly Freddie Mac, all in what I believe to be an effort to build momentum to ram through unsound public policy."[45]

The frontal assault did not work, and for the next two years I repeated the call for reform in many testimonies and speeches, but when legislative reform arrived, it was much too late.

There are many comments on the report. *The Wall Street Journal* in an editorial on May 26, 2006, went after the politicization of Fannie: "Fannie's board and executive ranks featured some of the most prominent names in Democratic Party politics, as well as a few big-name Republicans. . . . The larger story here is that Fannie Mae is less a corporate outrage than a political one. It is the tale of a company that has grown rich off an implicit taxpayer subsidy and then plowed those profits back into buying political protection in Congress and feckless regulation from the executive."

Peter Wallison in an AEI report of June 23 wrote that Fannie and Freddie's debts "are seen by US and foreign investors as nearly risk-free, and therefore not subject to market discipline. In effect, they are given a free pass to take risk. The name for this phenomenon—in which government backing reduces market discipline—is moral hazard, and the GSEs represent moral hazard on steroids."

The article may have been the first time I read a quote that I and many others used many times over the years—that Fannie and Freddie were "a classic example of privatizing profits while socializing risk and loss."

Wallison unkindly quoted OFHEO's 2003 annual report to Congress, saying, "In light of later events, it rises to parody: 'The Enterprises remain safe and sound through another year of exceptional growth in the housing sector.'" He also wrote OFHEO's "assignment was beyond the capacity of any financial regulator or supervisor."

I disagree with that comment, although we never had the powers until it was too late to prove it. He then asked, "[If] regulation alone is not able to revamp the loss to the taxpayers and systemic risk to the economy, what will? The only sensible course is to reduce the risk Fannie and Freddie are able to take. Fortunately, it is easy to do. The principal risk of the GSEs is what is known as interest rate risk," which was, from the enterprises' portfolios, funded by over a trillion dollars of debt.

Unfortunately, it was not easy. Credit risk, not interest-rate risk, turned out to be the principal risk.

CHAPTER 13

Market Discipline Missing

"In the case of the GSEs, market discipline is problematic. . . . [There is] a view among market participants that the GSEs are implicitly backed by the federal government, thereby weakening market discipline. Consequently, strong regulatory authority and controls on GSE risk-taking are needed to ensure that they do not create systemic risks. Unfortunately, the GSE regulator's constrained capital authority, the ineffective receivership process, and other limitations weaken regulatory oversight."

—Chairman Ben Bernanke answering a question from Senator Jim Bunning (R-KY) at his November 15, 2005, confirmation hearing to be reappointed as chairman

CRICKET IS A great fan of Ben Bernanke because of the way he handled the financial crisis. She was also pleased that he came to my farewell party in 2009. I was already a fan because he had talked about Social Security reform when he was chair of the Council of Economic Advisors. He asked me to lunch at the Fed in his private dining room on June 20, 2006. We had a good conversation about Fannie and Freddie. The next year he visited me at OFHEO.

On July 24, HUD secretary Alphonso Jackson, who would become a friend, swore me in at OFHEO. President Bush invited

me and most of my family to the Oval Office to commemorate
the occasion. My mother loved the Oval Office meeting. Also in
attendance were Cricket, JB, Graci, and her husband, Marko.
My sisters Joan (and her husband, Jim) and Annie attended.
Cricket's brothers, Biff and John, and John's wife, K, also were
there. POTUS was very gracious, giving us a tour and description
of the Oval Office. He posed with us for many pictures.

Two days later I was back in the Oval Office for a very different
meeting—a "principals meeting" to discuss the GSEs. The
president, vice president, Secretary Paulson (who had been sworn
in on July 10), Secretary Jackson, OMB director Portman, and NEC
chair Allan Hubbard. Bush did not like their quasi-governmental
structure, their management teams, or their potential risks. Josh
Bolten, Karl Rove, Keith Hennessey, and others attended.

POTUS had long worried about Fannie Mae and Freddie
Mac. Although the president had the power to appoint a few
board members at each enterprise, he had made the decision
not to do so. Over the years the two had become revolving doors
for prior presidential appointees. Franklin Raines, the Fannie
CEO during the scandal, had been Clinton's OMB director. His
predecessor, Jim Johnson, was a major Democratic fundraiser
and was on the Goldman Sachs, Gannett, and Target boards,
among others. Many have said that he helped create the culture
of arrogance that led to their accounting scandal.

One explanation I heard as to why Bush did not want to
appoint directors was that he did not want his administration
to be implicated if something went wrong with Fannie and
Freddie. He felt that they were already too political. And he knew
something could go wrong. At the time of the meeting, I was only
three months into the reform effort, but the Bush administration
had been pushing to rein in the GSEs since 2001.

Hennessey put together a PowerPoint. The first slide was as
follows:

✦   GSE Problems

✦   Systemic Financial Risk

✦   Bad accounting, weak internal controls and poor corporate governance

✦   Corruption in senior management

✦   Bad behavior in Washington (aggressive lobbying of Congress)

I gave the team an update on what was happening at Fannie and Freddie, including that we had frozen their portfolios. I mentioned their massive mortgage credit exposure as well as their interest-rate risk. That was on top of their accounting scandals, which meant that they could not produce accurate financial statements. At the time of this meeting, the GSEs were still very profitable according to their un-auditable financial accounts. However, the growth in housing prices had started to peak.

The systemic section of Hennessey's PowerPoint concentrated on interest-rate risk, mismatches between their investments and borrowings, and their strategy to hedge through derivatives only partially. Credit risk was not mentioned. It also said, "Banks and thrifts hold GSE debt and mortgage-backed securities as if they were Treasuries. In a crisis, the value of GSE debt drops, and these banks could find themselves with inadequate capital, forcing a sharp curtailment of lending across the banking sector."

Bush asked Paulson whether he felt that Fannie and Freddie were a systemic risk. Paulson replied, "They are not in my top ten." Bush pressed Paulson again, asking whether that was really true. Paulson said, well, "Not in my top five." Apparently, that was the street view at the time. Later, I was told by Treasury assistant secretary Emil Henry, who had taken part in preparing Hank for his confirmation hearing, that Paulson told him that

Goldman Sachs, which Paulson ran prior to accepting the Treasury nomination, did annual assessments of systemically important financial institutions. Fannie and Freddie were not on the list. Paulson did say to the president that he was concerned about their large derivative portfolios and that we needed legislative reforms.

Paulson was the fourth of the five Treasury secretaries with whom I worked. He was rightfully called a force of nature. He was on the cover of *BusinessWeek*'s June 12 issue with the title "Mr. Risk Goes to Washington." The article said he had grown Goldman Sachs rapidly and therefore increased their risks significantly. Having co-founded a risk management firm, I thought it was good to have a secretary who understood risk management. He also hired another Goldman partner, Bob Steel, who I knew from Greenwich and who was sworn in in late October as Treasury under secretary for domestic finance. Steel was a very strong ally for reform.

The "Our Position" slide called for a strong regulator with receivership powers, new activities authority, minimum capital standards (I commented that should include risk-based as well as leverage capital standards), and no presidentially appointed directors. The second bullet was "Reduce portfolios to limit systemic financial risk." The next slide, "Legislative Status," highlighted the support for Senator Shelby's bill and list of key allies and "key opponents," including Senators Sarbanes and Schumer and Representative Barney Frank. Barney was a longtime supporter of Fannie, but he had supported the weaker bill passed by the House. He was always good for a quote, saying, "The US Senate is clearly, infinitely morally superior to North Korea, but no easier to deal with."[46]

The last slide was labeled "Treasury Administrative Authority." It stated that the Treasury had "the ability under current law to limit the size of GSEs' debt issuance and, indirectly, their portfolios." The power was never used.

It was agreed during the meeting that we needed to work together to get GSE reform to rein in Fannie and Freddie. Time was running out for 2006 reform as Congress was going on their August break and congressional elections were looming in the fall. Senate Democrats led by Senator Sarbanes continued to fight the Senate Banking Committee's bill and would not allow a full Senate vote.

The same day as the White House meeting, I gave a luncheon speech at a Women in Housing and Finance event. I kept being pressed about whether I preferred the House or Senate bill on the ability to set portfolio limits. My response was, "The Senate bill provides stronger guidance. It is too tight, and we need some additional flexibility that could be delegated to the regulator."[47] I did say the flexibility would be used rarely and only to support troubled markets.

As at Social Security, Reuters wrote, I got pushback for leading a "blitz to push comprehensive reform." They quoted me,[48] "If someone was running an agency and was not worried about the long-term future of the agency, I'd be very worried."

The administration, Congress, commentators, and even OFHEO all focused on the risk of the GSEs' portfolios, emphasizing interest-rate mismatch and exposure to other financial institutions issuing derivatives (which is called counterparty risk) as a major source of systemic risk. The managements of both companies focused much more on interest-rate risk than credit risk, to their ultimate detriment.

Derivatives were used by the enterprises to manage interest-rate risk and, during their accounting fraud, to manipulate earnings. The enterprises' earnings management was a concern way back in 2000. In that year, Warren Buffett, who had been Freddie Mac's biggest shareholder, sold his shares. In his 2000 annual meeting he said: "I would stress we did not sell because we worried about more government regulation of Fannie and

Freddie. If anything, the opposite." He was more specific in his testimony to the 2010 Financial Crisis Inquiry Commission: "Any time a large financial institution starts promising regular earnings increases, you're going to have trouble. . . . [T]hey are going to do things, maybe in accounting—as it turns out to be the case in both Freddie and Fannie—but also in operations that I would regard as unsound."

Proponents of reform argued that the GSEs held too many derivatives, which increased their risk, especially systemic risk. The derivatives were used to hedge their interest-rate risk and resulting prepayment risk of their $700-plus billion each portfolios. The technical term is convexity risk. Thirty-year fixed-rate mortgages have very large convexity risk, as they are freely prepayable. If interest rates go down, homeowners refinance their mortgages. If interest rates go up, homeowners keep their mortgages. Therefore, investors do not know the real maturity of thirty-year, fixed-rate, fully prepayable mortgages or mortgage-backed securities.

As interest rates kept changing, the enterprises kept adding new hedges. The result was that they each had many trillions of dollars in derivatives. As they were sloppy, they did not legally offset the derivatives, which increased their counterparty (the bank issuing the derivative) risk dramatically. In fact, over a three-year period, their derivatives book tripled even though their portfolios only grew slightly. Their massive derivative portfolios increased their interconnectivity credit risk with other financial institutions.

Fannie and especially Freddie made several arguments why derivatives were not causing systemic risk and why it made sense for them, rather than other investors, to manage convexity risk. The enterprises claimed they were more sophisticated and better at hedging the convexity risk than the market.

We had imposed caps on Fannie Mae's portfolio by the May consent agreement at year-end 2005 levels ($727 billion), but the 2003 Freddie consent agreement had no cap. Their portfolio had been growing rapidly, and they had a larger PLS portfolio than Fannie. To level the playing field with Fannie Mae, I had to get Freddie Mac somehow to voluntarily consent to freezing their portfolio. Freddie always had an inferiority complex toward their elder sibling, Fannie.

In a June 6 memo, Dick Syron, Freddie's CEO, fired an opening salvo against a portfolio cap, mentioning all the remedial steps they were taking and the plan "to begin registering the company's common stock with the Securities and Exchange Commission." It took two years. Unbelievably, as one of the largest New York Stock Exchange–listed financial companies, Freddie had never registered with the SEC. It was one of the benefits of being a GSE. Another major benefit is that they do not have to pay state and local taxes.

To get Freddie's voluntary approval, I asked Syron to schedule me for their July 20 board meeting, which was held in New York City. It was tense and the first of many contentious board meetings. The Freddie board had many arrogant investment bankers who did not understand the regulatory process or, for that matter, the special benefits and responsibilities of being a GSE. They told me that their lawyers advised them their sole responsibility was to their shareholders. My reply was that being responsible only to shareholders was an outmoded idea for any large financial services company, let alone a GSE.

At my request, I was given talking points by the examiner in charge of Freddie Mac, Jeff Spohn, who was at the meeting with his boss, Len Reid. It was a long list of reasons why Freddie should freeze their portfolio. Interest-rate risk and derivative counterparty risk was on the list, but so was the inability to file financial statements with the SEC during their entire existence, internal control problems, noncompliance with Sarbanes-Oxley, operational risk, including systems issues, a long list of material deficiencies, and credit risk.

The board suffered sullenly through the long list. However, the lead director, Thomas Johnson, backed by several other directors, erupted at the mention of the growing credit risk in their own MBS and private-label MBS. They claimed credit risk was a core competency, citing their very low historical loss record. Freddie board members told me, "We understand credit risk. We don't have credit risk."

Despite the pushback, they knew they had to consent to freeze their portfolio. I gave them a small carrot: if they agreed to freeze their portfolios at year-end 2005 levels, OFHEO would allow them to grow them at 0.5 percent per year. On August 1 Freddie announced that they would freeze their portfolio.

The irony is that credit losses on their portfolios and mortgages in their guaranteed MBS were what brought the two firms down—not the interest-rate or derivative risks.

The myth that derivative exposure was their major problem persisted. The very suppliers of the private-label MBS and derivatives that hedged them kept the myth alive. JP Morgan's CEO, Jamie Dimon, wrote in his long and otherwise very informative 2008 letter to shareholders that the Fannie and Freddie problems were derivatives and a weak regulator. I agree that the regulator's powers were weak.

A great example of the weakness of the 1992 legislation was an October 1, 1992, letter by my old PBGC supporter, Representative Pickle, and Representative Bill Gradison to "Dear Colleagues." They wrote,

> We believe that Fannie Mae should not possess a veto over the form of its own supervision. . . . Fannie is using its political clout to convince Members that any attempt to question its own decisions on capital adequacy will raise mortgage rates and reduce support for low-income

> housing. Those scare tactics are unfounded. . . . Congress
> should have learned during the S&L crisis that strong
> capital requirements strengthen, rather than weaken
> financial institutions. . . . The time has come for Congress
> to protect the public purse, not Fannie Mae's profits.

While working on trying to get legislation, it was important to manage the agency. I was on a steep learning curve. We had a good team, but it was understaffed, and we needed upgrading. The policy team led by Pat Lawler was excellent. The capital oversight team was making progress, but we lacked a risk-based capital model, which was partially a result of the constraints of the 1992 legislation. The teams overseeing Fannie and Freddie were too thin and had a massive job overseeing the remedial activities and the growing risk levels as the housing market was sinking. We were putting out quarterly reports verifying the enterprises' capital and their too slow progress. I was also making a team to start working on the President's Management Agenda.

Meanwhile, we published the *2006–2011 OFHEO Strategic Plan*. The goals were as follows:

1. Enhance supervision to ensure the enterprises operate in a safe and sound manner, are adequate capitalized and comply with legal requirements.

2. Provide support for statutory reforms to strengthen our regulatory powers.

3. Continue to support the national policy of an efficient secondary mortgage market which promotes homeownership and affordable housing.

A big hole at OFHEO was the deputy director slot. It was a career position as OFHEO only had one political position—me, as director. The candidates were narrowed down to three good ones. I was scheduled to meet them but decided not to as I knew two of the candidates and was afraid that my selection might be considered prejudiced. Therefore, I deputized a three-person team.

They happily selected Ed DeMarco, who had been a key staffer at the Treasury with the responsibility of overseeing the GSEs, among other duties, before we hired him at the SSA. Legislation establishing OFHEO had required the Treasury to do a study on the privatization of Fannie and Freddie. DeMarco wrote the original study.

There were rumors in early 2006 that De Marco was the candidate for OFHEO director job. In fact, he was in the process of being considered when Ed Moy of Presidential Personnel, with some help, persuaded me to take the job. DeMarco did become the acting director when I left the FHFA in August 2009, a year after it was created. He did an excellent job as my deputy and then as my successor.

Dick Syron gave a speech in San Francisco on October 18, 2006. He questioned, "Why is the US the only major economy in the world where the fixed-rate, freely prepayable mortgage is widespread? The biggest reason is the GSEs." He was right, and that is a key reason why it has been so hard to reach a consensus on how to get Fannie Mae and Freddie Mac out of conservatorship. The thirty-year, fixed-rate, freely prepayable mortgage is as American as apple pie.

His speech continued,

> There are those who persist in trying to say we add risk to the financial system, in the guise of the concept—which is often imprecisely specified—called "systemic risk." . . . As a bank regulator and central banker [he had been president of the Boston Fed and CEO of the American

Stock Exchange] for the best part of twenty-five years, I've spent a lot of time on these issues. And I will continue to fundamentally disagree with and debunk the charge of systemic risk as it has been applied to the GSEs. . . . Simply put, the system is *safer* with the GSE playing our role.

He then claimed that they "supported legislation to strengthen regulatory oversight of the GSEs." And he added something I was going to hear many times from both CEOs a year later as the subprime bubble was bursting: "The GSEs have also stabilized the market on a *national* basis—as we did in 1998, after the Russian debt crisis and the collapse of Long-Term Capital Management."

Syron had earlier given me a paper trying to quantify "Exposure to Catastrophic Shocks." It totaled $26.8 billion. The total was conveniently under the $36 billion capital Freddie had at the time. As the board had pushed back so strongly on credit risk, it was interesting to see that credit risk was an $11.3 billion loss, assuming a nationwide 30 percent house price decline. When it did happen, the losses were many multiples of their estimate. The graph accompanying these numbers went up to a 50 percent house price decline, which showed losses of about $30 billion, still conveniently below their $36 billion in capital. If only!

Mudd also pushed backed at being considered a systemic risk. At that point I was having meetings monthly or every other week with the two CEOs. In December we discussed systemic risk. Mudd gave me a paper that Fannie published in 2003, written by the former comptroller of the currency, Eugene Ludwig.[49] Ludwig wrote, "The size of particular institutions is not necessarily related to systemic risk, and excessive concern about largeness can be counterproductive." Later in the paper he cited Citigroup, JP Morgan Chase, Fannie Mae, and Freddie Mac as large institutions.

I wrote back to Mudd:

> Some of the reason he cites for less systemic risk for large financial institutions, unfortunately, do not apply to Fannie Mae or Freddie Mac.
>
> "Regulated financial institutions now are subject of rigorous capital requirements." It is questionable how rigorous the capital rules set by Congress in 1992 are.
>
> "Larger entities typically are able to diversify in ways that materially lower their risk." Fannie Mae cannot diversify.
>
> "Larger entities tend to have greater market attention, have to meet higher standards of transparency and face greater market discipline." Fannie Mae has very limited, if any, credit market discipline because of its GSE status and "implicit guarantee."

Legislative reform did not happen before the congressional election. Portfolio limits, systemic language, and the affordable housing fund were the key stumbling blocks.

An October 2, 2006, *Wall Street Journal* editorial wrote: "The 109th Congress is going home to fight for reelection. . . . Social Security reform was never going to be easy. . . . But that still doesn't excuse such prominent Republicans. . . . So frightened were they that they never even brought the subject up for a vote. Power for its own sake also explains the GOP's decision to join Senate Democrats in killing serious reform of Fannie Mae and Freddie Mac, despite $16 billion in accounting mistakes or fraud. The members are in bed with the housing lobby."

The Republicans lost the reelection fight in both houses. Our hopes turned to somehow getting a deal in the one-week lame-duck session while the Republicans were still in charge. There was a National Economic Council (NEC) principals meeting scheduled in the Roosevelt Room of the White House on November 21 to decide next steps. The NEC PowerPoint and Treasury papers gave the reasons for reform. The PowerPoint highlighted the GSEs' systemic risk due to size, interconnectivity with other financial institutions, high leverage, and lack of market discipline.

The NEC also wrote, "Time Is Running Against Us," stating that the Senate bill was unachievable and the House bill unacceptable. However, the Oxley-Frank portfolio limit language was "workable (although imperfect), but far better than nothing at all."

As a result of the meeting, the NEC wrote a decision memo on November 26, 2006, to President Bush. The first paragraph stated:

> Treasury Secretary Paulson seeks your permission to attempt to negotiate a GSE compromise in the lame duck session. Your advisors differ on how far to negotiate at this time, particularly on the issue of systemic risk, when success in achieving legislation in the lame duck is unlikely.... Secretary Paulson and Jim Lockhart believed that, while it does not separately address systemic risk, the Oxley-Frank portfolio language enhances his current law authority to limit the GSEs' portfolios and it is an improvement in this respect over the House-passed bill.

I believed that by giving OFHEO much stronger "safety and soundness" powers, we could significantly lower the GSEs' systemic risk, and it would be unlikely to get a stronger bill in 2007. The decision memo laid out the arguments between the two groups as to whether to try to reach a deal. The pro group was Paulson, Jackson, Rob Portman, Candi Wolf (Legislative Affairs) and me. The con group was Bernanke, Edward Lazear (CEA), Harriet Miers (Legal), and David Addington (VP staff), who argued, "We should not negotiate away at this time the Administration's posture of strong regulation of the GSEs, particularly including the ability to control systemic risk." Bernanke was quoted:

> To assure that the GSEs do not pose risks to the financial system, they would need either to have adequate capital or to have some principle-based limits on expansion of their portfolios. The current capital ratios, at 2.5 percent, are well below the 8 percent or more that would likely be appropriate. . . . [N]either the politics nor the legislation would provide a basis for even a well-meaning OFHEO director to achieve a significant capital increase. These powers are much weaker than those that bank regulators have.

NEC added a parenthetical, which was "(Treasury lawyers disagree with the characterization that the powers are 'much weaker')."

The president did authorize Secretary Paulson to negotiate, but time ran out. The opponents in Congress were too entrenched; however, Paulson made the point that the attempt created some goodwill with Barney Frank, the incoming chairman of the House Financial Services Committee. I strongly supported Paulson's attempt as we had made good progress working with Congress. OFHEO needed stronger powers on capital, portfolio, mission, and other safety and soundness issues, and the funds to implement them—sooner rather than later.

In retrospect, it may have been too late even then to get the critically needed capital regulations through. Even though my team had been working on capital alternatives, the rulemaking process with comment period is slow. However, all the powers in the bill and the blessing of Congress on the bill would have made it much harder for the enterprises to continue to push back.

As Robert England wrote in his book *Black Box Casino*, "The failure of Washington to enact GSE reform in a timely manner . . . altered the course of financial history, according to Lockhart." He quoted me as saying, "If legislation had passed even when I arrived in May of '06, I don't think we would have prevented the crisis, but I think it would have been certainly less severe."[50]

The outgoing chairman of the House Financial Services Committee, Michael Oxley, summed up GSE reform failure (which could also be applied to the PBGC and Social Security): "Too many times when you permit the perfect to be the enemy of the good, you end up with the bad or the status quo—in this case, it's one in the same."[51]

CHAPTER 14

Cracks Appearing—Taking on Water

Mr. Lockhart
Very good presentation. You have a hard job and are doing
good work on the right side of history. There is a whole aspect
here around foreign central bank holding.
Good Luck,
Larry

—Handwritten note passed to me by Larry Summers, former
Treasury secretary, on December 2, 2006, at the 56th Plenary
Session of the Group of 30, Federal Reserve Bank of New York

I HAD BEEN invited to attend a three-day December 2006 session of the Group of 30, a highly respected international group. It was a foreshadowing of what was to come. The Saturday dinner was hosted at AIG, and Summers gave the opening remarks. Sunday at 9 AM there was a forum on "Risks in the Financial System." Tim Geithner, the host and president of the Federal Reserve Bank of New York, gave the overview remarks. After Summers's "Perspectives" presentation, my subject was "Housing Credit Risks," after which he passed the note above. Just a little over two years later, in January 2009, the three of us became united on that topic. Geithner was secretary of Treasury, and Summers was director of the National Economic Council.

Summers was right about the importance of central bank holdings. UBS put out a paper in June 2006 based on their annual Central Bank Survey, which showed that 84 percent of central banks held US agencies' debt and MBS in 2006 versus 54 percent in 1998. Agency MBS holdings almost tripled in one year. UBS projected that in 2006, central banks would buy over half the net new agency MBS issuance.

I may have been on the right side of history, but history started to turn against us in early 2007 as the housing markets showed cracks. William Poole, president of the Federal Reserve Bank of St. Louis and a student and harsh critic of the GSEs, gave a January 2007 speech on the GSEs.[52] He pointed out the failings and risks of Fannie Mae and Freddie Mac, but also the "other housing GSEs"—the twelve FHLBanks. He concluded, "I do not believe that a GSE crisis is imminent. However, for those who believe a GSE crisis is unthinkable in the future, I suggest a course in economic history."

The enterprises in early 2007 were facing four interrelated challenges: private-label mortgage-backed securities, exotic mortgages, subprime mortgages, and the too-high affordable housing goals imposed by HUD. Housing price sales were falling in some areas, home sales with slowing, and more exotic mortgages were starting to show stress. However, the biggest challenge was to pick up on our work to get GSE reform passed.

Barney Frank had been true to his word and introduced a bill in March 2007 that reflected the year-end 2006 Frank-Oxley compromise. He held a Financial Services Committee hearing on March 15. The first panel included Bob Steel, a HUD representative, and me. The second panel comprised Mudd, Syron, John Dalton (head of the Financial Services Roundtable's Housing Policy Council), and Gerald Howard (CEO of the National Association of Home Builders). A third panel was made up of five representatives from housing interest groups.

My OFHEO team, knowing that I like to be overprepared for a hearing, had outdone themselves by preparing a four-inch-thick binder. Steel's testimony was supportive of the legislation, but he expressed concerns about an increase in the conforming loan limit for higher-price areas and the Affordable Housing Fund. He mentioned the dreaded "systemic risk."

I stayed away from all three topics in my testimony. I said, "I am grateful for your hard work in reaching what I believe is a balanced approach to needed reforms. It is time for action." I added that "legislation provides all six building blocks" of reform—bank-regulator-like powers, combining the FHFB (Federal Housing Finance Board) and OFHEO, moving mission oversight from HUD to the safety and soundness regulator, stronger independence for litigation and funding, capital powers, and portfolio powers. On the latter, I pointed out that even with our portfolio caps, over the last fifteen years the portfolios had grown tenfold, while the mortgage market only grew threefold and their guaranteed MBS fourfold. I also commended Chairman Frank and Secretary Paulson for reaching a compromise. To no avail, I did ask for a better name for the new agency as its FHFA acronym was easy to confuse with FHA. It still is.

I thought Steel and I worked well together. My successor as head of the FHFA many years later, Congressman Mel Watt, accused me of leaking confidential enterprise information. The accusation may have come from residual bitterness at the accounting scandal investigations. He pointed to my January statement that Fannie Mae had a third-quarter loss based on a required public quarterly capital report. The only reason it was news was that Fannie (as well as Freddie) were not putting out timely financial reports. My comment hit the stock price but, of course, not the bond prices.

My congressman, Chris Shays, was focused on the enterprises' registering with the SEC. He also said, "OFHEO, everyone agrees, is doing a much better job under your management. . . . And I am not saying that because you happen to be a constituent. I note that is the consensus." He said that the House bill was good but worried what the Senate would do. Frank suggested, as Dodd was from Connecticut, that Shays should work with him.

The legislation did not mention systemic risk. While Chairman Frank was out of the hearing, Congresswoman Melissa Bean (D-IL) asked us: " Is your reading [of the legislation] such that systemic risk can be interpreted to be a factor or standard by which the portfolio can be reduced or capped?"

Me: "My reading of systemic risk is it is part of a regulator's job, it is part of safety and soundness, that you have to make sure that they do not have a problem that could spread risk to the rest of the financial system."

Mr. Steel: "Yes."

Mudd disagreed: "Legislation should identify the safety and soundness factors that would lead to the regulatory limits on the size or growth of our balance sheet. We believe 'systemic risk' should not be included in these factors." A cynic might suggest that Representative Bean's question was planted by a Fannie lobbyist.

Syron's testimony was a thesis of thirty-five pages with twenty-one footnotes. In his long section on systemic risk, he wrote, "We strongly disagree that the GSEs represent a unique, large, looming problem waiting to happen." He got carried away. "The assets the GSEs own are considered to be among the safest financial products." He added that the legislation "'could,' not 'would' . . . impair either our ability to remain financially viable or to serve our mission or both."

He showed a pie chart with Fannie and Freddie each only having 7 percent of the total mortgage debt outstanding of $10.5 trillion, ignoring their guaranteed MBS that allotted them well over 30 percent in total. An important statement was "We provide stability to the housing market by providing funds 'counter-cyclically' to lenders. That means that at the point in the business cycle when economic activity is contracting, Freddie Mac and Fannie Mae *increase* their relative provision of funds to the mortgage market, and vice versa."

The higher capital requirements we were calling for might have given the enterprises the wherewithal to act countercyclically. In the scores of speeches I have given about the GSEs and housing forms, I made countercyclicality the key element of any reform plan.

As with many government and quasi-government insurance companies, the enterprises' three missions of liquidity, stability, and affordability were inherently contradictory without adequate capital and controls. Fannie and Freddie always remained conflicted between maximizing profits and supporting their mission of stability and liquidity. As an example, in late 2007 they reduced their liquidity portfolios to invest in higher-yielding mortgages to meet their affordable housing goals.

Returning to systemic risk, Congressman Ed Royce (R-CA) placed into the record Bernanke's speech,[53] which highlighted the systemic risk of Fannie and Freddie. Bernanke's good definition was "Systemic risk is the risk that disruptions occurring in one firm or financial market may spread to other parts of the financial system, with possibly serious indications for the performance of the broader economy." Bernanke also cited me when saying that the housing GSEs' obligations exceeded the $4.9 trillion of US publicly held debt. Many years later, US publicly held debt is quadruple GSEs' outstandings.

As Frank was absent when Steel and I responded to Representative Bean's question, someone must have whispered in his ear. Barney sent a scathing letter, demanding to know why we could say that systemic risk was a safety and soundness concern for Fannie and Freddie. I responded politely the next day, quoting my response to Representative Bean. I wrote, "If for any reason the financial markets lose confidence in either Enterprise, it would be very hard for them to fulfill their critical mission. . . . You are correct. We did agree that the systemic risk outside of safety and soundness should not be part of the regulatory approach."

The committee passed Barney's bill later in March, by a bipartisan 45–19 vote.

On March 30, OFHEO published our 2007 report to Congress. I wrote in my transmittal letter, "OFHEO concludes that both companies remain a significant supervisory concern." We did say the enterprises were making progress but had many "matters requiring board attention," including that "continued close monitoring of credit portfolios trends is necessary as higher volumes of non-traditional credit products were purchased during 2006. Although these credit products are within current limits, these products exhibit higher than historical credit risk."

When the full House took up the bill, Representatives Bean and Randy Neugebauer (R-TX) introduced an amendment restricting the FHFA's constraints on the portfolios just to the enterprises' risk and not systemic risk. I was blamed for this change. A Dow Jones article reported, "'Mr. Lockhart kept talking about going beyond the bill,' Frank said. 'I asked that that amendment not be offered, but it becomes hard to argue against it because the administration—Mr. Lockhart in particular—said 'I am going to go after the portfolios.'"[54] The same article quoted me: "'I think the portfolios need to be right-sized, and I'm not sure they are right-size now,' he told reporters in January. 'Yes, there [are] a lot of arguments, and I've made them, and the Fed has made them, Treasury has made them, that these portfolios are too large. They represent too much risk.'"

The administration opposed the change, but the amendment

passed 383–36. Frank voted against it. The bill itself passed on May 22 with a vote of 313–104. Steel said, "Regretfully . . . [the amendment] significantly weakened the regulator's ability to examine systemic risk issues."[55] My statement was calmer, saying that "a few issues remain." I was less bothered by the new language as I felt that the authors did not understand systemic risk. Stopping risks in their portfolios would have prevented them from being a systemic risk.

Senate Banking Committee chair Dodd said he was "committed to addressing differences over the bill in a bipartisan, timely and thoughtful way."[56] As he was running for president, his thoughtful way took a long time. Shelby was opposed to softer House portfolio language.

The Bean-Neugebauer Amendment highlights the tightrope we were walking as we tried to get legislation. Being tough and truthful emboldened opponents of reform, the enterprises, and their lobbyists. As it turned out, the tightrope was over Niagara Falls.

Both CEOs in their testimony talked about the growing problems in the mortgage market. On subprime Mudd said, "If anyone wonders what the alternatives are to a market with well-regulated GSEs playing stability and liquidity role, we now have a reality TV with respect to subprime." He did not mention their growing private-label MBS problems.

Syron wrote rightly, "In the current environment, we are being reminded that housing that is not sustainable is *not* affordable housing" and "the confluence of strong borrower demand for low-payment mortgages and strong investor appetite for high-yielding securities fueled the origination of 2/28 and 3/27 hybrid ARMs."

Being in investment and risk management throughout my career, I thought I understood housing and mortgages. Way back at Gulf Oil, we were one of the first corporate buyers of Lew Ranieri's mortgage-backed securities.

In a 2006 meeting, a Fed governor spoke about bad 2/28 and 3/27 mortgages. Initially, I thought they were some numerical regulations. I quickly learned that they were toxic teaser mortgages that had either a two-year or three-year period of very low interest rate, but with much higher rates for the next twenty-seven or twenty-eight years. The shoddy underwriting assumed that they would be refinanced because house prices would rise. Most were not refinanced as house prices peaked in 2006. As a result, many of these homeowners were stuck with their toxic mortgages with increasing interest rates and faced foreclosure.

The 2/28 and 3/27 were nontraditional mortgages (NTM), as they were interest-only and adjustable-rate mortgages (ARMs). Some had negative amortization, meaning if interest rates go up and the payment does not go up as much as the interest rate, the principal amount of the mortgage increases. At year-end 2006, the enterprises each had 8 percent NTM.

Subprime mortgages are mortgages to borrowers with poor credit histories, sometimes defined as having a FICO credit score of 660 or below, but definitions were fluid. Fannie, for instance, only treated loans as subprime if they came from a subprime originator. Close to fifty of those originators—including the poster child, New Century—had failed by mid-2007. Under their definitions, Fannie had 2 percent of year-end 2006 book in subprime and Freddie 6 percent. In total they held about 14 percent of the estimated $1.2 trillion in subprime loans outstanding.

A third category of problem loans was Alt-A mortgages, which are loans to borrowers with an "A" credit rating who do not provide full documentation. A troublesome variety was referred to as NINA (no income, no assets) loans. Fannie reported that 13 percent of their year-end 2006 book were Alt-A. Freddie did not report a total number. There is overlap in these percentages as NTMs could be also subprime or Alt-A.

Many of these mortgages were packaged into PLS. The lowest-rated tranche was below investment grade (junk), but the largest tranches were rated AAA by the rating agencies. Unfortunately, in many cases the rating agencies were conflicted as they were paid an advisory fee to help structure the MBS.

Fannie and Freddie were the largest buyers of these AAA tranches because they were "safe" and rich in HUD-defined "affordable" mortgages. Freddie was much more heavily reliant on PLS, which met 34 percent of their total affordable purchase goal but only 10 percent of Fannie's.

A key flaw in the 1992 law was separating the mission and the safety and soundness regulator. In 2004, while setting the affordable housing goals for 2005 through 2008, HUD stated there were "millions of Americans with less than perfect credit or who cannot meet some of the tougher underwriting requirements of the prime market. . . . If the GSEs reach deeper into the subprime market, more borrowers will benefit from advantages."[57]

The enterprises struggled to reach these goals, which HUD kept increasing. They barely met them in 2007. At the peak in 2008, they were required to buy or guarantee affordable mortgages as 56 percent of their total annual mortgages. Just mathematically that was tough: 30 percent of the population could not afford to buy a house.

Meeting the affordable housing goals was a top priority of the two CEOs; it kept their congressional Democratic base happy. They were terrified that if they missed the goals, HUD would issue a damning public memo of understanding. Their search for affordable housing mortgages led to some questionable year-end transactions. Some commentators, especially Peter Wallison in his dissent to the *Financial Crisis Inquiry Report*, have said that these goals were the major reasons for the failure of the enterprises.

When the new agency, the FHFA, was created in 2009, I learned that the Federal Home Loan Banks were the third largest buyers of those formerly AAA PLS.

The regulators understood these toxic mortgages issues and the PLS that contained them, but it took several years to throttle them back. Part of the reason, as pointed out in the book by Bernanke, Geithner and Paulson, *Firefighting: The Financial Crisis and Its Lessons*, was that "these vulnerabilities were allowed to fester by America's balkanized financial regulatory bureaucracy, a hodgepodge of agencies and authorities and regulations that for decades had failed to keep pace with changing market realities and rapid financial innovation."[58]

To help overcome this hodgepodge, the regulators had created the FFIEC (Federal Financial Institutions Examination Council). It included the Federal Reserve, OCC, FDIC, OTS, National Credit Union Administration, and representatives of state bank regulators. But not OFHEO, even though I asked to join it several times. After all, Fannie was bigger than any bank they supervised.

In September 2006, the bank regulators put out guidance on NTM. We asked the enterprises to develop rules to implement the guidance by February 2007. Syron asked his team to show him examples of NTM loans in PLS. He reported to me that they were very nasty. He ordered his team to stop buying. Banks were still originating noncompliant NTM because the guidance was not enforceable regulation. In July 2007 we ordered the enterprises to stop buying these NTM directly or indirectly through PLS.

In March 2007, the bank regulators asked for comments on a rule for abusive subprime mortgages. The FFIEC final rule was not finalized until July 2008. Much too late.

To this day, the regulatory bureaucracy is still too fragmented. Dodd-Frank did away with the Office of Thrift Supervision but created a new agency, the Consumer Financial Protection Bureau.

Years later, at WL Ross, I was on the boards of two US banks. They and the other three US banks we invested in were very troubled. The first board I served on was the Bank of the Cascades, headquartered in Bend, Oregon, which had the highest house appreciation in the US in 2006 at 21.4 percent. The bank had the Fed, FDIC, and three state bank regulators looking over it. It was small enough not to draw the attention of the CFPB, but when it was acquired by a bigger bank, it got the CFPB as well. This morass of regulators needs to be streamlined. For instance, when I was on the board of Virgin Money in the UK, it had only a safety and soundness regulator and consumer protection regulator.

The day after President Bush's 2007 Fourth of July/birthday party, I met with him, Bolten, Hennessey, and Wolf. I thanked POTUS for the party. I said Cricket and I very much enjoyed having dinner with his parents and old Andover friends. It was a thrill watching the fireworks from the Truman balcony with the president and those friends. We were also honored to attend the "friends and family" holiday dinners. Cricket always made it down from Connecticut for the parties.

Throughout the meeting, the president called me Juice or Juicer. As usual, he was very busy, making three calls to congressmen throughout the conversation. He asked how my relationship with Fannie and Freddie was. I said it was okay—that we did get respect but also pushback at times. He said he did not like them and that they recycled political people. They were taking advantage of their subsidies to pay big salaries and dividends to shareholders. He also asked me if I thought Franklin Raines was guilty. I said I could not answer because I was supposed to be the judge. He laughed and then said for the record I should say, "No comment." We talked about the enterprises' lobbying strength. POTUS teased Wolf about wanting to go work there. She jokingly said no, but for several million dollars, maybe.

Turning serious, Bush said Fannie and Freddie could be a "house of cards." My first PowerPoint slide showed that the combined outstanding debt of Fannie and Freddie and their guaranteed MBS plus Federal Home Loan Banks' debt of $5.5

trillion exceeded that of the publicly held debt of the United States.

Hennessey reinforced the message that the regulator needed more power to curb the portfolios. The president was very interested in the risk in their MBS portfolios, especially the subprime exposure, and their low capital requirements, which I described as inadequate. He also questioned the risk of their derivatives.

I told him that Barney Frank had done a good job in getting legislation passed, but it needed some work. The president said, "Barney is good."

Turning to the Senate, I said it was a problem. Although Chairman Dodd was running for president, Republicans seemed willing to go forward, including Shelby, Mel Martinez, Hagel, and Carper. Bush corrected me, saying Carper was a Democrat. I said I meant Crapo, but that on the Democratic side Tom Carper and Jack Reed of Rhode Island seemed okay. I said we needed more push to get Dodd and Shelby to move.

Even though almost half the Republicans in the House had voted for the legislation, I pointed out that there was one big issue: the Affordable Housing Fund. Wolf called it a "slush fund." I said I didn't like the fund either, but one of Barney's arguments was that if the GSEs had to pay state income taxes, the money would have gone to affordable housing. Wolf responded negatively when the president questioned whether there was a veto threat. Bush said that was one of the few bills he had not threatened. I said I thought it could be bipartisan.

Maybe I was being too pushy because at one point he reminded me that he was the president. He laughed when I replied, "I was the manager of the [Andover] baseball team." My last PowerPoint was entitled "New, Stronger Regulator Needed." It was a slide I had used in many public presentations:

✦   More bank-regulator-like powers

✦   Strength through combining the GSE regulators (OFHEO and Federal Housing Finance Board) [43 said, "That makes sense."]

✦   Transfer mission and new product authority from HUD. [43: "You mean Secretary Jackson is approving new products?"]

✦   Stronger independence—litigation and budget [I told the president that unlike other regulators, OFHEO was appropriated by Congress even though we did not cost the taxpayers a penny as we were funded by Fannie and Freddie.]

✦   Ability to strengthen capital requirements

✦   Clear guidance to regulate portfolios

After my presentation, President Bush said, "I support the need for GSE reform. Keep working on it. You are my point man. Let's get it done." Bolten thanked me as well. As usual, at the end of the meeting the president asked me about my family. I wished him happy birthday. While there, he looked at the list of birthday presents he had received. I had given him the book *Fateful Choices* about key decisions in 1940–41 leading up to World War II. He wrote me a thank-you note on the spot. I told him JB was getting married in October and Graci in May. In my speech at JB and Virginia's rehearsal dinner, I said, "After being so embroiled in the subprime mess, I am so happy to be here with such a prime crowd!"

Bush also expressed his condolences on my father's passing in June. I had flown down to Florida when my sister Annie told me our father was failing. I felt very fortunate that I'd arrived just in time to be able to talk with him. On July 13 we buried him in his old Riegelsville cemetery.

Franklin Raines was a loose end from the Fannie accounting mess. In December 2006 we sued him for restitution of undeserved bonus payments of $84.6 million, as well as Tim Howard (CFO) and Fannie's controller. There were 101 allegations. As reported in a *Washington Post* article from December 19, 2006, I said that they "improperly manipulated earnings to maximize their bonuses while knowingly neglecting accounting systems and internal controls, misapplying over 20 accounting principles and misleading the regulator and the public."[59] Their lawyers, according to the article, said, "The allegations were false and politically motivated" and that I was "fatally biased." Their lawyers were being paid by Fannie. It was a strange process. The article noted that the SEC and Justice Department had taken no action.

A December 20 *Wall Street Journal* editorial wrote that I was "fortunately" at OFHEO: "[H]e's shown no appetite for tolerating the shenanigans of the two lobbying powerhouses." Gretchen Morgenson's *New York Times* year-end article, "A Year to Suspend Disbelief," gave me the "Follow the Money Award," saying, "Perhaps your suit will encourage similar actions at other companies."[60]

The money did not come quickly. Raines's lawyers, with an unlimited Fannie budget, sued for twenty-one million documents and tried to get me removed as the judge. I had "unbridled hostility" and waged "an unrelenting campaign of disparagement."[61] His lawyers said it was not fair that one person "serves as a prosecutor, the judge and the politician."[62] Politician? They claimed that we "hoodwink and bamboozle the court."[63] Given that OFHEO only had a $60 million budget to supervise two organizations with $4.5 trillion in assets, we had to get a midyear supplemental appropriation of $6.7 million to fund the litigation costs.

Freddie's ex-CEO in November settled for $16.4 million. The nuisance court cases went on with Raines. In December, district court judge Richard Leon threw out the request for White House records despite Raines citing in an article, "[Bush] administrative aides jokingly referred to their assault on the companies as 'Noriega,' a reference to the military's use of loud music to bombard the former Panamanian dictator . . . into submission."[64] In January the defendants were more successful as the judge ruled OFHEO in contempt for not producing all our privileged documents.

Meanwhile, potential settlements were being discussed. Raines had received $90 million in compensation, but much of it was in stock and options, which he still held. Their value was falling rapidly. We got back $24.7 million from Raines and $6.4 million from Howard. Given all the problems in the mortgage market and the drain on our resources, we thought it was prudent to settle. Not everyone agreed. On April 21, 2008, the *Wall Street Journal* editorialized that it was a "paltry settlement" with "underwater stock options" although they did point out that they "have never been charged with a crime."

As it turned out, we had much bigger underwater worries: the whole mortgage market was sinking. An article in the *Wall Street Journal* that same day was more supportive, saying OFHEO was no longer "toothless" and that there was a silver lining from the accounting scandals as they "probably spared the two government-sponsored mortgage investors from even worse losses in the current wave of defaults."[65]

CHAPTER 15

Submarining Subprime

"The most hated man in America you never heard of."

–Jim Cramer, CNBC, August 2007

JIM CRAMER WAS referring to me in the above quote. He followed up on RealMoney.com in an August 9 column entitled "Most Hated Man in the US or Savior of Homes":

> Should the most hated man in America be a faceless bureaucrat by the name of James Lockhart? You don't know him. Nobody outside the Beltway does. But he is at the heart of the chokehold on American mortgage markets. When the book is written, Director of the Office of Federal Housing Enterprise Oversight (OFHEO) Jim Lockhart might be the man who is responsible for making more unforgotten men forgotten (and here I refer to the title of the excellent book on the Great Depression) than anyone since Herbert Hoover. . . .
>
> But now there's a gigantic 1930s-like freezeup again. Think of it—American Home (AHMIQ) . . . and all the other ne'er-do-wells are no longer in the game. [As an aside, when I joined WL Ross, it had recently bought

the bankrupt American Home's mortgage servicing operation. It took some years for us to straighten it out.] We just can't rely on Countrywide Financial (CFC) for heaven's sake? [Countrywide was the biggest supplier of mortgages to Fannie Mae. Many turned out to be very ugly.] So Fannie Mae needs to get into the game, get its caps lifted and help people. Lockhart has the ability to step aside, or better, take a leadership role. . . .

We have a financial tsunami on our hands. Sure, some of it is caused by people who didn't know what they were doing and took down 2/28 loans that they can no longer pay. Some mortgage companies and homebuilders sold loans too aggressively to people who couldn't afford them. Alan Greenspan encouraged taking of the teaser rates—and then raised rates 17 times, making it a nightmare for those who took the bait. . . .

And Lockhart, the man who is a chokehold on the carotid artery of Fannie Mae, could allow this [lifting Fannie's portfolio cap] to happen.

With the subprime crisis hitting the news daily, pressure built to unleash Fannie and Freddie to save the housing market. By early August, the problem was starting to spread beyond subprime. The shoddy and predatory underwriting of the past several years was surfacing big-time.

Despite our 30 percent directed capital increase, the enterprises' thin and poor-quality statutory capital meant that they could not be the savior—poor quality because a major portion of their capital was an accounting concept called a deferred tax asset (DTA). That asset must be reserved against (subtracted from equity) if the company is money-losing into the future. The enterprises and many other financial institutions had to reserve against their deferred tax assets in 2008 and 2009. The emperor had no clothes.

Mudd told me several times in the summer of 2007 that there were three types of subprime loans of about equal size: ones that were bound to fail, ones that might make it, and ones that should not have been subprime to begin with. The enterprises targeted refinancing the latter group but also dipped into the middle one. Freddie committed in April to buy $20 billion in better-underwritten subprime mortgages, as did Fannie Mae. An *American Banker* article of May 23 expressed it well: "Fannie, Freddie Subprime Plans Seen for 'Cream.'" I was cautious, saying, "OFHEO wants to make sure that it's done in a safe and sound manner. It's a major part of their capital that they're committing."

On June 26, 2007, the *Washington Times* published my op-ed entitled "Homeownership ethos and subprimes" (you don't get to choose your titles in op-eds), which stated, "Delinquencies and potential foreclosures put some Americans at risk of losing their homes." Fannie and Freddie's "own securities [are] backed by $170 billion of subprime mortgages. Both are expanding efforts with lenders and consumer groups to avoid foreclosures and make safer subprime mortgages but need a strong regulator to oversee these efforts."

As we entered July, I was asked to give a speech at a NERA conference in Sun Valley, Idaho, which was hard to turn down. Presentations had to have a theme of a Broadway play. Getting creative, I changed *Monty Python's Spamalot* to *Mighty Python's Subprimealot*.

The playbill cover had a python that—having swallowed '04, '05, and '06 eggs—was trying to swallow '07 eggs, representing the bad subprime years. The subtitle was "Hard to Digest."

Most slides had in their title a song from *Monty Python's Spamalot*, including, "I'm All Alone," "Where Are You?," "Run Away," "Find Your Grail," and "Always Look on the Bright Side of Life." My favorite was "He's Not Yet Dead," where I pointed out that the subprime's market share of the total mortgage market had tripled from 2002 to almost 22 percent in 2006 ($600 billion), risk layering and fraud had increased, delinquencies and foreclosures were increasing, PLS prices (especially lower tranches) were falling, subprime hedge funds (Bear Stearns) were failing, and mortgage servicers were under pressure.

My plaintive call in "I'm All Alone" was for legislation. The "Find Your Grail" slide had what was to become our agenda for the next years:

✦   Encourage forbearance and loan modifications rather than foreclosures

✦   Encourage rescue mortgages without impairing safety and soundness

✦   Address PLS market and risk layering issues

On July 20, OFHEO jointly sponsored a conference with the key bank regulators entitled "Private Label MBS Outlook: Investors in the Subprime and Non-Traditional Mortgage Guidance." FDIC chair Sheila Bair and I gave opening remarks. Syron also spoke:

> Certainly, over the last month there has been much written and said on the subprime private label MBS market. Credit spreads on especially lower-rated MBS have widened dramatically . . . over ninety subprime lenders have shut down, originators are 30 percent off from last year, some hedge funds had been closed, and delinquencies, especially for adjustable-rate subprime loans, have risen dramatically. . . . There are many reasons why this mess has happened—excess liquidity, heightened demand, creative "teaser" mortgages, lower underwriting standards and a lack of market discipline.

The *Economist*[66] wrote that "Fannie and Freddie also hoped to regain credibility by portraying themselves as buyers of last resort in the subprime market, as private lenders belatedly tighten standards and investors run from toxic mortgage-backed debt."

In August the enterprises were not doing well, but the pressure continued to mount to rescue subprime and the rest of the mortgage market. They believed, as Frank was quoted in the July 30, 2007, *BusinessWeek*, that "Freddie and Fannie aren't the problem. [They] are the good part." The CEOs were pushing hard on me directly and indirectly. Senators Dodd and Schumer separately wrote me letters on August 7, asking me to temporarily raise the caps on the portfolios to stabilize the market. Perversely, the enterprises' stock prices increased over 10 percent because of the letters. Freddie was also asking to buy jumbo mortgages, those over the conforming loan limit of $417,000.

There were some mixed messages coming from the administration. President Bush quite rightfully said we needed reform legislation first. My boss, Secretary Jackson, made encouraging remarks about allowing the enterprises to do jumbo loans in a meeting with Mudd. I pushed back in an August 10 letter to Senator Schumer, saying that we would not raise the portfolio limits, but that we would "keep under active consideration [the] request for an increase in the portfolio." I also pointed out that most of the problems were in mortgages outside the enterprises' authorized businesses, such as jumbos and lower-quality subprime. The CEOs were not happy. The major mortgage and housing groups asked me to reconsider.

Dan Mudd suggested I call Angelo Mozilo, CEO of Countrywide, to reinforce Mudd's message that we should unleash Fannie. Previously, I'd been pushing Fannie to put back bad mortgages to Countrywide. They had the legal right to do that but were reluctant as Countrywide was Fannie's biggest mortgage originator by far. Some people called Countrywide

Fannie Mae's front office because of their tight ties.

As Mozilo's regulator was John Reich of the Office of Thrift Supervision (OTS), I thought it was appropriate to have him on the call. The OTS was in our building, so I went upstairs to Reich's office, right above mine. Mozilo assured me that Countrywide and Fannie had no problems, and therefore there was no need for changes.

The Bear Stearns hedge funds, after their fire sale of PLS, declared bankruptcy. BNP Paribas, the French bank, suspended redemptions in three funds holding MBS. The PLS market was tanking. Subprime lenders were failing almost weekly. A *Washington Post* August 11 editorial, "Bubble and Bust," wrote:

> Today's tulip bulb is the subprime mortgage: a loan to a not terribly creditworthy person in the United States to buy a house that he or she really can't afford. Hundreds of billions of dollars' worth of these paper commitments have been made, gathered together and resold as bonds to hedge funds and banks all over the world—which in turn have used them as collateral to obtain more loans, so they can buy more bonds, and so on. Now that home prices are falling and many unhappy US homeowners are, foreseeably, defaulting, the whole business is unraveling. . . . The world is in the grip of a liquidity crisis.

The editorial concluded that "it seems unwise to tap [Fannie and Freddie] for a bailout now."

It was a tough decision not to release the portfolio constraints, but the decision was revisited many times over the next year. I repeated in many responses that they were supporting the mortgage market. Given the low capital requirements for guaranteeing MBS, they issued over $700 billion in 2007.

"The fact that you have a regulator announcing economic

policy here while the president is up on his boat in Kennebunkport [Maine] is a little troubling to me," Dodd said in a conference call with reporters, according to a Dow Jones article.[67] The article also said, "Dodd spread criticism broadly, charging that missteps at rating agencies, brokers, lenders, and regulators combined to fuel a global credit crunch." It was very hard to disagree with his list—except he forgot to mention his lack of action as chair of the Senate Banking Committee to push for GSE reform.

Luckily, Senator Dodd did not know I was in Nantucket when he spoke. It was not a peaceful vacation for me. I was having daily calls with the office and regular ones with Mudd and Syron, as they kept pushing me to remove the portfolio constraints. On August 16, Fannie finally released their 2006 results with $4.1 billion in profits, a 36 percent drop from 2005. It turned out to be their last profitable year for many to come. The same day, Senator Schumer threatened to introduce legislation in September if I did not raise the portfolio limits.

The CEOs kept pitching me that they could save the mortgage market. I told them that they lacked the capital to support a $10 trillion market. Their combined equity at the end of the second quarter 2007 was only $64 billion. To be fair, they really did think that they could help stabilize the market and help some homeowners in toxic mortgages. But I am sure that they and their shareholders also liked seeing their stock prices go up when the rumors said that we would remove the cap.

Mudd, the ex-Marine, was always the tougher one. As it happened, he was also on Nantucket. One night he and his wife were dining at the same restaurant as Cricket and I. It was awkward, but we were civil.

After I returned from Nantucket on August 20, a policy time with the president on mortgage and credit issues and steps to avoid foreclosures led to a Rose Garden press briefing the next day. Bush said, "The recent disturbances in the subprime mortgage market are modest . . . in relation to the size of the economy. But if your family is . . . one of those having trouble making the monthly payments, this problem doesn't seem modest at all. . . . I strongly urge lenders to work with homeowners to adjust their mortgages."

The Senate continued to focus on raising the conforming loan limits and removing the portfolio caps instead of GSE reform. I wrote Senator Schumer another letter on September 6, telling him that the enterprises could buy $20 to $30 billion a month without hitting the portfolio caps because of the natural run-off in their portfolios. He then proposed legislation to increase the conforming loan limits and the portfolios by 10 percent.

The *Financial Times* had an article, "Fannie and Freddie to the rescue? Don't bet on it," which was an amusing way to answer Cramer:

> This is a problem. In a time when America, or at least Wall Street, needs a spineless hack as the head of the key agency, it is saddled with a credible man of principle: James Lockhart, OFHEO's director, Yale graduate, Harvard MBA, lieutenant in the nuclear Navy, risk management software entrepreneur, senior insurance executive, and former head of the Pension Benefit Guarantee [sic] Corporation. "A real hard-ass" in the words of a mortgage finance executive. It doesn't seem as though he can be intimidated by the threat of being sent back to Plano, Texas to work at his uncle's car dealership. Lockhart was appointed in the middle of last year to the directorship when there was no immediate, obvious cost to anyone of having a competent, effective regulator who actually knows what those buttons on his computer are connected to. . . . What is worse, his resistance to Fannie and Freddie ballooning their balance sheets and loosening their controls is reinforced by his experience in a previous

job. The Pension Benefit Guarantee Corporation, a thinly capitalized government insurance operation, which charged inadequate premiums for covering beneficiaries of failed pension funds, was in turnaround as they say in Hollywood, during his tenure from 1989 to 1993. Lockhart had to clean up other people's messes and one can guess he doesn't want to do it again.[68]

In September, we agreed to give Fannie and Freddie some more flexibility to manage portfolio fluctuations by increasing their portfolio by 2 percent. Dodd called the move "timid and inadequate."[69] The ever-quotable Schumer said, "Now that OFHEO has put its toe in the water, it is time to jump in." I said, "It would not be prudent at this time to allow any major increases." I should have added, "Or they will drown."

I did indicate, per our agreement with the GSEs, that the caps could be removed in February 2008 if they filed timely audited financials. Also in September, under pressure, Paulson and Bernanke agreed to a temporary increase in the conforming loan limit. I was against that.

All was not calm in the UK either. Northern Rock, a bank headquartered in Newcastle, had a "run on the bank." They asked for and got support from the Bank of England. They had a liquidity problem as they were borrowing short term and making thirty-year loans. At that point the UK government guarantee on bank deposits was very low. It had to be raised to stop runs. Later, I learned that Northern Rock was quite creative, even offering loans higher than a house's value. After failed rescue attempts by private equity, including WL Ross, the bank was nationalized in February 2008.

On a personal note, a year after I joined WL Ross in September 2009, we invested in Virgin Money, a very small UK mortgage bank, which had been almost fully owned by Sir Richard Branson until then. I joined the board. In 2012, Sir Richard Branson decided to have a Virgin Money board meeting on his private Necker Island to discuss the potential acquisition of Northern Rock from the UK government. Neither Richard nor Wilbur were members of the board, but their input was crucial. As WL Ross's funds were going to put up almost all the purchase price, we were more conservative in our pricing than the Virgin team.

Cricket and Wilbur's wife, Hilary, were included as guests. The Rosses and Lockharts arrived early. Richard decided to give us a tour of the island, including the highest spot. We trekked up the hill. Wilbur stepped on a thorn, which went right through his athletic shoe and into his foot. Sir Richard, being Sir Richard, took off Wilbur's shoe and sock. Then he bit the thorn and pulled it out with his teeth. Wilbur finished the tour and had no infection.

Between the board meetings, we swam, sailed, and did other water sports. We played tennis with Sir Richard and watched him parasail for miles. The meals and entertainment were elegant.

Necker has colonies of pink flamingos and lemurs as Richard is trying to preserve the species. The lemurs had a ten-foot fence surrounding their area. Richard said they could not jump out. Our villa, Bali Cliff, was at the tip of the peninsula at the western end of the island, about a mile from the lemur colony. The bedroom and deck had a fabulous 270-degree view of the Caribbean. To get to the bathroom required going down some steps. The bathroom was totally open to nature with only a back wall containing a sink and toilet. The shower was totally exposed. Luckily, a coral reef surrounded the peninsula, so no boats could come close when we showered. In typical Sir Richard tongue-in-cheek fashion, the toilet held a crown on its tank.

The lack of walls meant that animals could wander in, including a giant iguana. The highlight was when one of Richard's supposedly fenced-in lemurs joined us in the bathroom.

The Virgin Money board did decide to buy Northern Rock,

its seventy-five branches, and about £14 billion of mortgages and £16 billion in deposits, for less than £1 billion. The strong Virgin team led by Dame Jayne Ann Gadhia, using the Virgin brand, turned it around. Later we took Virgin Money public, and WL Ross eventually successfully sold our shares. Several years afterwards, Virgin Money was acquired by Clydesdale Bank, which assumed the Virgin Money name. It is now the sixth largest bank in the UK.

Back to Fannie and Freddie: Senator Schumer called a meeting in October 2007 with Dan Mudd, Patty Cook of Freddie (as Syron was abroad), and me to discuss subprime mortgages. I told Schumer it was a shame that their problems prevented them from doing more. I also said I did not buy the argument that somehow, single-handedly, the enterprises could save the mortgage market.

Congressional Democrats did not agree and again introduced bills to increase the portfolios by 10 percent, specifying that 85 percent had to be used to refinance subprime mortgages. The sponsors of the bill may have been undercut when the enterprises reported that their portfolios shrank in September.

House Financial Services chairman of the Oversight Subcommittee, Representative Paul Kanjorski (D-PA), asked for my thoughts on the legislation. I wrote back to him on October 31 that it "sets an unfortunate precedent of overriding the safety and soundness regulator's judgment."

In a June 2018 interview with the Yale Program on Financial Stability, which is a very important effort to prevent future crises, I said: "It was tough to get a majority to agree on new legislation. Some Republicans despised Fannie and Freddie—and didn't want to help them at all—while some Democrats wanted us to loosen additional restrictions on them. It really ended up being a balancing act. In the back of my mind, I always knew that if we were too tough on Fannie and Freddie, we might not have been able to get any legislation at all."

Out of left field, in November 2007, Fannie and Freddie got subpoenaed by New York attorney general Andrew Cuomo. He was doing an investigation of mortgage market appraisal practices and had focused on Washington Mutual (regulated by the OTS) and its mortgage appraisal company, suggesting they inflated home values. I wrote Cuomo a letter objecting to that subpoena as he had not gone through me as the regulator. Cuomo was using the 1921 Martin Act about securities fraud to go after Fannie and Freddie. He could not go after Washington Mutual as the bank regulators had "pre-emption" over the states on national banks. There was a question whether OFHEO had preemption for Fannie and Freddie. The enterprises were starting to comply with the investigation. I told them to stop.

Cuomo accused the enterprises of selling fraudulent MBS because of the Washington Mutual mortgages they had bought. He threatened to put the two CEOs in jail. Weirdly for a former HUD secretary, he said in a press briefing that he was "investigating Fannie Mae and Freddie Mac and other investment banks."[70] I pointed out in my response that he might not understand the difference between Fannie and Freddie MBS and other MBS issuers. Fannie and Freddie were guaranteeing the mortgage credit risk. Therefore, the investors in the enterprises' MBS that Cuomo was trying to protect did not have any exposure to mortgage credit risk, even if the appraisals were inflated.

Schumer weighed in with a letter urging me to cooperate with Cuomo and be "part of the solution not part of a perpetuation of the problem," as reported in a January 31, 2008, *Wall Street Journal* article.[71] As our team, led by General Counsel Alfred Pollard, reviewed the appraisal practices, we agreed with Cuomo that some of the practices were bad—loan officers leaning on appraisers to get higher valuations, brokers ordering appraisals, questionable compensation, and conflicting automated appraisal processes. By the end of February, I was talking almost daily with

Cuomo to reach a compromise to improve appraisals.

We did reach a good agreement with Cuomo in March 2008. Fannie and Freddie promulgated the Home Valuation Code of Conduct (HVCC), with a scheduled implementation date of January 1, 2009. The code was designed to eliminate fraud in the appraisal process and conflicts of interest. The enterprises also funded the Independent Valuation Protection Institute to monitor compliance with the code.

In OFHEO's March 3 press release I was quoted: "Accurate, independent appraisals are very important to ensuring safety and soundness of Fannie Mae, Freddie Mac and the mortgage market." Some of the bank regulators were urging me to wait for a joint appraisal code with them, which I thought would take much too long. However, we did add a comment period to the code to help appease the bank regulators. Nevertheless, the OTS put out a statement: "The closed-door fashion in which it was reached could result in negative unintended consequences."[72]

In Cuomo's blunt press release[73] he said, "Now national banks have a clear choice: immediately adopt the new code and clean up appraisal fraud in the mortgage industry or stop doing business with Fannie Mae and Freddie Mac—it is that simple." His release also quoted a pleased Schumer, who had been pushing the bank regulators as well as me: "This settlement represents one of the first major blows against the types of predatory lending that were so prevalent in the mortgage business of the last few years."

The bank regulators continued to fight back against the Home Valuation Code. It did seem strange to me that Fannie and Freddie did not have the right to insist that an appraisal should not be done by the same bank that was selling the mortgage to them.

At the end of March, Comptroller of the Currency John Dugan wrote me a twelve-page letter saying the code might violate federal law. He admitted, "OFHEO may well have a safety and soundness basis," but it "crosses the line into regulation of entities outside its domain." He was especially upset about Cuomo's involvement.

By June 20, 2008, we had united almost all regulators against us as the Fed, OCC, OTS, and National Credit Union Association sent a letter calling the code "unwarranted" and saying that it "would unnecessarily undermine the safe and sound extension of mortgage credit."[74] Sheila Bair sent a separate and softer letter. As we thought the code was important, it was finally implemented in May 2009.

A Federal Reserve Bank of Philadelphia paper[75] noted that Dodd-Frank in July 2010 superseded the code but "actually codified several of the HVCC's provisions." Their paper concluded: "The HVCC has done part of what it was supposed to do by reducing inflated valuations that were prevalent during the subprime boom . . . [but] caused the origination of purchase mortgages to be more difficult."

Back to November 2007, bad news continued to mount. Fannie and Freddie reported third-quarter losses of $1.4 billion and $2.0 billion, respectively, causing over 20 percent drops in their stock prices. OFHEO's House Price Index declined for the first time in thirteen years with a third-quarter drop of 0.4 percent. Twenty states reported declines, with California the steepest at 3.6 percent.

Knowing that the enterprises would continue to report losses in the fourth quarter, we put pressure on them to raise capital and lower their dividends, which they did. They issued preferred stock as they were unwilling to issue common stock at such a "low" price. Fannie raised $7.9 billion in December and Freddie $6 billion. Both companies would have violated our 30 percent directed capital requirement without those preferred stock issuances.

On December 6, 2007, Fannie Mae announced that it would introduce a new adverse market fee of twenty-five basis points on March 1, 2008, and reduce maximum loan-to-value by 5 percent for properties in declining markets. Fannie "also said it 'strongly urged' lenders not to solely rely on the information reflected in the appraisal and to validate housing prices trends using other sources as well."[76]

Also on the sixth, Bush met with a group of regulators and mortgage executives, the Hope Now Alliance. In his statement afterwards, he called for FHA modernization, tax forgiveness on mortgage reductions, and funding for mortgage counseling, saying, "Congress needs to pass legislation . . . that strengthens independent regulation of the GSEs and ensures they focus on their important housing mission. The GSE reform bill passed by the House earlier this year is good start. But the Senate has not acted."[77]

After the president's remarks, Paulson held a press conference with HUD secretary Jackson, Bair, Dugan, Reich, Fed governor Randall Kroszner, me, Mike Heid (Wells Fargo, representing the House Policy Counsel), and George Miller (American Securitization Forum, or ASF). Bair and Heid many years later were on the board of Fannie Mae.

Paulson's big announcement was that the ASF had "announced today a set of guidelines to streamline the process of refinancing and modifying subprime loans for able homeowners." The key was to freeze rates on those 2/28 and 3/27 before they reset at higher rates. Paulson said it was not a "silver bullet."[78] Unfortunately, the process was not followed as widely as we hoped.

Speaking last at the press conference, I applauded "the foreclosure prevention initiative" as Fannie and Freddie had about $160 billion in subprime MBS. I ended: "For the last six years, Congress has been considering GSE reform legislation. Given the problems faced by Fannie Mae and Freddie Mac and the current market condition, it is time to act to ensure that they will be here to support the mortgage market, especially affordable housing for lower-income people, now and in the future."

As the PLS market had dried up starting in the summer and banks were pulling back, Fannie and Freddie's mortgage market share in the fourth quarter of 2007 was 76 percent, which was double their market share of 38 percent for 2006. The enterprises were now serving their countercyclical role, but without enough capital to promote stability and liquidity. It had been a year since Paulson had pushed for a final year-end reform deal. Barney Frank and the House had delivered in March, but the Senate was MIA on serious reform. They were concentrating unsuccessfully on increasing the portfolio limits and the conforming loan limits.

In the year-end, December 21 *American Banker*, I expressed my 2008 New Year's wish for OFHEO: "'Hopefully, it doesn't have a future,' Mr. Lockhart said, only half-joking [hoping there would be a new agency created by Congress soon]. 'It'll be very tough to manage this agency with one or two hands tied behind your back.'"[79]

Chapter 16
Searching for Lifeboats

"The GSEs have become the dominant funding mechanism for the entire mortgage system in these troubling times. They are fulfilling their missions in providing liquidity, stability and affordability to the mortgage market. In doing so, they have been reducing risk in the market but concentrating more risks on themselves."

—James B. Lockhart III testimony to the Senate Banking, Housing and Urban Affairs Committee, February 7, 2008

MY NEW YEAR'S wish looked promising as 2008 started. Chair of Senate Banking Dodd was returning from his unsuccessful presidential campaign and making noises about passing GSE reform. Both President Bush and Paulson were calling for reform. Bush repeated the call in his State of the Union as well as mentioning Social Security reform. I was giving speeches and meeting with senators to push for reform.

One of the potential carrots for the Democrats in GSE reform was an increase in the conforming loan limit. They were concerned that the cost of "jumbo" mortgages rates were about 6.7 percent versus the 5.7 percent for a conforming mortgage. In normal markets, the spread was much smaller. The carrot was given away to get the House Democrats to agree to the $150 billion stimulus bill, composed primarily of tax reductions. The February stimulus act contained a 75 percent increase in the conforming loan limit from $417,000 to $729,750 for higher-price areas. Very many of those mortgages were concentrated in Speaker Pelosi's California. Paulson, leading the negotiations, said he had been a victim of a "bipartisan steamroll."

Despite Bush's and Paulson's reluctant agreement, I remained opposed to increasing the conforming loan limit without GSE reform. I repeated my disagreement in the Senate Banking Committee hearing on February 7. I said that as a new product, jumbo mortgages would require new systems and controls as credit risks were different and concentrated in California. Answering a Dodd question, I said, "A jumbo mortgage takes three times as much capital as their normal mortgage, so that's a concern to us from a safety and soundness standpoint."

With me on the first panel of the Banking Committee hearing was Treasury assistant secretary David Nason and FHLB chairman Ronnie Rosenfeld. The second panel was Mudd and Syron. I, of course, made my strong pitch for reform, saying that they had grown by 16 percent in 2007 with now a $5 trillion book of business. They were expected to report fourth-quarter losses and were "stretched." I had charts showing that they were "huge;" between the enterprises and the FHLBanks, they had $6.3 trillion in obligations.

I showed a chart demonstrating that the enterprises' guaranteed MBS and portfolios at fair value market prices were highly leveraged—Fannie Mae was eighty-one times capital and Freddie Mac was eighty-five times. As I added, "If you look at it the other way around, there is only 1.5 percent of equity backing their mortgage exposure." I noted that they were "securitizing almost $100 billion per month in mortgages, which has led to a dramatic reversal in their market share, from 38 percent to 76 percent, so they are effectively the mortgage market, and it might be 90 percent if you added in the FHLBs."

The two CEOs testified that they were in favor of reform as in the House's 2007 bill, but they made it clear that the stronger capital and portfolio constraints were not appropriate. Mudd testified: "Regulation should not impose arbitrary limits, including a so-called 'systemic risk' standard, on the GSEs' portfolios." Syron agreed with Mudd, saying, "The focus should be on managing the risk the portfolios posed to our financial safety and soundness." He rather rashly said to a Shelby question, "The subprime MBS mortgages were bought for our [Affordable Housing Fund] goal. We do not, at this time, expect to take any losses in those mortgages." He also noted that they had $100 billion in subprime PLS.

On capital, Syron testified, "Requiring the GSEs to have the same leverage ratio as banks would make the GSE business model unviable." Mudd testified, "As I have said before, the normal capital levels established by Congress for the normal time should be the norm."

Senator Schumer said, "Fannie and Freddie have not lived up to my expectations. We had to push them forward every step of the way." My interpretation was pushing them off a cliff. He added, "I expect in return for allowing the enterprises to enter the jumbo market the companies will also make a commitment to fund additional refinancing or modification resources to lower-income borrowers who are having difficulty affording their payments."

Senator Shelby, the ex-chair and then the ranking Republican, was not happy with the enterprises, but especially Paulson, as he had agreed to increase the conforming loan limit after he told them he would not. He said to Nason, "I know Mr. Lockhart is committed to [GSE reform] and I know Mr. Rosenfeld is, but I am not sure about Secretary Paulson. You know he says one thing and does another."

Nason's answer was right: Paulson was very committed to reform. The question between the Senate Republicans and Democrats was how strong the reform should be. I had said in my testimony that the House bill needed to be strengthened, especially on portfolios and capital. An *American Banker* article[80] reported on Dodd's and Shelby's comments after the meeting: "Senator Dodd said he was confident the deal on the GSEs could be reached quickly, but Senator Shelby was pessimistic. 'It's going to be very difficult,' Senator Shelby said in an interview. 'We don't need reform that is going to be a sham.'"

This tension lasted for the next several months. I spent that time meeting with key senators, giving speeches and interviews to push the GSE reform message as the housing and mortgage markets continue to deteriorate. The Fed was very supportive. Chairman Bernanke came to visit me on February 20. I was in regular contact with his point person, Governor Kevin Warsh, whom I knew well and respected because he was at the NEC when I was working with the White House on Social Security reform.

The day after the hearing, there was a Freddie Mac board meeting at their McLean, Virginia, headquarters, which I attended. It was another contentious meeting. In their 2004 consent agreement, they had agreed to split the chairman and CEO positions. Syron had refused to modify his contract, which did not allow that. The term of the contract was now over. Worst yet, Freddie's COO, a very capable banker, Gene McQuade, resigned in 2007. One of the reasons was that he did not like the political fishbowl of Washington. Syron was trying to do three jobs at once but was stretched too thin to do them properly. A search for a CEO was underway, but the headhunter said it was hard to get people to leave New York for Washington. That was believable.

A second issue was a serious but arcane accounting disagreement. All of Freddie's derivative losses and gains were wiped out in the required restatements of their financials after their accounting scandals, except closed-off losses in "cash flow" hedges. As those $5 billion in losses were part of accumulated other comprehensive income, they were not deducted from statutory capital. When reviewing the 2007 accounts, OFHEO's accountants recommended, with strong outside accounting opinions, that the $5 billion should be charged to income. If so, it would have put Freddie's capital below our 30 percent imposed extra capital requirement. The issue was critical. I had attended several heated but inconclusive meetings with the Freddie team.

The board pushback was strong. The lead director, Tom Johnson, asked me to meet separately with him and two other directors, Bob Glauber and William Lewis, who had been a trustee at Andover. He reminded me of the school's motto, *Non Sibi,* "Not for one's self." He suggested that I was being selfish and unpatriotic for questioning Freddie's accounting.

As we had strong accounting opinions on both sides and nothing from the SEC, the decision was pushed off until the SEC scrubbed their accounts as part of the upcoming registration process. When Freddie did register with the SEC in the second quarter of 2008, the entry was allowed. However, the $5 billion was later written off.

On February 8, 2008, I was invited to a breakfast at the Four Seasons Hotel in Washington with the Federal Advisory Council of the Federal Reserve System for their quarterly meeting. The twelve participants were bank CEOs representing the twelve Federal Reserve districts. I used my standard PowerPoint presentation about Fannie and Freddie's huge size, their massive market share, and their extreme leverage.

Ken Lewis—chairman, president, and CEO of Bank of America—commented that Fannie and Freddie "were the mother of all systemic risk." I'm not sure the CEOs enjoyed their breakfast. The irony was that the Bank of America had, the year before, invested $2 billion in Countrywide and later acquired it.

I eventually saw numbers indicating that 22 percent of Fannie's mortgages came from Countrywide and 5 percent of them were in default.

At the end of February, Fannie and Freddie reported their 2007 results. It was not pretty: *underwater*. Fannie reported a $3.6 billion loss for the fourth quarter, and Freddie's losses were $2.5 billion. The losses were a combination of credit losses and losses on the much-feared derivatives as interest rates fell in the quarter with the Fed's interest-rate cuts. Fannie's losses for the year were $2.1 billion, and Freddie's were $3.1 billion. It was Freddie's first ever annual loss. Their core capital continued to exceed our 30 percent imposed requirement because of their preferred stock offerings in the fourth quarter.

Despite the losses, I had to live up to our agreement, which was that if they produced timely, audited financial accounts, we would remove the portfolio caps. On announcing that the caps would be removed on March 1, I said that the filings "constitute an important milestone in remediation of their respective operational and control weaknesses." Schumer, always willing to give a quote, "praised the action as 'a long overdue step, but certainly a welcome one.'" But Shelby called the action "ill-advised."[81]

To me, the portfolio restrictions were becoming less important. Without more capital, it was going to be hard for them to grow their portfolios. Bernanke, Paulson, and I said they should raise more capital. The two CEOs agreed on the importance of capital. Mudd said, "The number one priority is capital." In sync with the theme of this book, Syron told investors, "We're treating capital a little bit like a scuba diver treats oxygen."[82]

The headline on the March 7 *Washington Post* business section was "Investors Dump Securities from Fannie, Freddie— Mortgage Sector Strongholds Falter." It reported that investors were selling both their stocks and MBS. The spreads about Treasuries were the highest since 1986.

Barron's March 10, 2008, giant front-page headline was "Is Fannie Mae Toast? . . . A government bailout ahead?" The cover illustration was a toaster with houses going into it. The article[83] was hard hitting and gave an in-depth accounting analysis of Fannie. The first sentence was "It's perhaps the cruelest of ironies that in the US housing market's greatest hour of need, the major entity created during the Depression to bring liquidity to housing, Fannie Mae, may itself need a bailout."

The financial analysis was based on a leaked White House NEC memo by Jason Thomas, which was very upsetting to me—but apparently not upsetting to the author: he sent an email to Steel notifying him that his memo was the source of *Barron*'s article. As I told Thomas later, the analysis was reasonable, but I thought the message was very harmful as there was no legal way to bail them out. The memo started:

> Any realistic assessment of Fannie Mae's capital position would show the company is currently insolvent. Accounting fraud has resulted in several asset categories (non-agency securities, deferred tax assets, low-income partnership investments) being overstated, while the guarantee obligation liability is understated. These accounting shenanigans add up to tens of billions of exaggerated net worth.
>
> Yet, the impact of a tsunami of mortgage defaults is yet to run through Fannie's income statement and further annihilate its capital. Such grim results are a logical consequence of Fannie's dual mandate to serve the housing market while maximizing shareholder returns. In trying to do both, Fannie has done neither well. With shareholder capital depleted, a government seizure of the company is inevitable.

He did have a good description of their capital:

> The primary regulatory capital measure for Fannie Mae
> is core capital. As pointed out by OFHEO director James
> Lockhart, "The statutory core capital is shareholders
> equity excluding Accumulated Other Comprehensive
> Income (AOCI), which is primarily marking their
> Available for Sale portfolios to market. As AOCI is a large
> negative number, core capital is significantly higher than
> shareholder's equity, especially at Freddie Mac, which
> also has losses on some old, closed hedges in AOCI."
>
> In addition, Lockhart notes another capital measure,
> fair value capital, which is calculated by marking all
> assets and liabilities to market. Fair Value is considered
> by many to be a superior estimate of net worth, as it is
> unsullied by sometimes arbitrary accounting choices.

However, what he did not point out is that unlike bank
regulators, OFHEO had no discretion in how to define core
capital. It was defined by Congress. For instance, he mentioned
the deferred tax asset, which bank regulators only treated as
regulatory capital up to 10 percent. All of Fannie's 29 percent
and Freddie's 27 percent reported DTA were treated as part of
core capital calculation.

Another issue was the valuation of the PLS. There were few
trades. Those that happened tended to be "fire sales." An index—
ABX—was traded. Its AAA index started to fall in spring 2007.
By March 2008 it was down 40 percent. In the spring of 2007,
Freddie started to buy some of the index. We stopped them.
Starting in fall 2007, we had been having regular, very tough
meetings with the management teams on putting more realistic
marks on the PLS. We also wanted them to classify some of those
marks as permanent rather than temporary AOCI, which would

have reduced core capital. We were making some progress, but the pushback was strong.

The NEC paper ended, "A nationalized Fannie Mae would be refocused to directly address the various problems of illiquidity, affordability and sustainability in the mortgage market." *Barron's* article picked up the same theme: "Just maybe a bailout of Fannie, in effect the nationalization, would be a good thing. A retooled Fannie could pursue its important social mission without the distraction of Wall Street."

The pressure was building to reduce the extra 30 percent capital requirement to give the enterprises more firepower to securitize loans, especially for the newly authorized jumbo loans. The Treasury was pushing for it. Steel and I had been negotiating with the two CEOs separately and together. The terms of our negotiations had three elements: a reduction in the excess capital requirement, an agreement by Fannie and Freddie to raise more capital, and their promise to call off their anti-reform lobbying efforts. Despite the CEOs' prior promises, we were hearing from senators that the enterprises' congressional teams and lobbyists were still talking down reform.

Mudd was arguing that he had now fulfilled all eighty-one requirements in the consent agreement. Freddie was still missing one: the separation of the chairman and CEO jobs. They also said that they needed their board's approval to raise capital. As always with Fannie and Freddie, the process was frustrating.

Paulson, Bernanke, and Geithner were working on the sale of the troubled Bear Sterns to J. P. Morgan the weekend of March 15 and 16. Hank wanted to announce a Bear Stearns deal and a deal with Fannie and Freddie the Sunday evening before markets opened in Asia.

In a Sunday-morning email, which I only saw years later, Bob Steel wrote to his team,

As I think all of you know, we are being leaned on as part of the plan for today's series of afternoon announcements to deliver a GSE "plan." Just to summarize, the idea would be to announce a grand bargain of capital raise and beginning the relaxation of the capital surcharge for housing GSEs. Also, some ideas about "commitment" to legislation but that's a bit fuzzy. . . .

I have spoken to Mudd, and he is good. . . . He expressively said Lockhart needs to ELIMINATE the negative rhetoric. I have emailed and called Syron and waiting to hear back.

In the email Steel also wrote that he "was leaned on very hard by Bill Dudley [NY Fed deputy] to harden substantially the gty [meaning a US guarantee]. I do not like it and it has not been part of my conversation with anyone else. I view that as a very significant move, way above my pay grade, to double the size of the US debt in one fell swoop." To harden the guarantee would have required congressional action.

The Bear Stearns deal was announced, but Fannie and Freddie did not get nailed down. Monday afternoon there was a meeting in the Roosevelt Room with President Bush and his Working Group on Financial Markets. I had graduated from one of the chairs against the wall to the president's side of the table, albeit at the end, next to Chris Cox. Next to him was Paulson, then Bush and Bernanke. The PowerPoint focused on overall liquidity challenges, banks, and Bear Stearns but did have one bullet: "GSEs: need to see counter-cyclical activity."

Steel mentioned Fannie and Freddie, and so Bush asked him how I was doing. He said "great," and then Bush told the crowd we went to college together. We chatted afterwards with him. In his media statement he said these were "challenging times," but "we've taken strong and decisive action." He added Paulson had

"reaffirmed the fact that our financial institutions are strong."
He ended by saying, "In the long run, our economy is going to be
fine. Right now, we're dealing with a difficult situation."

Still working on the deal with Fannie and Freddie, earlier
that Monday I had a call with Fannie Mae's chairman. Monday
evening, Mudd sent me a proposed statement that he and Syron
had agreed upon. I am afraid I had "negative rhetoric" again in
my reply. I wrote,

> At first read it appears that OFHEO is being asked to
> be first, last and only [to lower capital requirement]
> with no firm commitment by you to raise capital. The
> idea strikes me as perverse, and I assume it would seem
> perverse to the market. If you believe that 2008 business
> is very profitable, it is not credible that you would not
> raise accretive capital to build profits and future capital.
> Not only would it be good for your shareholders, but it
> also would be good for the markets in fulfillment of your
> public purpose.

The final negotiated statement changed the language to
"Both companies announced that they will begin the process to
raise significant capital," leaving out the language that I found
offensive—that it had to be accretive. Instead of their proposed
quote of "Both companies are well capitalized and have adequate
reserves," I said, "Both companies have proven cushions above
OFHEO-directed capital requirements and have increased their
reserves."

The CEOs finally agreed to raise capital. I lowered OFHEO-
imposed capital requirement by 10 percent to a requirement of
20 percent, which released almost $6 billion in capital. With
their very low leverage requirement, that meant that they
could provide additional hundreds of billions of liquidity to the

markets. Importantly, they also agreed to keep a cushion well above the new 20 percent requirement.

On Wednesday the nineteenth, I had a press conference with the two CEOs to announce the deal. In OFHEO press release we stated, "All parties recognize the need for world-class regulatory structure and have renewed a shared commitment to work for comprehensive GSE reform legislation." Syron's statement reflected the inherent conflicts with the GSE model: "This approach . . . balances our mission to provide stability, liquidity, and affordability consistent with safety and soundness while enhancing the interests of our shareholders."

The markets liked the deal, with their MBS spread over Treasuries falling from 3.68 percent to a still-high 2.78 percent. Their stocks popped almost 30 percent. The Associated Press[84] quoted Schumer calling the deal "a day late and a dollar short," saying again we were "beginning to put our toe in the water." I rashly said that the control improvements made "bailout talk nonsense."

Senator Martinez called it "a huge gamble on the backs of the US Treasury."[85] He was right, but as the PLS market had disappeared and banks were pulling out, the GSEs were the only support for the very troubled mortgage market. There was no other countercyclical force available. As all this was happening, Martinez's successor, HUD secretary Jackson, was in the process of resigning, and there were rumors that I was one of the candidates for the job. As I had my hands full, I knew it was just rumors. Bill Maloni, Fannie's former top lobbyist, who hated me, wrote in a blog: "It's a shame Jim Lockhart didn't get the top job. If his remaining few months in town were spent running the agency [HUD]—often called '11 floors in a basement'—it would have been just reward for his regulatory debasement of Fannie and Freddie."[86]

The Fed cut its main lending rate by three-quarters of a percentage point to 2.25 percent. Although lower than traders anticipated, it was the sixth decrease since September. Former Federal Reserve chairman Paul Volcker called for Fannie and Freddie to draw down on their Treasury facility rather than relying on the Fed to do everything. It is not clear whether he realized the lines were only $2.25 billion each.

On March 20, 2008, the *Wall Street Journal* weighed in with an editorial entitled "A More Honest Socialism." They liked the idea of Fannie and Freddie raising capital but did not like how it could be leveraged: "Yesterday's capital expansion merely lets the companies continue their double lives as profit-making companies [but they were not anymore] backed by taxpayer guarantees—and do so by taking even greater risk at a very risky time." They suggested that the Treasury buy convertible subordinated debt in Fannie and Freddie; then, "once the crisis ends at least the taxpayers would get some upside. . . . Yes, this amounts to nationalization, but at least it's honest socialism."

Surprisingly to me the editorial ended, "With a couple of brave exceptions (Mr. Lockhart, Alabama Senator Richard Shelby), Fannie and Freddie own Washington. It'd be better for the housing markets and taxpayers if Washington finally admitted it and bought Fannie and Freddie." The editors knew that would not happen; Congress was addicted to off-balance-sheet insurance companies.

Meanwhile, Freddie was already reneging on their agreement to raise capital. Our announcement said significant capital, but I later said I expected it to be in the range of $5 billion to $10 billion each, which hit their stock price. Syron said no more than $3 billion after saying he would not raise any. The CFO said any capital raising would be "non-dilutive" at a Citi analyst meeting. That was hard to believe.

I met with Larry Summers on March 14. Two weeks later, in a *Financial Times* article,[87] he wrote that Fannie and Freddie should eliminate their dividends and raise substantial capital. If they "refused, policymakers should put them into an appropriate form of administration that ensures that their obligations will be met." We had "conservatorship" powers but no ability to "ensure" their obligations. The implicit guarantee had no legal backing or guarantee fund like the FDIC.

On April 15, 2008, OFHEO published our required annual 2008 report to Congress on our 2007 examinations of the enterprises. It highlighted Fannie and Freddie's many problems and OFHEO's actions. My summary letter said, "Significant progress was made in the remediation process, but OFHEO concludes that both companies remain classified significant supervisory concerns. The primary reason for this classification has changed from previous years. The extraordinary declines in the housing and mortgage markets have greatly increased their credit and interest-rate risks, which have put additional pressure on their credit management, interest-rate risk management and financial modeling processes."

As their core capital remained above OFHEO-directed extra 30 percent at year-end 2007, they were classified as "adequately capitalized." I concluded in my letter to Congress, "The time to act on legislation is now."

The same day, Paulson had a meeting in Dodd's office with Shelby and the two CEOs, but not me. In his book, Paulson describes it as a breakthrough meeting, leading to a Senate banking bill a month later. I thought it was unusual that I was not included in the meeting, but I assume Paulson thought my tough approach with the CEOs might not be helpful.

Fannie Mae reported on May 6 a loss of $2.2 billion for the first quarter, but their core capital of $42.7 billion still well exceeded the previous 30 percent OFHEO-directed capital requirement. A week later, Freddie reported a much smaller loss of $0.2 billion. Their core capital of $38.3 billion was also well above the 30 percent level. By law, they were adequately capitalized, which was a statement I repeated many times. Paulson was optimistically quoted in the *Wall Street Journal* on May 7 as saying, "I do believe the worst is likely behind us." But he added there will be "further bumps along the road."[88]

I also pointed out many times in the ensuing months that, including their guaranteed MBS, they were extremely leveraged, with Fannie Mae's core capital percent being 1.4 percent and Freddie's 1.7 percent. Fannie's fair value of net assets was only $12.2 billion, and Freddie had a negative $5.2 billion.

Fannie Mae kept their promise and raised $7.4 billion in common preferred stock on May 13. As they had met all eighty-one requirements in the 2006 consent agreement, we released them from the agreement and reduced our directed capital requirement to 15 percent. I did hear after the conservatorship that not all the preferred was placed with investors. J. P. Morgan's Jamie Dimon was not happy with me as they still had $1 billion of the preferred at the time of the conservatorship.

In our regular meetings, Syron kept promising to raise capital but worried about diluting returns to shareholders. He was even getting squishy on supporting legislation, wanting more information on "capital and mission policies."[89] We did approve a capital raise of $5.5 billion on May 15, but then Freddie's lawyers decided that it was too dangerous until they registered with the SEC. They were intensely working on the SEC filing.

The Senate Banking Committee passed a bill on May 20. It was a reasonable compromise, and I endorsed it. It lacked the systemic language from 2005 bill but was stronger than the House bill. Senator Shelby was okay with it. In my statement, I congratulated both Dodd and Shelby, optimistically saying, "The legislation should give the new regulator the tools necessary to ensure the safety and soundness of the GSEs so they fulfill their congressionally established mission of providing stability, liquidity and affordability to the housing market."

The Economist[90] said there was "lofty talk of bipartisanship." Replacing "the feisty but toothless Office of Federal Housing Enterprises Oversight (OFHEO) has long been a White House goal. . . . Some worry that their vastness poses a systemic risk: at $5.3 trillion. . . . GSEs' share of monthly issuances of mortgage securities has doubled to 84%, since 2006. . . . James Lockhart, OFHEO's director and the putative first boss of the new agency, recently called them a 'point of vulnerability' because of their lofty leverage."

CHAPTER 17

Lessons Learned from Turmoil

"Fannie Mae and Freddie Mac have continued to be a point
of vulnerability for the financial system because they are so
highly leveraged relative to their risks."

–James B. Lockhart III, 44th Annual Conference on Bank Structure
and Competition, Chicago, Illinois, May 16, 2008

THE ABOVE QUOTE was from a speech I gave at the Chicago
Federal Reserve Bank, entitled "Lessons Learned from Mortgage
Market Turmoil." Despite being on page seven, it was picked up
by many media sources. Most of my speeches were PowerPoints
with commentary. I had OFHEO's team do the first draft, which
was too negative. I toned it down and added some personal
background. Nevertheless, I received quite a bit of criticism from
Fannie and Freddie's CEOs and others.

Even though it was a formal speech, I could not resist using
PowerPoint. The slides showed the massive size and market share
of Fannie and Freddie and their loss history. The one positive
slide showed that their MBS spreads over Treasuries had come
down: "The combination of OFHEO's actions, the Fed's and J.
P. Morgan's actions with respect to Bear Stearns, and the Fed's
new liquidity facilities had the desired effect of quickly reducing

MBS-to-Treasury spreads although they still exceed prior market spreads by 100 basis points."

The slide that went with the vulnerability quote had their first-quarter 2008 core capital leverage at 1.4 percent for Fannie and 1.8 percent for Freddie, but their fair value leverage was much worse. Fannie's was 0.4 percent, and Freddie was negative 0.2 percent. My words were "With that leverage, the enterprises could pose significant risk to taxpayers as well as to financial institutions and other investors that invest in and count on the liquidity of their debt and guaranteed MBS. Such leverage has also limited the ability of Fannie Mae and Freddie Mac to fulfill their mission of supporting secondary mortgage market stability and liquidity in good times and bad."

It may have been early to talk about lessons learned, as we were in the middle of a growing crisis. However, since this book is about underwater lessons learned and how to surface, I think it is worthwhile quoting portions of the speech:

> Unfortunately, many of those lessons should have been learned long ago from previous blow-ups. The most fundamental lesson is this: what goes up too far goes down too far.
>
> In other words, bubbles burst. Another lesson, as I heard Jamie Dimon say recently, is that mortgage securities are risky and that there is a long list of financial firms that have had problems with those securities, including problems related to model, market, credit, and operational risks. . . .
>
> Another lesson ignored is that in bull markets investors and financial institutions tend to misprice risk, which can result in inadequate capital when markets turn.
>
> The lack of transparency all along the long chain of mortgage financing is, in retrospect, mystifying. From

low- or no-documentation "liar loans" and no escrow accounts, all the way through constructing and rating MBS, collateralized debt obligations (CDOs), and "CDOs squared"—it is hard to comprehend.

A new lesson that should be learned is that putting subprime mortgages, which almost by definition need to be worked, into a "brain dead" trust makes no sense.

Another lesson is that overreliance on sophisticated, quantitative models promotes hubris that has frequently caused serious problems at many financial institutions. As a former partner in a risk management software and consulting firm, I believe management judgment—common sense, if you will—must act as a check on, and sometimes must override, those models.

Financial institutions need both. Management decisions must be informed, not dictated, by models.

Looking at the junkyard of previous periods of financial turmoil, the common theme is that pushing the envelope too far, often with the aid of models, eventually leads to problems.

Long-Term Capital Management was the landlord of our risk management firm [NetRisk] in Greenwich, Connecticut . . . but they were never a client. Their models did not capture the correlation of risks on the downside. Their name was right. Financial institutions should be run for the "long term," but their strategy and models failed during a short-term problem. As chair of a corporate pension committee in 1987, I still remember the failure of portfolio insurance.

But financial institution risk is not all about institutions; it should be about people—investors, borrowers, and—in the mortgage market—homeowners.

I am proud to say that over the last six-plus

years I have been involved in President Bush's push for the Ownership Society. . . at the Social Security Administration, with the key responsibility of working for Social Security reform, and now at OFHEO, trying to balance homeownership with the safety and soundness of the secondary mortgage market. In "Bush 41," running the Pension Benefit Guaranty Corporation (PBGC), we struggled to find a similar balance between promoting defined benefit pensions and protecting their safety and soundness.

I then mentioned my father's "Successful Society" and its call for better education and financial literacy. Continuing:

Mortgages got too complicated for individuals to understand the risks. Even with simple products, like thirty-year loans, less financially literate homeowners sometimes fail to exercise their prepayment options. Efforts to promote financial literacy must be increased. In the meantime, a lesson to be learned is that complicated, risky mortgages should not be marketed to people who do not understand them. . . .

There are also some very important lessons to be learned from the current mortgage crisis, which some have called the worst since the Depression. . . . [The] GSEs do fulfill a very important role in the mortgage market, which means that they require a strong regulator. . . . Fannie Mae and Freddie Mac grew rapidly during the housing and mortgage lending boom that began after the 2001 recession. During that boom the enterprises' combined share of residential mortgage debt outstanding reached its peak in 2003.

That growth slowed after Freddie Mac in 2003 and

Fannie Mae in 2004 had to begin restating their earnings following the discovery of serious accounting, control, and other management weaknesses. In response to those discoveries, OFHEO increased the enterprises' minimum capital requirements to 30 percent more than the statutory minimum requirements.

In 2006, we imposed limits on the size of their retained mortgage portfolios. . . . If the limits had not been in place, Fannie Mae and Freddie Mac almost certainly would have had larger retained portfolios and fared far worse in recent quarters.

Nonetheless, the house price and mortgage lending boom tended to increase the risks of Fannie Mae and Freddie Mac in several ways that are not difficult to discern today but were not widely appreciated during the boom.

First, home price appreciation during the boom raised the average homeowner's equity in his or her house, facilitating widespread equity withdrawals via cash-out refinances and home equity loans. At the same time, the risk of a sizable house price correction increased, especially after interest rates began rising in late 2005 . . . [even] for properties financed with the prime conventional loans in which Fannie Mae and Freddie Mac specialize. . . . A growing share of borrowers whose first mortgages the enterprises purchased also took out second, "piggyback" loans, yet the enterprises did not have complete information on those seconds. . . .

Second, subprime, Alt-A, and other nontraditional mortgages and the private-label MBS they backed were relatively new and untested financial products whose performance in a period of rising interest rates and low or negative house price appreciation was quite uncertain.

Those securities posed credit risk . . . not fully reflected in the enterprises' initial pricing. At mid-year 2007, before the start of the current market turmoil, Fannie Mae and Freddie Mac together held $257 billion in private-label MBS backed by subprime, Alt-A, and home equity mortgages. By the end of the first quarter of this year, that total had declined to $206 billion.

Third, the growing risk of a house price correction and the risks posed by subprime and nontraditional mortgages also affected the servicers, mortgage insurers, bond insurers, and even the derivatives providers that are major counterparties of Fannie Mae and Freddie Mac. Thus, the enterprises' counterparty credit risk increased as well.

Fourth, the models Fannie Mae and Freddie Mac use to manage risks were increasingly inadequate. . . .

Those increased risks became evident after the mortgage market turmoil began last August [2007].

There are three lessons that should be learned and applied immediately. The first is about procyclical behavior during the credit cycle. When financial institutions practice and their supervisors allow overly liberal underwriting standards and mispricing of risks during a credit and asset boom, the build-up of risks makes it more likely that, during the inevitable correction, institutions will experience solvency problems and tighten underwriting standards more than warranted by credit considerations alone.

An important issue for supervisory agencies is how to create incentives for institutions to behave in a less procyclical manner without interfering with their ability to earn reasonable returns on capital.

That lesson is particularly relevant to supervision

of Fannie Mae and Freddie Mac. The enterprises' statutory mission is to provide liquidity and stability to the secondary mortgage market at all points in the credit cycle. . . . To do so, they should limit their risk exposures and build up sufficient capital, relative to their risks, in periods of housing and mortgage market expansion, to be able to absorb losses and maintain sufficient capital while expanding their activities during contractions in the housing sector or the broader economy. That will be good for their mission and their shareholders.

As we seek to apply that lesson, an interesting question is whether Fannie Mae and Freddie Mac could have been a more countercyclical force during the recent house price and mortgage lending boom.

For example, as the largest buyers of private-label MBS, could they have brought a long-term view and more stability to a very liquid MBS market? . . .

A second lesson from recent experience is the importance of capital. Capital at individual institutions not only reduces their risk of experiencing solvency and funding problems and of contributing to financial market illiquidity, but also helps them avoid the need to retrench in bad times and miss what may be very attractive opportunities in weak markets. . . . Capital reduces the risks the enterprises could pose to taxpayers and the financial system and enhances their ability to support the secondary mortgage market.

Those two lessons provide compelling arguments for a third: legislation needs to be enacted soon that would reform supervision of Fannie Mae and Freddie Mac and, specifically, give a new agency authority to set capital requirements comparable to the authority the bank regulatory agencies possess. The legislation that created OFHEO in 1992 requires the agency to set very low minimum capital requirements and greatly limits OFHEO's flexibility with respect to risk-based capital requirements. . . .

Reform legislation passed by the House of Representatives last year and now scheduled to be voted on by the Senate Banking Committee Tuesday would create a new agency to regulate Fannie Mae and Freddie Mac that would have authorities comparable to those possessed by the federal banking agencies, including broad flexibility to set minimum and risk-based capital requirements for the enterprises.

Other bank-regulator-like powers of the new regulator would include receivership authority, independent litigating powers, removal from the congressional budget process, and stronger oversight of enterprise directors and officers. . . .

Through regulation the director could give Fannie Mae and Freddie Mac incentives to operate their retained mortgage portfolios in a countercyclical manner, consistent with their mission. In conjunction with appropriate capital requirements, standards with respect to enterprise portfolio holdings could encourage them to build up capital in periods of housing and mortgage market expansion. The standards could be reduced during periods of mortgage market distress to allow the enterprises to use that capital to support the liquidity and stability of the secondary mortgage market. . . .

The new agency created by the legislation would result from the combination of OFHEO with the Federal Housing Finance Board, which supervises the Federal Home Loan Bank System, and the mission oversight performed by the Department of Housing and Urban Development. . . . Since the housing GSEs combine to finance or guarantee three-quarters of the nation's mortgages, the new regulator would largely oversee the secondary market. . . . As the largest issuers of non-government debt, they also share liquidity or funding risks. . . .

A combined regulator could greatly enhance the government's ability to ensure that each housing GSE accomplishes its mission with respect to affordable housing.

To conclude, Congress created the housing GSEs with a common mission to support mortgage lending and housing markets throughout the credit cycle.

Frankly, OFHEO, Fannie Mae, and Freddie Mac were fortunate in recent years in that OFHEO's regulatory responses to accounting, control, and other management weaknesses constrained enterprise growth and risk-taking at the height of a boom, and those constraints have limited the magnitude of the enterprises' losses in the subsequent downturn. . . .

The present market turmoil has brought to a boil long-simmering policy issues related to the appropriate roles of the housing GSEs and the federal government in supporting mortgage markets and the housing sector.

Those issues include . . .

✦   the allocation of risk bearing between the public and the private sectors,

✦   the ability and willingness of shareholder-owned firms to act against financial services industry trends,

✦   the appropriate size and structure of GSEs; and

◆ the ability of the new housing GSE regulator to encourage countercyclical behavior to reduce the severity of credit cycles and their macroeconomic consequences in ways that do not shift risks to the public sector and increase moral hazard.

Many years later, we are still simmering with no signs of a boil.

CHAPTER 18

HERA to the Rescue

President Bush: "Hello, Lockhart. Have you reformed the GSEs
yet?"
JBL: "Not yet. That is what you're signing. We will do it after
we have the powers."

—Oval Office conversation, July 30, 2008

AFTER TWO YEARS working with Congress, the Treasury,
the press, and many interest groups, July 30, bright and early
at 7 AM, was the big day for the signing of the Housing and
Economic Recovery Act (HERA) that would create a new agency,
the Federal Housing Finance Agency (FHFA), to oversee Fannie
Mae, Freddie Mac, and the twelve Federal Home Loan Banks.

Secretary of the Treasury Paulson, HUD secretary Preston,
FHA commissioner Brian Montgomery, assistant Treasury
secretary Nason, and I stood behind President Bush as he signed
HERA at the Resolution Desk in the Oval Office. The president
mockingly asked, "Where are all the senators and congressmen?"
The legislation was so controversial that a decision had been made
not to do the typical Rose Garden ceremony. Maybe it was too hot
in late July? Of course, key staff, including Bolten, Hennessey, and
others, were in the Oval Office; but no press was included.

Even though the Senate Banking Committee passed a bill on May 20, it was not smooth sailing in the Senate or the House to get to that Oval Office signing ceremony. The House wanted higher conforming loan limits than those in the Senate bill. The other, bigger sticking point was whether the new agency would start on the day the president signed the bill or, as the House wanted, six months after signing.

Part of the date of enactment issue was that Barney Frank and other House members wanted a new head of the agency to write the new regulations. Speaker Pelosi was more straightforward, saying that the six-month delay would allow the next president, presumably Obama, to name the head of the new agency. Under the Senate's immediate effective date, I would be head of the new agency until replaced by a Senate-confirmed successor. Therefore, I could begin to write new regulations quickly in hopes of strengthening Fannie and Freddie.

Shelby held fast to the immediate date. He was still talking about systemic risk even though the Senate bill used less explicit language. The Senate bill specified that the new regulator was to consider in policy making "the ability of the Enterprises to provide a liquid secondary market" and "the portfolio holdings in relation to the overall mortgage market,"[91] according to an article in *American Banker*. The article did quote experts suggesting that the language opened the consideration of systemic risk. It also quoted me from an interview I gave after the Chicago Fed speech: "I don't see how the safety and soundness regulator cannot consider systemic risk." Paulson and Bernanke were also using the S-word from time to time.

I met with Barney Frank in his office on June 19. He eventually relented on having an immediate effective date, but he could not resist taking a shot at me. After the House had passed the bill, "asked if he had confidence in the current regulator, Frank said, '. . . [I do], at this point. I've had some disagreements with Mr.

Lockhart. . . . Jim Lockhart's expertise is not in financial markets, and that's more of an issue these days. On the other hand, the first thing that has to happen is, the regulatory structure has to be set up . . . and I think he will do that well.'"[92]

As it turned out there was no time to set up the regulatory structure. As to my lack of financial markets expertise, I must not have spent much time talking about my background with him. The irony is that none of my successors had any private-sector financial market experience.

Throughout June and July, there were reports of housing prices continuing to fall, Fannie and Freddie's stock prices kept falling, and their debt and MBS spreads were widening.

Earlier in 2008 we had reorganized our enterprise examination teams around risk categories. We had had separate teams for Fannie and Freddie. Many of the team members spent most of their time at the enterprises. There is a concept of "regulatory capture" where an examiner gets too comfortable with an institution. We had set up a new rating system, GSEER. It stood for governance (management and boards), solvency (capital), earnings, and enterprise risk (market/liquidity, credit, operational, and model risks). Therefore, the credit team could look at the practices, portfolios, and risks across Fannie and Freddie. They came up with interesting findings: for example, Freddie was seeing higher delinquencies on mortgages they bought based on Fannie's underwriting system versus their own system.

In a letter to Dick Syron on June 13, I wrote that first-quarter losses were a "trigger" for action and "Freddie Mac should move expeditiously to meet its capital raising commitment. . . . Key OFHEO safety and soundness concerns:

✦   Freddie Mac has not separated the CEO and Chair functions.

✦   OFHEO views Freddie Mac's application of accounting literature regarding Other than Temporary Impairments

[OTTI] as aggressive, with respect to Alt A and subprime PLS. . . .

✦ Freddie Mac should move with haste and place a higher priority on the remediation of remaining internal control problems."

The two CEOs were making brave comments in our regular meetings but also in public. In a June 13 interview with *American Banker*,[93] Dan Mudd had some rather colorful quotes: "People say, 'Yeah, they're [the enterprises] pretty damn relevant in the market, and they're key to the recovery and the future of these markets.' . . . If you weren't putting the eggs in the GSE basket, the eggs would land on the floor, because there is no other basket right now."

The article continued, "He dismissed published reports that suggest Fannie might be taking on so much risk that it requires a federal bailout. 'We now have more capital than we've had at any time in our history, and . . . so I think we're in a sterling position." Mudd also took issue with my statement "If you're going to have these enterprises, they have to be there through thick and thin, and that means that they should be building up excess capital in good periods and using it in the bad periods."

Mr. Mudd countered, "If OFHEO can tell me with certainty the day the cycles begin and the day that they end, I'll be happy to follow that guidance. . . . When the good times are and when the bad times are is immensely clear in retrospect but never has been clear in prospect in 2,008 years of financial history."

The article did end with a constructive quote after saying "Mr. Mudd has expressed concern over provisions [in the Senate bill], but he acknowledged that OFHEO is not an effective model of regulation.' . . . This regulator will oversee a fifth of the economy, so this is a huge deal, and if you're going to give a single regulator that much authority, then they certainly ought to have the set of powers and the capabilities and the budget and the quality of staffing to go with it."

Meanwhile the legislation in the Senate was in trouble as several Republican senators wanted to offer amendments. There was also a furor about the special loan treatment Senator Dodd had gotten from Countrywide.

During the latter part of June, I started to meet with many of the presidents of the FHLBanks and with their Office of Finance in hopeful anticipation of the passage of the GSE legislation. I worked with our staff on developing a risk-based capital framework and supported the President's Advisory Council on Financial Literacy, co-headed by John Hope Bryant. On the twentieth I did a housing event with my congressman Chris Shays in Connecticut. The stories of mounting foreclosures were not encouraging.

On June 30 I visited Cuomo regarding our appraisal code and then the president of the Federal Reserve Bank of New York, Geithner. He rightfully was very concerned about Fannie and Freddie and their impact on the markets and the banks, which he regulated. I explained that they were in a very tough position. Without them the mortgage markets would crater. Although they were adequately capitalized according to the law, the leverage levels and the risk-based capital standard were much too weak.

He pressed me hard about whether they should have government support. That was the hardening of the guarantee that his deputy had mentioned to Steel in March. I said I hoped with the powers of the new pending legislation that it would not be necessary. I'm not sure whether Geithner ever forgave me for that optimism.

Cricket drove down for Bush's Fourth of July/birthday picnic and fireworks. I had a brief chance to talk with him. The topics included how expensive weddings were as Graci, our daughter, had just been married, and naturally the GSEs. I mentioned a housing event that I'd done with Representative Shays. I told

Bush the housing market was not looking very good, and it was starting to see many foreclosures. He said, hopefully, that the stories were probably "exaggerated."

The stories were not exaggerated, but the next week we needed all the optimism we could gather. On Monday, Fannie and Freddie's stocks plunged to the lowest level in sixteen years. A Lehman Brothers stock analyst wrote that a proposed accounting principle, Financial Accounting Standard 140, would require Fannie and Freddie to raise an additional $75 billion in capital. The principle was designed to bring guaranteed assets such as the enterprises' issued MBS onto their balance sheets.

The timing of the proposed accounting principle was bad—it was procyclical rather than countercyclical, as I told the head of the FAS board—but the principle itself was right. Too many financial institutions had been allowed to bury in their footnotes these fully guaranteed, off-balance-sheet assets. *The Wall Street Journal* on July 9, 2008, speculated that the three biggest banks had $1 trillion in off-balance-sheet assets. Fannie and Freddie had 3.5 times that.

Ironically, as Lehman Brothers later triggered the big meltdown, the Lehman analyst wrote, "We believe any threat of [a Fannie or Freddie] failure could trigger a meltdown in the credit markets that would make the movements in credit markets that we've seen over the last year look like a hiccup. . . . Needless to say, the impact of dislocation of that order could cause serious harm to the global economy."[94]

On Tuesday I attended an FDIC forum at their campus in Arlington, Virginia. Reporters wanted me to respond to the Lehman analyst. On CNBC's *Squawk Box* I said, "I have to tell you, an accounting change should not drive a capital charge. If the [securities] were brought on balance sheet, it would make no change to the risk of these firms. It would make no sense to me for it to imply a capital raise."

Speaking at the conference, Paulson called Fannie and Freddie "a constructive force." Bernanke called for GSE reform. Dimon, CEO of J. P. Morgan, was upbeat, saying, "The future is very, very bright."[95] His stock, and especially Fannie and Freddie's, surged. But the week was just starting. Wednesday and Thursday, the enterprises' stocks took massive hits.

Thursday, July 10, started with another *Wall Street Journal* anti-GSE editorial ("The Price of Fannie Mae"), piling on:

> The message from markets is that both companies are in danger of exhausting their capital and becoming insolvent if home prices keep falling and mortgage losses mount. . . . So how do we get out of this mess? The worst option would be to let the situation erode until the Fed and Treasury panic amid market pressure and issue an explicit taxpayer guarantee. . . . Our own proposal, made months ago, is to require a more honest form of socialism by injecting taxpayer money now in both companies . . . to weather the current storm. This would prevent a US balance sheet debacle. . . . Then as the crisis passed, the taxpayers would at least get something for their money.

The editorial asked, "Why is there so little Washington or Wall Street alarm about this?" We in Washington were alarmed but were missing critical tools.

The same day, Paulson and Bernanke testified at the House Financial Services Committee. They were being pushed hard. Paulson quoted me as saying that they were "adequately capitalized." *The New York Times* said, "Mr. Bernanke said that Fannie and Freddie 'are well-capitalized in the regulatory sense' but added that they, and other major financial institutions, needed to raise their capital levels further."[96] The article also said, "Senior Bush administration officials are considering a plan to have the government take over one or both the companies and place them in a conservatorship if their problems worsen."

The Treasury may have been considering that, but I was not as I did not see how one could execute a conservatorship without financing, which would require legislation. The AEI's Wallison had surprised me in a June meeting when he suggested we should add to the legislation the ability to fund Fannie and Freddie. I thought that might kill the chances of any reform legislation.

On Thursday, July 10, I got calls from Mudd and Syron pressing for reassuring statements from me to go along with theirs. I released a statement: "As I have said before, they are adequately capitalized, holding capital well in excess of OFHEO-directed requirement, which exceeds the statutory minimums. They have large liquidity portfolios, access to debt markets and over $1.5 trillion in unpledged assets."

The last clause was optimistic; most of those assets were mortgage assets, which were becoming harder to borrow against. We had been having sessions with the enterprises to encourage them to increase the liquid assets, such as Treasuries, in their portfolios. As their borrowing cost was much higher than Treasury interest rates, they were resisting.

My "adequately capitalized" statement figures in many books about the crisis, not always positively. In Andrew Ross Sorkin's book *Too Big to Fail*, he writes that after I said on *Squawk Box* that they were adequately capitalized, "Paulson had a one-word judgment of that assessment that he later shared with his staff: 'Bullshit.'"[97] I never knew what the alternative was for me to say at the time.

That statement was based on their March financial statements. Even when they filed their June quarterly statements, they were statutorily adequately capitalized. Of course, the 1992 law was inadequate. As I said in a July 23 Bloomberg TV interview, "They are adequately capitalized according to law. Many argue that the law is weak." I noted that the new law would give "the regulator power to change those capital requirements" and that "we need to look at how you build up rainy day capital . . . so they can cope with these kinds of markets."

July 10 became an even busier day as the presidential candidates weighed in. Senator Obama called them "essential."[98] Senator McCain said the enterprises were "vital to Americans' ability to own their own homes. And we will do what's necessary to make sure that they continue that function."[99] But two weeks later in a Larry Kudlow interview, McCain called HERA a "sweetheart deal."

Earlier that morning, Tim Geithner and I had received an email from the Treasury to review immediately Paulson's planned comments about "contingency planning" with the goal of downplaying the rumors about potential conservatorship. These comments included the statement "OFHEO has made clear that these firms are adequately capitalized and will remain vigilant in supervising the safe and sound operations." I signed off.

Geithner responded, "No reference to them being adequately capitalized now, and no reference to vigilance in oversight. The former is not credible, the latter goes without saying." Geithner did suggest positive alternative language in brackets that "Treasury and OFHEO would work together [to ensure they are capitalized at a level that allows them] [to ensure that these firms have a sufficiently strong financial foundation that they are able] in their present form to carry out their important mission in the housing and mortgage markets."

Paulson put out a statement saying, "Today our primary focus is supporting Fannie Mae and Freddie Mac in their current form as they carry out their important mission. We are maintaining a dialogue with regulators and with the companies."[100] Many articles took "in their current form" to mean the government was not considering conservatorships or nationalization. The enterprises' stocks and securities gyrated wildly.

Later Friday afternoon, the FDIC took over IndyMac, a California bank with $32 billion in assets. It was a very busy weekend of calls. On Saturday I talked with Paulson. On Saturday and Sunday, I talked with Mudd, Syron, Warsh, and Ryan, among others. And on Sunday, July 13, Paulson called to tell me about an impending statement that afternoon.

Meanwhile, on Sunday, Dodd was saying on CNN, "They have more than adequate capital. They're in good shape. The chairman of the Federal Reserve has said as much. The secretary of Treasury has said as much."[101] For once, I was not quoted. Later Sunday, on the steps of the Treasury Department, Paulson asked Congress, on behalf of the Bush administration, for the right to increase the $2.25 billion lines of credit to Fannie and Freddie, the right to buy equity in them, and the ability for the Fed to have a consultative role with the new regulator. It was a brave request but very necessary. As he wrote, "We face the catch-22 of crisis policymaking. There was always the chance that by asking for these powers we would confirm just how fragile the GSEs were and spook investors."[102]

Also on Sunday, the Fed put out a press release announcing that they would lend to Fannie and Freddie on a collateralized basis "to help ensure the ability of Fannie Mae and Freddie Mac to promote the availability of home mortgage credit during a period of stress in financial markets."

There were many editorial cartoons. One (created by Heng Kim Song of Singapore) had a fat Freddie Mac sitting on a house that was flooded up to the attic (not totally underwater). A fat Fannie Mae woman was jumping off the roof into a small boat labeled TAXPAYER. Given my experiences, my favorite cartoon[103] had a young girl talking with an old bald guy sitting in an easy chair. She asks, "Fannie Mae Bailout . . . Freddie Mac Bailout . . . Medicare Bailout . . . Social Security Bailout . . . What Happens

When the BILL Arrives??" The man answers, "Not My Problem, Kid . . . I Plan to Bail Out Before Then."

On Tuesday, July 15, in a Senate Banking hearing, Paulson was "hammered by lawmakers."[104] CNN wrote, "Paulson told the committee that the two firms had adequate capital to continue operating," and that he was asking for a "backstop." The ask was for an unlimited authorization through 2009. In Senator Shelby's opening statement, he said, "The GSEs, even when they are deemed safe and sound, compose systemic risk."

Paulson uttered his famous words, "If you've got a squirt gun in your pocket, you will have to use it. If you have a bazooka in your pocket and people know it, you probably won't have to use it."

On the sixteenth, Ben Bernanke did his required semiannual Humphrey Hawkins testimony in the House. He mentioned several possibilities, including "nationalization" of Fannie and Freddie. He also said that they were in "no danger of failing." He added that OFHEO had assured him that they are "fine and they can continue to operate and there's nothing about to happen."[105]

On my copy of the article, one of my deputies scribbled, "Need to get Ben to not say stuff like this."

As Congress was deliberating, we welcomed in senior OCC and Fed bank examiners to begin looking at the enterprises' books. We were also working with the CBO to help them score the cost of the potential funding of Fannie and Freddie. They estimated that there was less than a 50 percent chance of the need for Treasury funding, and the average cost, if utilized, was $25 billion. However, in their severe house-price-drop scenario, CBO estimated that there was a 5 percent chance of needing $100 billion in funding.

On the twenty-third, Bush dropped his veto threat, and the House responded by passing the HERA bill 271–151 with the "bazooka." The Senate passed it on the twenty-sixth.

The night before the HERA signing, I got an eight-page fax

from the always proactive Mudd, including an early draft of their second-quarter "executive summary" and proposed "talking points" for me. It was a follow-up to our regular meeting on July 22. We had discussed their forecast, which was showing that they would barely meet their reduced capital requirements in the third quarter. He had also said that the debt markets were broken, with the FHLBanks' borrowing requirements "backing up the market." Other worries included the ongoing asset impairments, potential deferred tax asset reserves, and the deteriorating finances of the mortgage insurance companies.

In his fax, Mudd wanted me to announce "a two-year capital plan that calls for the company to operate with a counter-cyclical capital regime. . . . Under this plan, the regulator will expect us to access the capital markets as available." I assume the countercyclical was thrown in to appease me, but it was too late. Capital was not available.

On the twenty-fifth and twenty-ninth, I had meetings with Syron. The concerns we discussed were the same ones I had discussed with Mudd the week before. His comment was "Problems don't age well." But the big question was when they were going to raise the capital to fulfill our March agreement. Several board members were still resisting. He was getting mixed messages from their investment bankers, J. P. Morgan and Goldman Sachs, regarding whether they could do it. We also discussed reducing their portfolios to lessen their capital needs, but he admitted he could not sell without taking losses. Syron also told me that the reason they had been growing their portfolio was because of pressure from the Treasury. Somehow, he did not mention his board's pressure.

Although there was no Rose Garden ceremony on July 30, there were nice pictures. It was a first for me. PBGC and Social Security reforms never got that far. After the short ceremony, I was the last one to leave the Oval Office. I thanked the president.

He said, "Thanks, Juice." We chatted for a while.

As I was leaving, he said, "So, you are the guy."

I replied, "Yes, I get all the fun jobs."

CHAPTER 19

Battle Stations Bazooka—All Hands-on Deck

"From the fall 2007 to the conservatorships, it was a tightrope
with no safety net."

–J. B. Lockhart III, Testimony to Financial Crisis Inquiry
Commission, April 9, 2010

THE TIGHTROPE WAS rapidly fraying. Two enterprises were
two too many for the tightrope. HERA would have allowed us to
build a strong bridge, but that would have taken years.

As August 2008 started, both CEOs were admitting problems
but saying that they could raise capital at some point in the future
to plug any holes. Fannie called the first week of August a "critical
week" as they and Freddie reported second-quarter earnings.

The week was full of meetings and calls with the FHLBanks'
presidents and chairmen, Fannie and Freddie's CEOs and
directors, and Treasury assistant secretary Tony Ryan (Steel
had left to become CEO of Wachovia Bank), and speeches. We
were putting the brand-new FHFA team in place. I was quoted
as saying that we were going to have to write twenty to twenty-
five new regulations.

Monday the fourth, Dan Mudd, his team, and their banker,
Lazard, made presentations to us. They provided an updated

forecast showing pretax losses of $14.1 billion for 2008. Optimistically, they reduced the expected losses to $8 billion assuming a tax credit. That kept Fannie slightly above the expected 10 percent FHFA-directed capital requirement at year-end. According to the presentation, there was "no apparent availability of new capital" and "regulatory uncertainty [was] raising questions for current shareholders about the equity proposition."

They were pushing for clarity around capital management by the FHFA that would give them a chance over the next several years to "move towards more robust capital structure." I appreciated Mudd's call for regulatory certainty, but there is no way to do that with the markets in a freefall.

He was now pushing for the FHFA to reduce their capital requirements so they could countercyclically support the mortgage market. Being an ex-Marine, to him the alternative was "managing to the line of death."

On August 5, I was in Chicago speaking to the twelve FHLBank presidents. The next day was reporting day for Freddie. It did not start well for Syron; a front-page *New York Times* article was entitled "At Freddie Mac, Chief Disregarded Warning Signs." It cited a mid-2004 report from Freddie's risk manager.

Freddie reported only a $0.8 billion loss after putting up a $2.5 billion reserve. They blamed most of the loss on the Alt-A mortgage book. Despite their 2007 capital raise, their shareholders' equity had fallen from $29.9 billion at year-end 2006 to $12.9 billion. With the law's perverse definition of core capital, which excludes AOCI, it rose from 2006's $35.4 billion to $37.1 billion. In contrast, the fair value of assets was a negative $5.6 billion. To go back to Syron's analogy about capital being like oxygen in a scuba tank, there was no oxygen left. And yet, they still met the directed capital requirement.

The report itself was a major accomplishment as it was the

first time ever that Freddie had become an SEC registrant. The NEC's Thomas, who had written the emails that inspired the damning March *Barron* article, wrote an email the same day to Hennessey, his boss, and other White House officials; Ryan, Nason, and Jeremiah Norton in the Treasury; Warsh; and me. The email's title was "FRE Insolvent based on GAAP, -$30bn FV Basis." That email pointed out issues with the deferred tax asset, reserving, and fair value calculations, among others.

My reply the next morning was "Jason, that is a good instant analysis. GAAP does allow some broad choices. . . . We have examinations going on in most of these areas. . . . It may be small comfort, but they just completed their SEC registration process which means they [SEC] did not object to the GAAP practices."

Always sure of himself, his reply was "I do appreciate that the SEC signed off on the accounting practices, but I doubt the Commission wishes to be the regulatory body that ultimately pushes them below the minimum capital threshold. . . . Freddie already looks like a zombie to me."

Friday was Fannie's turn in the box, announcing a $2.3 billion loss with credit expenses of $5.3 billion. Despite their two capital raises since year-end 2006, their shareholders' equity was about the same as 2006 at $41.2 billion. Core capital was higher at $47.0 billion. However, their fair value of net assets had fallen from 2006's $43.7 billion to $12.5 billion. As with Freddie, there were questions on whether their fair value pricing was too optimistic.

Like Syron, Mudd blamed Alt-A for most of their problems. He announced he was exiting Alt-A and undertaking a dividend cut, 10 percent cost reductions, and a credit reserve build. Fannie's PowerPoint stated, "We expect that 2008 will be our peak year for credit-related expenses as we build our combined loss reserves in anticipation of charge-offs that we expect to incur in 2009 and 2010." The peak turned out to be much higher than they or the FHFA, Fed, and OCC examiners expected.

It was not an upbeat earnings call. Mudd said, "Conditions which many of us had described as the worst in a generation took a turn for the worse after the quarter ended." He said, "None of the plans that we have advanced contemplate access to any Treasury line. . . . [T]he GSE model requires a 'competitive return' for private investors."

As I was a "businessman" and Paulson "ran an investment bank," we understood the need for competitive return, according to Mudd. He added rather hopefully, "It's very important that there be an attractive shareholder proposition so that the investment comes into the company so that the capital is built, so that we can . . . defray the cost of US housing and keep all markets liquid."[106]

Secretary Paulson did a *Meet the Press* interview on August 10 with Tom Brokaw as they were both in China for the Olympics. Paulson could not escape Fannie and Freddie, even on his family vacation. Some of his quotes were "The housing correction is really at the heart of our economic problems as a nation right now" and "Well, we have no plans to insert money in either of those institutions." He went on to say, "What we have now is a legislation calling for a strong new regulator with real powers to deal with, with capital adequacy, to deal with systemic risk. . . . And it's very important that Freddie Mac and Fannie Mae continue to play their very important role. . . . I also understand the importance of moral hazard, market discipline."

Brokaw threw back a quote of Paulson's from April 2007: "I don't see subprime mortgage markets imposing a serious problem. I think it's going to be largely contained." In April 2007 most people believed that, including Bernanke and myself.

The next week I was having conversations with the two CEOs as more and more questions were raised about the viability of Fannie and Freddie. Although Paulson was in China, his team was very busy. On Thursday the fourteenth, I had a meeting with

Ryan and his team. We discussed a variety of options on how to create a more stable mortgage market while protecting the taxpayer. As usual, there was a conversation about raising capital and clarifying how much capital was needed to "muddle through." But we also began to discuss the new power of receivership we had received in HERA as a "strawman."

On August 14, Fannie announced it was going to increase the adverse market fee on October 1 to fifty basis points from twenty-five. Freddie joined in. In hindsight, to be countercyclical, they should have done it years before.

I was in New York on Friday the fifteenth. My first meeting was with Al DelliBovi, the president of the New York Federal Home Loan Bank. He was one of my favorites as he knew the system well. His bank had had problems several years earlier. The resulting risk aversion led him to stay away from the private-label MBS, unlike some of the other FHLBanks.

The next meeting was with a subgroup of the Freddie board that was working on the much-promised capital raise. They were still hopeful that they could raise $5.5 billion publicly or from private equity. We then met with their bankers at the Park Avenue office of J. P. Morgan. They made it very clear that it would be impossible to raise the capital publicly but thought there might be a private possibility.

Sunday was to be the start of my two-week vacation in Nantucket. Cricket drove one car, and I drove the second. Sunday and Monday were spent constantly outside on the phone because the reception was so poor in 'Sconset.

Saturday, August 18, *Barron's* had an article, no doubt inspired by Thomas. Its title was "The Endgame Nears for Fannie and Freddie."[107] It emphasized the fair value of capital and many of the other issues in Thomas's emails. The article noted that their stock prices were down 90 percent and dividends on their preferred stocks, which had been downgraded, were yielding 14 percent. The only solution was "quasi-nationalization" as "by some calculations each company is around $50 billion in the hole."

The Wall Street Journal's August 19 editorial was entitled "When Henry Met Fannie." It noted, "Treasury claims it has no plans to inject taxpayer money directly into the companies. Even so, Mr. Paulson has quietly hired Morgan Stanley, the investment bank, to look into 'appropriate capital structures' if he does decide to sign the blank check the Congress has given them." Very heavy-handedly, it said if either the shareholders or management "survive after the taxpayers are forced to inject capital, the Treasury chief should be run out of town."

Early in the morning of Tuesday the nineteenth, I flew back from Nantucket for a meeting at the Treasury with Paulson and Ryan. I also had conversations with the two CEOs as we were pressing for more loan level information for the examiners. On a call with Bernanke, we discussed the possibility of raising private capital, but he was hearing from his team that $10 billion was too small. In the Fed and Treasury discussions, three options were laid out for a Treasury investment:

✦ Consent agreement with a memorandum of understanding (MOU) requiring many remedial actions and timelines

✦ Conservatorship in which the enterprises retain some public ownership, but as conservator, the FHFA would have all the powers to return Fannie and/or Freddie to a safe and sound condition

✦ Receivership, which would liquidate the enterprises, wiping out common and preferred shareholders. The FHFA would then have the option of transferring assets and liabilities in equal amounts to a limited life regulated entity (LLRE).

My legal team had given me a memo the day before outlining the FHFA's powers under HERA to place a GSE into conservatorship or receivership. It listed twelve possible criteria, many of which were related to capital, unsound and unsafe conditions, violations of law, and inability to pay bills. From our standpoint, an important criterion was the consent of their board of directors. We had a strong legal team but had hired the law firm Arnold & Porter to supplement their efforts. They produced several very helpful papers.

I was not in favor of receivership because I thought it would spook the markets even if the LLRE were set up quickly without any problems. As I was quoted in *The Fateful History of Fannie Mae*, "We felt it would scare the hell out of the market."[108] Some of my staff preferred the consent agreement approach. I did not think that was strong enough.

On Wednesday the twentieth, calls continued with Bernanke and Paulson. Hank was pushing to move quickly to get the board's voluntary agreement. He used the phrase "time-out." Bernanke and Warsh were supportive of acting. Bernanke told me he was "completely on board" and advised it should be a step-by-step, orderly process. I also discussed with John Oros of the private equity firm J. C. Flowers whether a private equity solution was available. John Fiske, head of the FHLBanks' Office of Finance, told me all six of his major GSE debt dealers expected Treasury intervention.

On Thursday the twenty-first, Mudd's top lieutenants told me that a private capital solution was not available but again asked for a lower capital rule. I had a conversation with Bair about IndyMac and updated her on Fannie and Freddie.

The big event was lunch with Secretary Paulson in his private dining room. He was pushing for receivership. In my talking points, I said no matter whether it was a conservatorship or receivership, it had to be done carefully and be well documented as "grounds must be strong as capital [in their second-quarter reports] was well above minimum capital requirements, let alone significant and critically undercapitalized." I also said we needed "to let Freddie find out private equity was not there," and that both needed new management. I noted another concern was that I had to be more comfortable about the impact on the FHLBanks and the US banking system as banks owned a lot of Fannie and Freddie preferred shares.

On the management issue, Hank had brought in Ken Wilson, the former head of Goldman's Financial Institutions Group. Wilson knew many senior financial executives and was extremely helpful in gathering a list of potential CEOs, chairmen, and board member replacements.

At the lunch, Hank advised me not to go back to Nantucket to finish my vacation. I said I had already made that decision. In between the next weekend of calls, I did make a quick trip late Saturday to a family dinner. I wanted to see my son, who had been in an accident. On the return flight early Sunday morning, I met Dan Mudd and his family returning to Washington. It was awkward because I knew why I was going back. As I had left Cricket on Nantucket, she had to recruit her brother, Biff, to fly in and drive off the second car.

On the Friday before my quick weekend trip, Syron told me his liquidity position looked good. He also reported that private equity understood the credit risk but could not deal with the political uncertainty. I also spoke with the Treasury about the receivership LLRE structure. In an Arnold & Porter meeting, I asked the key question: could we do a receivership or conservatorship even if they were still "adequately capitalized" at the end of June? The answer was that a case could be built upon "unsafe and unsound" conditions and practices. They emphasized that it had to be a strong case to prevent being challenged as "arbitrary and capricious."

That Friday, the FHFA's deputy for enterprise regulation sent the regular draft quarterly-capital letters to Fannie and Freddie for comment. Some of the books written about the crisis questioned how we could call them adequately capitalized even though they well exceeded the statutory requirements. We had not done enough work to thoroughly document the issues with their June 30 accounts, nor were we ready to put them into receivership or conservatorship.

It was too early to show our hand; they would have had to disclose to investors a downgrade. We did have a big caveat in the letters to both firms as in the Fannie letter: "Despite the statutory classification of 'adequately capitalized,' and Fannie Mae's capital issuance last quarter of $7.4 billion, further deterioration in housing markets leaves us seriously concerned about the current level of Fannie Mae's capital. As a reminder, FHFA's director has discretionary authority to downgrade the capital classification."

Over the weekend I updated Paulson on my Arnold & Porter conversation and that we were continuing to develop a road map, including the pros and cons of all three alternatives. We were also drafting a safety and soundness justification, working with the Fed and OCC examiners. He reported to me that Syron had told him three board members wanted him to fight back. Syron had also been stirring up his old boss from his Fed days, Volcker. Hank told Syron to stop.

An FHFA report dated August 24 contained a revised forecast for a stress test based on a 21 percent drop in OFHEO's House Price Index. It forecasted 2008 pretax losses of $28.2 billion for Fannie and $14.1 billion for Freddie. Unrealistically, it assumed that those losses would be tax affected. The forecasts showed that they would barely meet the statutory minimum capital test. The report also forecasted three to four more years of losses.

The week of August 25 continued the series of calls with the

Fed and Treasury. BlackRock's risk group was doing a deep dive into Freddie's and Fannie's MBS books. Hank told me one of his Goldman predecessors, Bob Rubin, then at Citibank, said that the GSEs could not raise capital and it was time to nationalize them.

On Tuesday, Mudd updated me on a personnel restructuring plan he was discussing with his board. I also met with Fannie's chairman, Ashley. Both were hoping for a Treasury line of credit. He mentioned that the audit committee was looking at the deferred tax asset issue. Syron told me that J. C. Flowers wanted to go to the next step. In my conversations with Flowers and their advisor, they expressed concerns that $5.5 billion was not enough capital. They hoped to have an answer in a week.

We had drafted the semiannual examination letters downgrading the composite rating for the two to "critical concerns" but decided not to send them as we were still building a stronger case. Freddie's lead director, Johnson, told me they had three good CEO candidates. He said to me that a "critical concerns" letter would mess up everything. He was still positive on the business model.

Hank and Ben suggested that Fannie and Freddie were each $20 to $25 billion short on capital. Although they believed we could make a case on capital alone, we also needed a safety and soundness case. Paulson reported he had talked to the president, who advised him that we should make a strong case. Despite our friendship, Bush had been advised that he should not talk directly with me because I was an independent agency head.

Wednesday's conversation with the Treasury started to flesh out some of the conditions imposed on the enterprises. The idea was a "keepwell" financing in the form of senior preferred stock to ensure assets would equal liabilities so that the enterprises would not have a negative equity.

Larry Fink and his BlackRock team came in and gave us an update on the MBS portfolios. The number of issues was growing.

Wilson continued to help me on CEO and chairman selections.

On Thursday the twenty-eighth, I met with the FHFA's accounting and examination teams and the Fed and OCC examiners to discuss reserves. They stated that the enterprises were still slow in providing information. Fannie and Freddie were suggesting GAAP would not allow them to increase their reserves for bad debts. Preliminarily, the Fed and OCC examiners were suggesting that the pretax losses should be doubled. They were also worried about the mortgage insurer exposures and the under reserving for real estate owned (REO) which are foreclosed, homes.

The OCC's final damning report dated September 4 expanded on these problems. The key issue was that the enterprises put up reserves after ninety-day defaults rather than "expected losses." They pointed out weaknesses in risk-management practices, lack of model discipline, and credit reserving "decisions unduly influenced by financial, accounting and other concerns." It was hard to argue with those conclusions as we had cited many of those issues in our exams. Unfortunately, Fannie and Freddie were not the only financial institutions with those weaknesses.

I also had another awkward call with Fannie's chair, Ashley, telling me the board was pushing very hard to get all problems properly resolved. Mudd told me that they had overemphasized market risk and ignored credit risk. Ryan reported that the rating agencies thought banks and insurance companies had almost $9 billion of Fannie and Freddie preferred stocks.

By Friday I was starting to interview potential CEOs. That week I'd had more meetings with the FHFA's accounting and examination teams, focusing on reserving. There was some pushback from the team but not from Wanda DeLeo, the FHFA's chief accountant. Obviously, it was not easy for our team to admit that Fannie and Freddie had been under reserving, as Paulson wrote in *On the Brink*. Given my experience on TWA when I was at the PBGC, I thought it was imperative to get the team on board and get it right. Very importantly, we wanted to make the case so strong that the two boards would consent to the conservatorships. It took longer than Paulson would have liked, but we made an ironclad case.

The next three days was Labor Day weekend as well as the Republican Convention. There were large Saturday, Sunday, and Monday meetings at the Treasury Department with the Treasury, Fed, FHFA, Morgan Stanley, and legal advisors—Wachtell Lipton and Arnold & Porter. There was very thorough discussion of the legal situation and the grounds for action. Morgan Stanley reported that both Fannie and Freddie had holes in their capital. Paulson said, "No one thinks they have enough capital." No one disagreed. Concerns were again expressed about the draft August 22 letter, despite the strong caveat it contained.

We were discussing whether receivership or conservatorship was the best alternative, as well as a consent order. As some members of the FHFA team were still pushing for a consent order, I asked if the FHFA's general counsel could present that proposal, knowing that it would be turned down. Richard Alexander of Arnold & Porter presented the consent agreement approach. Paulson rejected it and made it clear that without conservatorship or receivership, there would be no financing. He said both CEOs had approached him directly asking for financing with only a consent agreement.

I'd hoped that the softer alternative of a consent agreement would help the Treasury to compromise on conservatorship rather than receivership. The form of action taken was the FHFA's decision, but the financing was the Treasury's. It was agreed the conservatorship was the better, less risky alternative.

I thought I had been too outspoken in the meeting. I called Paulson later explaining that I was trying to be constructive in the meeting and thought that giving my FHFA team its day in court would help. Hank said he understood. He added that he had briefed the president, who called me a "good man" several times.

There were still questions about the impact of the enterprises' $36 billion in outstanding preferred stock, which would be junior to the Treasury preferred. The Fed, in conversation with the FDIC, thought preferred losses would only hit a handful of banks badly. To my question, Morgan Stanley said existing preferred stocks might lose about half their value.

We had always thought that the subordinated debt would be wiped out in the conservatorship, which was why we had a requirement for a prescribed level of subordinated debt. After the lawyers reviewed the loan documents, they said stopping interest payments on the subordinated debt could cause a cross default on all the enterprises' debts, which would have been a calamity.

We sent short letters to the enterprises on Labor Day. The key part read, "You are aware that FHFA is currently conducting a review of the adequacy of . . . reserves. . . . As such, the August 22, 2008 classification remains under review." That was a serious shot across their bow.

By Tuesday the plan was in place for conservatorship, but many details had to be completed. All the teams continued to work flat out. Fink updated me on the reviews of the MBS. Hank was hammering, saying Wednesday was "D-Day."

Wednesday and Thursday, I continued to interview CEO candidates. One dropped out when he heard that the pay was going to be cut by two-thirds to "only" $5 million. Tuesday afternoon, in a long meeting with Mudd, we discussed the full range of issues, including impairments, mortgage insurers, deferred tax assets, capital classification, personnel issues, and the upcoming midyear letters. He also said that using banks' reserving practices did not make sense, but he was going to shorten Fannie's ninety-day default rule.

The next day I had another call with Johnson and Glauber, the

Freddie directors. They admitted that things had not gotten done under Syron, and they were still trying to hire his replacement. They claimed again that private equity could get their arms around credit and housing if the price was right; but private equity could be "chumps" due to the political risk. They also said that they were working on asks for Treasury financing. They admitted that there could be a "buyers' strike" on their securities. Later, J. C. Flowers's Oros said there was no way to "stick" capital into a "four way" (meaning the Treasury, the FHFA, Freddie, and themselves) as Freddie's reserves were not adequate.

On Thursday the fourth, we released the draft midyear letters to the enterprises' CEOs to share with their boards. The hard-hitting letters had twenty-plus pages of specific problems and risks. The opening paragraphs of the two letters were similar:

> [Your] composite rating is "Critical Concerns." This rating reflects critical safety and soundness concerns with the Enterprise. The financial condition of the enterprise is vulnerable to continuing adverse business conditions, and it cannot raise additional capital to cover a potential significant increase in credit losses and related expenses. . . . Given the unsafe or unsound practices and conditions that gave rise to the Enterprise's existing condition, the deterioration in overall asset quality and significant earnings losses experienced through June 2008, as well as forecasted future losses, likely require recapitalization of the Enterprise.

The critical concerns rating was our lowest. It was defined as "enterprises with critical safety and soundness concerns. . . . In absence of immediate corrective measures, these situations could result in government action such as conservatorships."

There were very compelling cases for the downgrade. It was

backed up by a draft memo sent to me on September 6 from the FHFA's deputy for enterprise regulation, Chris Dickerson, laying out the justification for the conservatorships. As Paulson wrote in his book, "They were tough letters, accompanied by affidavits from their examiners, that dissected capital and management deficiencies and noted all of the corrections the companies had been asked to make and hadn't."[109]

The CEOs knew that the letters marked the beginning of the end. Syron told me he was "stunned" and "in shock." He and his board wanted to know if they could remediate. I gave heads-up calls to Reich, Dugan, Cox, and Warsh. I placed calls to the two CEOs to come to meetings Friday afternoon. Hank told me that President Bush wanted to thank me in person for pulling this all together, but his White House counsel said he could not.

It was great to hear the president was thankful, but as I prepared for the meetings with the CEOs, I thought on what we could have done earlier to prevent the mortgage mess and the conservatorships. For almost two and a half years we fought hard for legislation, which came much too late. President Bush in *Decision Points* said he had called for reform eighteen times. He started asking earlier than I did, but I am sure I beat him in the number of times I asked.

We had been tough on Fannie and Freddie, pushing them to reform their accounting, install better internal controls, strengthen risk management, freeze their portfolios while supporting the mortgage market, increase the capital requirements, and raise capital several times, but that was not enough. Even as we were taking those actions, I was getting criticism for being too tough on Fannie and Freddie, with critics saying it was hurting the housing market. Loosening the constraints would have only produced higher losses. Others suggested I was too soft on the enterprises or had been misleading by calling them legally adequately capitalized.

The fundamental problem was that of many other government and quasi-governmental insurance programs. Fannie and Freddie were created to serve a noble purpose to provide stability, liquidity, and affordability to the American mortgage market, but their structure was fundamentally flawed. In *Firefighting: The Financial Crisis and Its Lessons*, Bernanke, Geithner, and Paulson wrote that Fannie and Freddie "were basically the corporate embodiment of moral hazard, enjoying the upside of their risk taking while taking comfort that taxpayers would cover any downside. They did not cause the crisis, as some have suggested; until late in the boom, the underwriting for mortgages they bought and backed was relatively conservative for the industry."[110]

Of course, by the end, they were the industry. PLS had disappeared, and banks were withdrawing. Their hybrid structure of being government chartered and shareholder owned did lead to an inherent conflict—privatized profits and socialized losses.

The push from shareholders, directors, and managers for growth, market share gains, and higher profits was exacerbated by HUD over two presidential administrations' push for higher affordable housing goals. Homeownership was pushed up to 69 percent, but when it fell, the result was that millions of Americans' life savings and credit ratings were destroyed by foreclosures.

It was a structure designed for failure at some point. The tightrope finally snapped. Fannie and Freddie helped enable skyrocketing housing prices and participated in far too many poorly designed Alt-A and subprime mortgages through their own purchases and private-label MBS. Then, when the housing market inevitably started to submerge, they did not have adequate countercyclical capital to lessen the impact.

CHAPTER 20

Torpedoed—Biggest Financial Rescue

"We had just pulled off perhaps the biggest financial rescue
in history. Fannie and Freddie had not been able to stop us,
Congress was supportive, and the market looked sure to accept
our moves . . . and we had, I thought, just saved the country—
and the world—from financial catastrophe."

—Henry Paulson, *On the Brink*

"WHY ARE YOU putting us in conservatorship when Freddie
is much worse?" The question came from Beth Wilkinson, Fannie
Mae's general counsel, at our 3 PM meeting on Friday, September
5, 2008. Also in attendance were CEO Mudd, Chairman Ashley,
and their outside counsel, Rodgin Cohen, at the meeting in the
FHFA director's conference room.

The day's economic news was bad. The Mortgage Bankers
Association reported that mortgages over thirty days delinquent
and in foreclosure hit 9.2 percent in the second quarter, the
highest rate in the thirty-nine-year history of the survey. The rate
for subprime was 30 percent, but even the prime delinquency rate
was 5.4 percent. The unemployment rate had increased to 6.2
percent in August. The enterprises' stock prices continued to sink.

Seated between Paulson and Bernanke across the table from

the Fannie team, I gave my opening remarks. Our side of the table also included the FHFA's Pollard; Richard Alexander, our outside counsel; and others. I was somewhat nervous given the size, importance, and arrogance of Fannie Mae. The goal was to have their board consent to the conservatorship by noon the next day.

Speaking from handwritten notes, I outlined the many problems and risks Fannie posed. The list summarized the "critical concerns" letter of the day before, including unsafe and unsound conditions relating to earnings, solvency, liquidity, credit and counterparty risk, and accounting. There were many holes in the hull, and the ship was sinking fast.

Following me, Paulson was forceful in citing the Fed's, the OCC's, and Morgan Stanley's reviews, which all supported the FHFA's conclusions. He said he had spoken to foreign central bankers who were losing confidence in Fannie Mae. (A Fed paper in 2015[111] stated that on June 30, 2008, central banks had holdings of the enterprises' MBS and GSE debt, including FHLBanks, of almost $1 trillion. In total, foreign holdings were $1.46 trillion, of which $527 billion were held by the Chinese.) As the fair value capital was very low, Paulson said a large capital infusion was necessary and that he could not support committing taxpayer funds without a conservatorship.

Bernanke made it clear that the markets were very troubled, and the troubles were spreading globally. Fannie and Freddie were needed to help calm the markets. The way to do that was an orderly and consensual conservatorship.

Paulson's planned ambush worked as we had built up such a compelling case. The Fannie team appeared stunned but pushed back strongly. Mudd questioned how I could repudiate my July statement of their strong capital position. I said, "We have changed conditions—there was a tidal wave of events," and we needed to provide clarity to Fannie's MBS, senior debt, and subordinated debt holders to ensure market stability. Mudd asked again why it could not be done with a capital plan and a Treasury backup line of credit, which was the "moral equivalent of conservatorship." He also wanted to know how big we thought the hole was.

Wilkinson, pushing back again, asked where the notice of unsafe and unsound conditions was. I thought the September 4 critical conditions letter and my statements at the start of the meeting made that very clear. She said conservatorship would "destroy the investor proposition" and was a move to nationalization.

The pushback continued. Cohen noted that the board could be sued if they consented to the conservatorship. Wilkinson wanted to know why only Mudd was going to be let go and not the rest of the senior management as they were a team. My response was that the team was needed to ensure a smooth conservatorship and that we wanted Mudd to help in the transition. Mudd bluntly said, "We have material factual disagreements." Ashley wanted to know why we were doing it.

Paulson and Bernanke were very strong. Even Fannie could not stand up to the power of the US Treasury and the Federal Reserve Bank. Cohen helped calm things down, and Ashley agreed to schedule a Saturday board meeting. We made it clear that consent to the conservatorship was the only option for the board.

In Hagerty's book he wrote: "Mudd still wasn't ready to surrender. 'Our board will want to take a close look at this,' he said. Alexander replied, 'I need you to understand that when these gentlemen [Lockhart and Paulson] come to your board meeting tomorrow, it's not to have a dialogue.'"[112]

Next up were separate calls from my office to the two key Democratic lawmakers, Frank and Dodd. Paulson handled the calls well. Early Saturday morning, CBS News (September 6, 2008) reported that "Frank said the company's financial position was better than Wall Street investors assume but 'it just plainly became clear that elements of the market wouldn't accept it.'"

Wall Street was right. Dodd was always eager to place blame: "Any government action must help to strengthen our economy, which is suffering a crisis brought on by the administration's failure to stop predatory lending." He failed to note how many times he had pushed us to get Fannie and Freddie to do more subprime lending.

The 6 PM Freddie meeting was almost anticlimactic because they knew there was no way out; they had failed for six months to raise capital and even longer to hire a CEO. The news was also starting to leak out. Syron was joined by his general counsel, Lead Director Johnson, and a couple of other board members. They pushed backed less than Fannie. They knew that they had a weak case. Many of the questions were more procedural—about how a conservatorship worked and about the requested board meeting. It was quite a change from the usual pushback I got from Freddie and their board. Syron appeared somewhat surprised but at the end looked visibly relieved. Doing three jobs was wearing him down. He seemed happy to be relieved of command.

After the Freddie meeting, there were calls with Shelby and Schumer. Shelby said Sunday night that if Congress had acted earlier, "we could have avoided our current situation. Now that the old structure has failed . . . we now need to begin a vigorous debate about the future of these entities and the role of government in our private housing market."[113]

The Saturday Board meetings were scheduled at the FHL board's offices in hopes of keeping the conservatorships secret. The room was much larger and nicer than OFHEO's as the FHLBoard used it for their public meetings. I proudly read in Paulson's book that he described OFHEO's conference room as "drab and cramped," and Bernanke's description was "unprepossessing." I liked my office next door to the conference room, with its view of the Old Executive Office Building and the Washington Monument. Jimmie Brand, my friend and driver, used to drive a tour bus and told me that he would tell tourists that the stones changed color halfway up because the monument was lowered at night.

The press did not show up Saturday, but the news was already out. The enterprising *Wall Street Journal* reporter Damian Paletta staked out our offices Friday afternoon and saw Ben Bernanke arriving. His September 6 article was entitled "US Near Deal on Fannie, Freddie—Plan Could Amount to Government Takeover; Management Shakeup Expected." He quoted PIMCO's Bill Gross statement: "Investors are saying we want to see [the Treasury] in there with us" and that the Treasury needs to "swim in the pool, not just be a lifeguard." As it turned out, it was more like the North Atlantic in the winter with thirty-foot waves.

Both boards had a full set of advisors and members present. The bald-guy team of Paulson, Bernanke, and I ran again through the problems and our request for consent. The boards, management, and their advisors knew the topic and the answer. Fannie's board was much feistier than Freddie's. Doing their fiduciary duty, they asked questions for the record. Freddie's board reluctantly consented to the conservatorships after we left. Fannie's board took longer. We had to call for their answer. As I told the Financial Crisis Inquiry Commission, "The companies' opposition to legislation for so long was a major mistake. The boards focused on maximizing shareholder profitability. In the end they failed both the shareholders and the taxpayers."

With Wilson's and Paulson's help, we had selected two good CEO candidates. They were ready to get started. Herb Allison, the former chairman of TIAA-CREF and former vice chairman of Merrill Lynch, agreed to be Fannie's CEO. David Moffett, a Carlyle senior advisor and a former vice chairman and CFO of US Bancorp, became Freddie's. We were also selecting new chairmen and directors. In a conservatorship, boards were not required, but we thought it was a good practice and necessary for the eventual exit from conservatorship.

We scheduled a press conference for 11 AM on Sunday. It was in our building, upstairs in the OTS's amphitheater conference room. It was a fitting location as it was the room where we'd had the press conference announcing the Fannie Mae settlement agreement in 2006. We also had our quarterly risk assessment meetings there with the full OFHEO team. Those meetings tended to be intense; the list of issues kept growing as the housing market deteriorated.

Before the press conference began, Hank pulled me aside, saying, "This is going to be an adventure, as I am not good at this." I was not sure whether he thought that his confession would calm me down or not, but I think it did.

It was a big crowd with lots of cameras. Rewatching the C-SPAN video, I believe we got our message across relatively smoothly. Secretary Paulson led off by saying we had been "closely monitoring financial market and business conditions and have analyzed in great detail the current financial condition of the GSEs. . . . As a result of this work, we have determined that it is necessary to take action."

Before introducing me, he tried to differentiate Fannie and Freddie from other financial institutions as their conditions were obviously worrying him. He said the GSEs were "unique" and "their statutory capital requirements are thin and poorly defined as compared to other institutions. Nothing about our actions today in any way reflects a changed view of the housing correction and the strength of other US financial institutions."

In my remarks I said we did an "exhaustive review" and laid out the case for action, saying that their ability to balance mission with safety and soundness "has been lost. Unfortunately, as house prices, earnings and capital have continued to deteriorate, their ability to fulfill their mission has deteriorated."

I announced the conservatorships, adding that they were consented to by the boards. I thanked the boards, CEOs, and other managers for their service, noting that they "did not create an inherent conflict and flawed business model embedded in the enterprises' structure":

> The goal of these actions is to help restore confidence in Fannie Mae and Freddie Mac, enhance their capability to fulfill their mission, and mitigate the systemic risk that has contributed directly to the instability in the current market. The lack of confidence has resulted in continuing spread widening of their MBS, which means that virtually none of the large drop in interest rates over the past year has been passed on to the mortgage markets. On top of that, Freddie Mac and Fannie Mae, in order to try to build capital, have continued to raise prices and tighten credit.

They did need capital, but these actions were the opposite of the countercyclical activities needed to save the housing market.

I announced that "Monday morning the business will open as normal, only with stronger backing for the holders of MBS, senior debt, and subordinated debt and with new CEOs." DeMarco, my deputy, had been doing yeoman's work with the Treasury to ensure that there would be a smooth transition. Later that Sunday, there were separate meetings with the two management teams and the new CEOs.

A key point I made in my press conference speech was "as conservator, FHFA will assume the power of the board and management." I also announced the suspension of their common and preferred dividends and the halting of "all political activities—including lobbying activities." There were a lot of lobbyists mad at me for that, including some friends. I also said we would allow the portfolios to grow through year-end 2009 and then begin reducing them 10 percent a year.

Before turning it back to Paulson, I ended:

This decision was a tough one for the FHFA team as they had worked so hard to help the Enterprises remain strong suppliers of support to the secondary mortgage markets. Unfortunately, the antiquated capital requirements and the turmoil in housing markets over-whelmed all the good and hard work put in by the FHFA teams. . . . I want to thank the FHFA employees for their work during this intense regulatory process. They represent the best in public service. I would also like to thank the employees of Fannie Mae and Freddie Mac for all their hard work. Working together we can finish the job of restoring confidence in the Enterprises and with the new legislation build a stronger and safer future for the mortgage markets, homeowners, and renters in America.

After I turned the podium back to Paulson, he stated that he supported my decision and had advised me "that conservatorship was the only form in which [he] would commit taxpayer's money to the GSEs." He described the keepwell, the preferred stock purchase agreements (PSPA), which "ensures that each company maintains a positive net worth." I had signed the two PSPAs with him earlier that day as the conservator of Fannie Mae and Freddie Mac.

The accompanying fact sheets detailed that the PSPAs were $100 billion each and that "the number is unrelated to Treasury's analysis of the current financial conditions of the GSEs." In fact, we thought that the usage would be much lower. There was a 10 percent dividend and a potential commitment fee on the PSPA. In return for supplying the financing, the Treasury received from each enterprise $1 billion of the senior preferred stock and warrants for 79.9 percent of their common stock. The percentage was as high as it could go without consolidating the enterprises' $5.4 trillion debts on the US government books. The very creative part of the PSPAs was that they were of "indefinite duration," which was the way to protect the MBS, which had thirty-year maturities.

As the new preferred stocks were senior to the existing preferred, he said the banking regulators were reviewing the situation and would work with banks holding a significant amount of Fannie and Freddie's preferred stock. With a 20 percent risk weighting and high-dividend yields, the enterprises' preferred stocks had become a favorite of many banks. The rating agencies immediately cut their ratings for a third time—this time to "junk."

A March 2012 Federal Reserve paper[114] estimated that "more than 600 depository institutions in the United States were exposed to at least $8 billion in investment losses" from the Fannie and Freddie preferred stocks, and "in addition, 15 failures and two distressed mergers either directly or indirectly resulted from the takeover." The paper did not point out that US banks held over $1 trillion of Fannie Mae and Freddie Mac MBS and debt. Their hit would have been catastrophic if no action were taken.

A second facility was secured lending for Fannie, Freddie, and the Federal Home Loan Banks as an "ultimate liquidity backstop." The third facility was a Treasury program to purchase GSE MBS, which Paulson said "could produce gains" for the Treasury. It did produce gains, as did the other two facilities.

Paulson was perceptive to address what became a major postmortem theme of the Great Recession—"Wall Street versus Main Street":

> And let me make clear what today's actions mean for Americans and their families. Fannie Mae and Freddie Mac are so large and so interwoven in our financial system that a failure of either of them would cause great turmoil in our financial markets here at home and around the

globe. This turmoil would directly and negatively impact household wealth: from family budgets to home values, to savings for college and retirement. A failure would affect the ability of Americans to get home loans, auto loans and other consumer credit and business finance. And a failure would be harmful to economic growth and job creation. That is why we have taken these actions today.

He concluded by saying that as the GSE lending and MBS purchase facilities would expire at the end of 2009 and as the PSPA would start charging a commitment fee starting in 2010, that "should give momentum and urgency to the reform cause. Policymakers must view this next period as a 'time-out' where we have stabilized the GSEs while we decide their future role and structure."

His "time-out" is probably even more quoted than his "bazooka." I know I have used it in scores of speeches after leaving the FHFA when calling for reform. Less quoted is his conclusion: "We will make a grave error if we don't use this time-out to permanently address the structural issues presented by the GSEs."

The "grave error" was made, as despite lots of debates and proposals, the enterprises' structural issues have not been reformed. The Obama administration put out a thought piece, but Secretary Geithner did not push reform strongly. Bills introduced in the House and Senate did not get far. The Trump administration did not push for legislative reform, nor has Biden.

The conservatorships were all over the papers the next day. The top of the *Wall Street Journal*'s front page was filled with two stories as well as a picture of an intense Hank and a fuzzy me. The headline was "US Seizes Mortgage Giants." The opening line was "In its most dramatic intervention in years, the US government seized two of the nation's largest financial companies, taking direct responsibility for firms that provide funding for around three quarters of new home mortgages."[115]

The *Journal's* editorial board got their "more honest socialism" but still had lots of complaints, saying it was too late and it should have been a receivership wiping out all equity holders and subordinated debt investors. They worried that "the biggest risk here, however, is that the companies could still emerge with their business models intact." The editorial ended, "The least we can do now is bury these undead monsters for all time."

The Asian, European, and US markets all popped. Some financial stocks saw double-digit gains, but Lehman's stock fell 14 percent, portending the coming weekend. More directly, the enterprises' bond yields fell thirty basis points, and the MBS tightened by fifty basis points. The *Financial Times*[116] wrote that there was a "buying frenzy in mortgage bonds."

On Tuesday, the *Financial Times* editorialized, "There was no alternative. This weekend, the US government effectively nationalized Fannie Mae and Freddie Mac. It was the right decision. It will save the world from a financial catastrophe, and it means that the absurd quasi-private structure of Fannie and Freddie can now be put to bed, at long last."

The editors wrote the Treasury "should devise plans for splitting up and privatizing the GSEs. As in other countries, the secondary mortgage market ought to have no public participants. This is a distant prospect—a decade at least—but planning should start now."

On *PBS Newshour with Jim Lehrer* on September 9, Shelby and Dodd gave dueling interviews. Shelby, accusing Democrats of killing his 2005 bill, said it "was a debacle waiting to happen. We knew for a number—four or five years—that they were thinly capitalized, questionable accounting practices and, in a lot of instances, poorly run, although they did do some good." Dodd said, "The fact that there was no cop on the beat, predatory lending, subprime, all this went on over the last eight or ten years. In a sense, Fannie and Freddie are almost victims of what happened."

There was a cop on the beat, but he was unarmed. As a *Washington Post* journalist wrote,[117] "Lockhart spent much time warning that he lacked the tools of other regulators and urging Congress to create a new, more powerful overseer for the companies."

Not surprisingly, Fannie's common stock fell 80 percent, and Freddie's sank 73 percent.

Unfortunately, many of the investors were individuals. A Dow Jones article, "Investors Say US Govt. Misled them on GSEs,"[118] quoted a Treasury spokeswoman saying the week of August 18 that "as the Secretary has said many times, we have no plan to use this authority [bazooka]."

The article also cited me: "Lockhart, in a July 8 televised statement, said the firms were 'adequately capitalized.' That's a technical term referring to the complex internal measures that were taken by some investors as a statement of Lockhart's faith in the firms." The article cited the FHFA's press person saying that I had not done a television interview in August to reaffirm that statement but was not happy that some equity investors relied upon my technical statements. Like Paulson, I was trying to be reassuring to prevent a panic "run on the bank."

On Monday, September 8, I gave a series of interviews. On NPR's *All Things Considered*, the interviewer, Melissa Block, asked if I was concerned about the common shareholders. I said it was "very unfortunate," and that the enterprises "took on too much risk for too little return."

She then asked, "Is it wrenching for you?"

My response was "Well, yeah. I mean, it is not a happy day. But you know, I think we had to make the right decision for the country. And the right decision for the country [and] the financial markets was to do this."

She also asked about the future of Fannie and Freddie.

I said, "My personal view is there should be a way to get them back into the private sector."

She then asked: "What do you think the price tag for this takeover is? One number that's been floated is $25 billion. Do you think that's about right? Do you think that's too low?"

I responded, "Well. It's hard to say that there will even be a price tag at this point. The US government has gotten a preferred stock of a billion dollars, has warrants of almost 80 percent. You know, we'll be buying mortgage-backed securities that should be very strong. So, they may need money put in, but over the long term, you know, the hope would be that it would be repaid."

That was a very optimistic statement. A Fed paper[119] of March 2015 summarized the results:

> From 2008 to 2011, Fannie Mae and Freddie Mac posted total combined losses (in terms of comprehensive income) of $266 billion and required $187.5 billion of Treasury support. The biggest contributor to these staggering losses was single-family credit guarantees, which generated about $215 billion in losses over this period, almost all due to provisions for credit losses. . . . A second contributor was the dividends on the senior preferred stock held by the US Treasury (paying 10 percent per year), which totaled $36 billion over this period. Perhaps surprisingly, Fannie Mae's and Freddie Mac's investment portfolios, which at first had suffered large losses ($83 billion in 2008), actually generated $2 billion in comprehensive income over this entire period.

The presidential candidates were happy for the time being. It did not last long as Senator Obama wrote Paulson and me a letter on September 9, starting with "News reports indicate that the chief executives of Fannie Mae and Freddie Mac will stand to reap millions of dollars in severance payments. . . . I recognize that intervention is necessary to maintain liquidity for the housing market. . . . It would be a gross violation of the public trust not to block the severance payments."

A deluge of letters and press followed. Senators Schumer and Reed (D-RI) wrote a letter, as did Senators Dick Durbin (D-IL), Ben Nelson (D-NE), Hagel (R-NE), and Bunning (R-KY). The latter introduced legislation to stop the severance payments. Representative Waxman, chair of the House Oversight Committee, and other members of the House weighed in. I had conversations with Hagel several times, well before the conservatorships, about Mudd and Syron's pay. Under the 1992 law, OFHEO had some powers over pay, but those were more to ensure that the executives were not paid above comparable financial executives, which they were not. HERA gave us stronger powers, which the legislators were asking me to use, to block Mudd's and Syron's severance and pension payments.

Cricket and I flew to St. Louis the weekend of the twelfth for a wedding. JB, Virginia, Graci, and Marko also attended. The lawyer representing Mudd on his payments was there. The devilish host, our friend Dick Grote, introduced us. We had an awkward conversation. By the end of the week, we decided to eliminate the "golden parachutes" for the two CEOs for a total of $12.6 million, but not their pensions of $6.8 million for Mudd and $4 million for Syron.

Schumer was pleased and put out a statement on the fourteenth. The next day Senator Obama commended us, reminding everybody about his letter. The other compensation issue we were working on with outside consultants was retention payments for the enterprises' employees as it was critical to retain them to keep the mortgage market functioning. Paulson was helping with morale, visiting both Fannie and Freddie headquarters on Tuesday.

Barney Frank tried to define the conservatorships of Fannie and Freddie by saying that "they were being torn between their private activities and their public mission. Now that's finished— it's the public mission."[120]

Prior to the conservatorships, the enterprises were working slowly on modifications of troubled mortgages to lower interest rates or stretch out payments. As I said to the *American Banker*,[121] "We have prodded them to be creative and aggressive [on mortgage modifications]." As we were the conservator, the ball was now in the FHFA's court. The article cited Sheila Bair's announcement in August of an aggressive mass modification program for IndyMac's $184 billion servicing portfolio as a potential model for us.

The *American Banker* article quoted many commentators pushing back on mass modifications, which they thought would disturb the markets going forward. To me it was shortsighted. An effective modification would prevent an expensive and disruptive foreclosure from hurting individuals and their neighbors.

Developing a streamlined modification program would not be easy. Fannie and Freddie had more than $5 trillion in mortgages, and they relied on third-party servicers, most of which were not well staffed or trained for modifications. An even tougher question was how to force modifications in the private-label MBS in which the enterprises were the largest investors.

Personnel retention and mortgage modifications were not the only challenges the new conservator and CEOs faced. There were questions on the FHFA's new powers transferred from HUD on setting affordable housing goals and funding the new Affordable Housing Fund. We were recruiting new directors and nonexecutive chairmen. On the sixteenth, we announced that Philip Laskawy, former head of Ernest & Young, would be the Fannie chair, and John Koskinen, turnaround executive and Clinton's OMB deputy for management, would be Freddie's.

Market participants kept prodding us on what actions we were going to take on multifamily housing, reverse mortgages, putting back bad mortgages to originators, low-income housing tax credits (LIHTC), state housing finance agency funding, and mortgage insurers. Fannie and Freddie were some of the largest buyers and securitizers of multifamily housing loans. As the programs were very successful, I put a statement out on September 12 supporting their multifamily programs. The same day, in a letter to me and the two CEOs, Senators Schumer, Bob Casey (D-PA), Sherrod Brown (D-OH), and Bob Menendez (D-NJ) called for a ninety-day foreclosure freeze and more rapid mortgage modifications.

That was an opening salvo for a Senate hearing on Tuesday, September 16, in which Paulson and I were asked to testify about the conservatorships. I met with Paulson on Friday to prepare, but the hearing ended up being postponed for a week—Lehman failed on Sunday.

CHAPTER 21

The Lender of Next-to-Last Resort

"During the early part of the financial crisis, the FHLB system
played an important stabilizing role as a 'lender of next-to-
last resort' by providing funding—collateralized by mortgages
and mortgage related assets—to banks, thrifts, insurance
companies, and credit unions."

—"The Increased Role of the Federal Home Bank System, Part 1:
Background. Board of Governors of the Federal Reserve System," by
Stefan Grissler and Borghan Narajabad, October 18, 2017

WITH THE SIGNING of HERA (Housing and Economic
Recovery Act) in late July 2008, OFHEO was merged with the
Federal Housing Finance Board (FHFB), which oversaw the
twelve Federal Home Loan Banks, to create the FHFA. The FHFB,
which was effectively abolished after the passage of HERA, had
been established in 1989 in the aftermath of the savings and loan
crisis as the successor agency to the Federal Home Loan Bank
Board (FHLBB), which also oversaw the savings and loan banks.
In 1989 the Office of Thrift Supervision took over responsibility
for S&L oversight only to be abolished with the passage of the
Dodd-Frank Act in 2010.

The FHLBoard had five members: a Republican chairman,

Ronnie Rosenfeld, who previously had been the president of Ginnie Mae; three other full-time board members apportioned to be equally divided by party; and the HUD secretary, which ensured that the president's party had the majority. As with other government agencies run by full-time boards, it was subject to the government under the Sunshine Act of 1976. That meant that any time more than two members of the board met, there had to be a public notice and public meeting. The act plus the political split made it hard to interact and reach consensus. As a result, decision-making was slow and cumbersome.

The then twelve (now eleven) banks were chartered by Congress at the end of the Hoover administration in 1932 during the Depression to support "buildings and loan" institutions. The twelve were headquartered in Atlanta, Boston, Chicago, Cincinnati, Dallas, Des Moines, New York, Indianapolis, Pittsburg, San Francisco, Seattle, and Topeka.

The FHLBanks are also GSEs. In total they are much smaller than Fannie Mae and Freddie Mac, but their combined assets exceeded $1.4 trillion in September 2008. The banks are cooperatives owned by their members—banks, thrifts, credit unions, and insurance companies. Their boards are composed of bankers and other community leaders. The key function of the FHLBanks is to make "advances" to their members/shareholders. Advances are loans well over-secured by assets pledged by the borrower, and as a result, the FHLBanks have never taken a loss on advances. The FHLBanks were often the only lender left for troubled banks.

In 2008 there were many vacancies for the independent director positions as they had to be appointed by the finance board's cumbersome process. HERA changed that to allow the individual FHLBanks to appoint the directors. One of our first priorities was to implement that rule.

The FHLBanks paid dividends to their shareholders and

therefore were under pressure to produce profits. They issued debt with joint and several liabilities through the FHLBanks Office of Finance, based in Reston, Virginia. Reston was a real estate development established by Gulf Oil when they were trying to diversify. I attended a Gulf Oil meeting there when we were in the process of moving to London. Cricket was characteristically efficient but not happy as I was not around for the move. It seemed I was always in another city or country whenever we had to pull up stakes. Cricket thought I planned it that way.

As was the case with several other GSEs, the banks had problems over the years. Poole, the president of the Federal Reserve Bank of St. Louis, said in his previously quoted January 2007 speech that the FHLBanks "were enduring accounting and control issues of their own. Two of the 12 FHLBs signed written agreements in 2004 with their supervisor, the Federal Housing Finance Board (FHFB), to rectify portfolio risk management deficiencies. Then, in 2005, 10 of the 12 FHLBs failed to meet their agreed deadline to register their stock with the SEC. Like Fannie Mae and Freddie Mac, all of the Federal Home Loan Banks restated their earnings in recent years."

Chairman Rosenfeld was supportive of the HERA legislation, which did away with his agency. However, the two Democratic directors were adamantly opposed to the reform bill and worked to get the FHLBanks excluded. One said, "If you combine everyone in one agency, I think you're looking at the possible demise of the Federal Home Loan Bank system." He called the board "a world class regulator." The other Democratic member said that they had "every single conceivable legal authority" and there was no benefit to having a new regulator.[122]

In 2007 there was talk of merging the Dallas and Chicago banks because of their problems. The GSE Activity Report in August 2007[123] pointed out a problem that I inherited a year later: "Most of the [FHL]Banks are also sitting on big positions in private-label paper that may require significant mark-to-market reductions. None is well enough capitalized to absorb this without a sharp hit to dividends. These will, in turn, exacerbate earnings problems at small members, worsening bank regulators' fears about the system." For instance, Chicago had "$5.8 billion in AAA-rated private-label MBS of which $1.8 billion is composed of home-equity ABS."

While juggling the enterprises' massive problems, we had to integrate the ex-FHFB team and review the FHLBanks' financial status. DeMarco did a great job in spearheading this effort to merge the teams to create the new FHFA. He arranged an all hands meeting at the Mayflower Hotel the day after the HERA signing for a team-building event.

Funnily, I was the only employee of the FHFA the way the legislation was written, as the two agencies had a year to wind down. We ignored that as we had to create a united team in face of our massive challenges. In my speech, I invoked Andover's motto, "The end depends on the beginning." Rosenfeld gave a very gracious speech. I thanked him for his FHFB leadership and his strong support of the HERA legislation.

I spoke on August 5, 2008, at a meeting with all twelve of the FHLBanks' presidents in the offices of the FHLBank of Chicago, saying:

> FHFA is only six days old, but there is no day of rest yet. On the day after President Bush signed the bill (at 7:05 a.m., I might add), we had an all-hands meeting designed to get everybody up to speed and lessen the uncertainty. I'll give you a streamlined version.
>
> The key message I gave them: our mission is critical, especially in this market. It is to ensure the safety and soundness of the fourteen GSEs so that they can provide liquidity and stability to the mortgage markets

and financial institutions. And so that they can provide affordability to homeowners and renters. . . . I told them that I am a strong believer that good management is based on good plans, well executed. And that I am hands on and like lots of input, but I am impatient to get results.

In August, John Fiske, the head of their Office of Finance, told me borrowing spreads were widening and it was hard to extend maturity beyond six months.

Concerns about capital levels were spreading to many financial institutions, including the FHLBanks. As the lender of next-to-last resort to the banking system, that was very worrisome to me. The capital of the FHLBanks was supplied by their member banks and insurance companies. They had a risk-based capital test and a leverage ratio of 4 percent, much higher than Fannie and Freddie.

A member requesting advances had to invest 4 percent of that advance into the FHLBank's equity. They had very small retained earnings as most of their earnings were paid out in dividends, which made their stock attractive to their members. When a member reduced their advances, they could get their capital back after five years, but the FHLBanks often waived that requirement, returning the capital immediately.

An *American Banker* article[124] of September 4 reported that there was a proposal moving to my desk to require the FHLBanks to build capital by retaining more earnings. Community bankers were especially unhappy because that meant lower dividends.

A similar proposal was made by the examination team led by Steve Cross in 2006. The article said, "After receiving 1,066 mostly angry letters from bankers, the Finance Board ultimately decided in December 2006 to table the plan." The examination team was probably leaking the proposal because the FHFA's "structure puts the decision solely in Mr. Lockhart's hands."

JAMES B. LOCKHART III

The timing was not good: it was procyclical as more banks were starting to fail.

Part 3 of the Fed study quoted at the beginning of the chapter stated: "In fact, investors lost confidence in GSEs in 2008 due to the substantial troubles facing Fannie Mae and Freddie Mac. The FHLB system found itself 'guilty by association.' . . . A spike in funding costs reduced the FHLB system's ability to act as lender of next-to-last resort and FHLBs' advances and interest income dropped significantly. The FHLB system's access to funding markets was only restored when the Federal government signaled support for the GSEs."

That support was the Treasury GSE credit facility. That helped reassure the market. Unlike Fannie and Freddie, they did not have to tap it. The Fed could also buy their debt, but by April 2009 they had only bought $17 billion.

At the end of November, FHLBanks' Office of Finance reported their third-quarter 2008 results. Unlike Fannie and Freddie, they reported a profit, about half a billion dollars, albeit down 30 percent from the previous quarter. They took a loss on Lehman Brothers' investments and other-than-temporary impairment (OTTI) on their PLS investments. Their advances were up 10.7 percent to a still record $1.01 trillion.

I spent a lot of time with bank presidents, chairmen, and occasionally with their boards. They have an effective Washington-based Council of Federal Home Loan Banks, which had a meeting September 8 and 9, 2008, in DC.

A month later, the bank presidents were back in DC. Despite the growing PLS problems, they were all trying to figure out what more they could do to help the mortgage market and their members. Almost weekly there were meetings or calls with one or more of the presidents to hash out issues, sometimes lobbying me against the tough stance the examination team was taking. On December 9, the presidents had their major annual meeting in Key Biscayne, Florida. I flew in and out for a working lunch.

In January 2009, Moody's wrote a piece questioning the FHLBanks' soundness. They reported Seattle would miss its capital requirement in December and Pittsburgh might as well. They also estimated another six banks might fail the capital test. The report said the twelve banks had $76.2 billion in PLS at the end of September with unrealized losses of $13.5 billion versus total capital of $57 billion. A *Wall Street Journal*[125] article reported that the president of the Pittsburgh Bank "said it may have to ask its members to provide more capital if auditors and regulators require a major write-down." He said, "The home-loan banks are being hurt by 'Alice in Wonderland' accounting rules that exaggerate the likely size of eventual losses on the mortgage securities."

As to "Alice in Wonderland" accounting, I told Bloomberg, "Conceptually, I'm a big believer in fair value, but it's tough in a market like this where there's that fear factor, lack of confidence and lack of liquidity. . . . Applying fair-value accounting to privately backed mortgage bonds is somewhat problematic at the moment. It's really hard to get a good market based fair value because so few of these securities are trading."[126]

I was being asked whether the FHLBanks should be placed in conservatorship or receive TARP funds. I said there was no need for TARP. As to conservatorship, I was quoted, "I don't see what purpose it would serve at this point. They are continuing to be able to fund themselves as a system."[127]

In total the banks were the third largest holders of PLS after Freddie and Fannie. Almost all of the formerly AAA PLS were downgraded to junk. Several banks, including Boston, Pittsburgh, Chicago, and Seattle, had much higher percentage holdings than the system average of 5 percent of assets. Having drilled down on the enterprises' PLS for over a year, we were well prepared to review the banks' portfolios.

In March 2009, the FHFA published our first annual report to Congress. The introduction was a "Federal Housing Oversight Board Assessment" by the FHFA's board, composed of Geithner as Treasury secretary, Shaun Donovan as HUD secretary, and Mary Schapiro as chairman of the SEC. I was chair of the board. The new board was strong and supportive, as was the original board of Hank Paulson and Steve Preston and—not as much—Chris Cox.

We wrote:

> As financial markets seized in 2007 and 2008, the FHLBanks played a critical role in providing liquidity (advances) to their members, with advances growing to more than $1 trillion at September 30, 2008. The FHLBanks' advance business continues to be a safe and sound business, with no credit losses. . . .
>
> In contrast, the quality of the FHLBanks' investments in private-label mortgage-backed securities was revealed to be far worse than their initial triple-A credit ratings would have suggested. By the end of 2008, six FHLBanks had voluntarily or by regulatory requirement ceased paying dividends and repurchasing member stock as means for conserving capital. . . .
>
> Overall, the FHLBank System with its joint and several liability for System debt remains safe and sound, but actual and potential losses associated with these private-label securities is a cause for safety and soundness concerns at certain FHLBanks.

One very troubling aspect about their PLS investments was that the different banks were marking the same security at different prices. A cynic might reflect that the mark might have been related to how large their capital surplus was. The different pricing was especially problematic because, as they jointly issued debt, they had to produce a combined, audited financial statement compiled by the Office of Finance. We pressured the Office of Finance to force common pricing. The chair of the Office of Finance was Charles Bowsher, who had been the comptroller general of the GAO. As mentioned earlier, after he compared the PBGC to the S&L crisis, I had asked him to do the PBGC audit as required by law. He did the audit under some pressure.

Disappointingly, Bowsher decided to resign from the Office of Finance rather than to enforce the required discipline. Reuters on April 8, 2009, reported a quote from Bowsher: "I decided I didn't have confidence in the financial statements." The FHFA's response was "As Mr. Bowsher recognized, the difficulties in establishing valuation in inactive and distressed markets are significant. We are sorry he chose to resign. We will be seeking a replacement who is prepared to work with the 12 banks and FHFA."

As I wrote in the *FHFA Focus* on July 2009,

> At the end of 2008, there were 10 different approaches to write-downs in the Federal Home Loan Bank System. The fourth quarter produced widely varying estimates of expected losses on OTTI bonds and several late filings— including the System's combined financial statements.
>
> After many meetings with the Presidents and Chairmen of the Banks, installing a new Chair of the Office of Finance, and clarification by the Financial Accounting Standards Board of OTTI accounting, we got the job done during 2009. It was a team effort of the FHLBanks, our two examination teams and our Chief Accountants group."

I finished my *FHFA Focus* note, "I am certain that this effort will prove to be just one of many instances when FHFA synergies enhance the supervision and regulation of the 14 housing GSEs."

FHLBanks Office of Finance was responsible for not only publishing the combined audited accounts but also marketing the banks' debt worldwide. The selling of debt was critical; their debt had almost doubled to over $1 trillion in four years as they responded to their members' funding needs. A May 29, 2009, Office of Finance report to the FHLBanks' presidents reviewed the Office of Finance's marketing efforts: "The overall focus of most investor meetings remains credit risk management related to collateral and the private-label MBS portfolios. . . . While our stellar record of no losses on advances resonates well with investors, some continue to show concern."

As the Fed study quoted at the beginning of this chapter pointed out, "All FHLB advances are subject to the statutory super-lien, which means that in the case of a borrower's insolvency, any security interest granted to the FHLB has priority over the claims and rights of any other party. The super-lien on collateral has facilitated FHLB's ability to lend to a variety of institutions . . . that might otherwise not have ready access to funding from investors who cannot secure such protections."

The super-lien was not without critics, especially FDIC chair Bair. As the FHLBanks had priority over the FDIC in bank failures and oftentimes held the best collateral, she felt that the FHLBanks had an unfair advantage, causing the FDIC to book larger losses. She and I had long discussions about how unfair it was, especially in relationship to the big July 2008 failure of IndyMac Bank.

As Bair put it in *Bull by the Horns*,[128] "The FHLBs lend only on a secured basis and typically demand a bank's best loans as collateral for their lending. When the bank fails, the FDIC must turn all of that collateral over to the FHLB. We cannot sell those high-quality assets to recoup our losses, so our costs for a bank that relies heavily on FHLB loans are typically high as we saw with IndyMac." What really happened was that the banks repaid the advances and retained the loans. Chairman

Bair was especially upset because when the FHLBank advances were repaid by IndyMac, the FDIC had to compensate the San Francisco FHLBank for the prepayment penalty as well.

IndyMac was sold in March 2009 to a newly formed bank, OneWest, whose investor group was led by Steven Mnuchin. At the time of its failure, IndyMac had $10 billion of advances from the San Francisco FHLBank, about a third of its total liabilities. Another troubled bank, BankUnited (which was purchased from the FDIC by a consortium that included WL Ross before I joined them), lived off the Atlanta bank's advances. At their September 2007 year-end, advances of $6.2 billion represented 45 percent of their total liabilities. Countrywide, the biggest supplier of mortgages to Fannie Mae and a major supplier to Freddie Mac, had $51 billion in advances from the Atlanta bank when it was acquired in distress by the Bank of America.

That advance capability, which can extend maturities up to thirty years, made the FHLBanks the waiting room for troubled banks before the FDIC could find a buyer. Bair's FDIC team did a great job of working through the many hundreds of bank failures. Despite her comments, the FHLBanks served a very important function of providing credit when critically needed because of the strength of the super-lien. The FHLBanks played a crucial countercyclical role in lessening the pain of the Great Recession.

Bair was averse to private equity. In July 2009 she proposed a rule that would have made it impossible for private equity to get any returns from rescuing troubled banks. She wrote in her book, "Some of the funds really went after us, including the Carlyle Group and WL Ross & Co."[129] She had to back down. As it turned out, private equity funds were a key component in the rescue of many troubled banks over the next three years.

After I joined WL Ross in September 2009, I brought Ross down to meet with Bair to help her understand that private equity could be a very useful tool for the FDIC. I am not sure that we convinced her, but as it turned out, we were very helpful at turning around troubled banks. Starting in 2009, we alone participated directly or indirectly in rescuing over fifteen community banks. We also bought loans from troubled banks in partnership with the FDIC in our Mortgage Recovery Fund.

The countercyclical capability of the FHLBanks, which was backed up by the Treasury's credit facility, is often overlooked, even though advances exceeded TARP's $700 billion. As mentioned, advances peaked at $1.01 trillion on September 30, 2008. The advances were very concentrated, with the top ten borrowers representing 32 percent of their total advances. True to FHLB's status as lender of the next-to-last resort, the top four borrowers were all troubled: Citibank ($83.5 billion), Washington Mutual ($63.3 billion), Countrywide ($43.5 billion), and Wachovia (through two entities, $57.5 billion).

The May 2009 Office of Finance memo reviewing their marketing efforts went on:

> The FHLBanks announcement about the movement to a common framework for OTTI analysis for the MBS portfolios to bring consistency to the financial reports and the adoption of the new FSPs [financial stability plan] in the first quarter generally met with a positive response from investors. . . .
>
> Our current marketing presentation includes a discussion of strong government support for the FHLBanks as shown in the HERA legislation, inclusion in the GSE credit facility and the Fed's support for the Agencies through the debt purchase program. . . . In addition, many investors ask how we might be affected by the coming debate around the future of Fannie Mae and Freddie Mac.

In the same memo, the Office of Finance mentioned a weeklong visit to Europe to meet with the central banks of France, Germany, the Netherlands, and the European Central Bank (ECB) and other investors. They wrote: "The ECB remains comfortable with the FHLBanks' credit outlook but did express some concern over capital levels and the ability of the FHLBanks to strengthen capital positions."

Two banks did breach the 4 percent capital requirement: Seattle fell to 1 percent and Chicago to 1.5 percent. At the request of the Chicago bank and with some pushing from a plugged-in Washington friend, Rick Hohlt, we allowed the banks to buy federally guaranteed student loans, which were selling at high yields. That helped reduce the capital hole, and the Chicago bank eventually recovered. Seattle did not survive their PLS write-downs and the demise of their largest customer, Washington Mutual. In 2015 it was merged into the Des Moines bank.

The FHLB team's office was four blocks from OFHEO's office. To build teamwork and to better understand the challenges the FHLBanks faced, we had weekly senior staff meetings at the former FHFB office. We also had weekly meetings at the FHFA for the combined senior staff. The ex-FHFB team chafed initially as the former board structure had meant that most of the week-to-week issues were handled by the staff. But the issues faced by the US banking system and many of the FHLBanks were much too large not to have the leadership of the FHFA involved. We developed a good working relationship, but the head of the FHLB team, Steve Cross, said in his speech at my goodbye ceremony that we had too many staff meetings.

The FHLBanks, with the Treasury backstop, weathered the global financial crisis, but not without some scary times. If the FHLBanks had had more serious troubles, the financial crisis would have been much worse. Their loss-free advances allowed financial institutions to continue lending. They also provided life preservers before the FDIC could act. If they became troubled, their member financial institutions would have had to write down their equity investments. In June 2009 I had proposed a pre-funded mutual insurance fund for the FHLBanks to back up their joint and several guarantees. It could have been another countercyclical tool, but the insurance fund did not happen.

The cooperative GSE structure worked better than Fannie and Freddie's public ownership, but pressure to produce dividends for their members did lead them, in several cases, to imprudently increase their PLS investments. The days of "building and loans" are long gone. The Fed study quoted at the beginning of this chapter points out that only 2 percent of the system's advances were to banks with over $50 billion in assets in 2000, but by 2017 they were 50 percent of all investments. Insurance companies over that time frame went from about 1 percent to over 15 percent of advances. As a result of money-market-fund reform, almost 50 percent of their debt is held by government money market funds. In a future time of turmoil, these concentrations could become areas of concern.

As a postscript, as COVID-19 hit in 2020, the FHLBanks served their countercyclical role well. In March 2020 they grew their advances by over 30 percent to $807 billion from February. By May, advances were down to February levels as the Fed, the "lender of last resort," again flooded the market with liquidity.

CHAPTER 22

To TARP or Not to TARP

"The committee gathers this morning at an extraordinary and perilous moment in our nation's history. . . . This plan is stunning in its scope and lack of detail."

–Chairman Dodd (D-CT)

"This may be the most important hearing that this committee has conducted, at least in the twenty-two years I have been a member."

–Ranking member Shelby (R-AL)

"This massive bailout is not a solution. It is financial socialism and it is un-American."

–Senator Bunning (R-KY)

"We are in uncharted waters."

–Senator Hagel (R-NE)

THE ABOVE SENATORIAL quotes are from the respective senators' opening remarks at the Senate Banking Committee hearing on September 23, 2008. The US economy was definitely in uncharted waters—deeply underwater.

The postponed September 16 hearing to review the conservatorships had been hijacked as Paulson proposed the $700 billion Troubled Asset Refinance Program (TARP). He had submitted a three-page TARP proposal. TARP was the response to the chaos after the September 14 Lehman bankruptcy, which was quickly followed by Bank of America's proposed acquisition of Merrill Lynch, the Fed's AIG rescue, a money market fund "breaking the buck," and the requests of the two remaining big investment banks, Goldman Sachs and Morgan Stanley, to become bank-holding companies.

The panel in order was Paulson, Bernanke, Cox, and me. It was a marathon of five straight hours with most questions centered on TARP—how it can work, was it enough, and would the bank sellers of troubled assets give up some equity? Schumer waxed poetic, saying we were sailing between Scylla and Charybdis and that TARP needed THOR—taxpayer protection, housing, oversight, and regulation.

Bernanke in his testimony said the combination of Lehman and AIG "contributed to the development last week of extraordinary turbulent conditions in global markets." However, he did note that the conservatorships had led to "lower mortgage rates, which should help the mortgage market." He called the "downturn in housing the key factor" in causing the economic slowdown and market problems.

Paulson went farther in his testimony, alleging that "the root cause of this turmoil . . . is the housing correction which resulted in illiquid mortgage-related assets choking off the flow of credit." He blamed "bad lending practices by banks and financial institutions and by borrowers taking out mortgages they couldn't afford. These bad loans have created a chain reaction, and last week our credit markets froze." He said that the steps taken were "necessary but not sufficient." He proposed, and Bernanke supported the plan, to buy troubled and illiquid assets from financial institutions to stabilize the markets. Bernanke said, "Purchasing impaired assets will create liquidity and promote price discovery in the markets for these assets, while reducing investor uncertainty about the current value and prospects of financial institutions."

Cox agreed that the problems "have their roots in the subprime mortgage crisis—which itself was caused by a failure of lending standards." He was pushed hard in the hearing due to the failures or conversions of the five major investment banks.

My testimony focused on the reasons for the Fannie and Freddie conservatorships and the action taken since. I did not mention TARP, although Senator Carper (D-DE) asked me and the others whether TARP should have an inspector general and GAO oversight. He started with me, saying I should "earn my keep" as I had not been asked many questions. I was supportive, as were the other three.

I emphasized in my testimony the topic many senators were worrying whether TARP would address:

> If we are to address the problem of mortgage delinquencies, a systematic approach to loan modifications is essential. Well before last week's actions, we had already asked the enterprises to facilitate the loan modification program the FDIC has undertaken with IndyMac Federal. I expect the ongoing work on loan modifications . . . to be a high priority for the conservatorships, both as a matter of good business and as a matter of supporting the enterprises' mission.

It was lonely at my end of the table. Senator Tim Johnson (D-SD) asked me about the futures of the enterprises. My response was "how they will look, to a large extent, may depend as where the Congress wants to go." Optimistically, I said it "may take a year or even longer."

Bernanke and Paulson were grilled. A major theme of the questions was how TARP would prevent foreclosures and help homeowners. Dodd said, "Homeowners are watching the value of their homes plummet," citing 9,800 foreclosures a day. "It would do nothing to help a single family to save a home."

As the *Washington Post* wrote an hour into the hearing: "No one on the committee missed the opportunity to: A) Lash out at Wall Street fat cats and B) Lash out at Washington regulators who they said let the fat cats get away with their fat cattery."

Chairman Dodd said the regulators were much too late and timid, causing the "calamity" with a "combustible combination of private greed and public regulatory neglect."

Many senators wanted oversight, pay limits for bankers, and equity warrants from the banks that sold assets. Paulson pushed back, saying that the thing was to get "lenders to lend." Senator Bunning told Bernanke that Bernanke's predecessor had come up to the Hill that day and said that "the $700 billion in this plan is chicken feed and it won't take care of the problem."

Cricket sat through the hearing after driving down to DC with me on Sunday. On Friday, I had a long-postponed operation for hyperparathyroidism to remove a large benign tumor on my parathyroid gland. Although it did not affect me, a symptom of hyperparathyroidism is depression, so, just in case, given the markets, it was time to eliminate a potential source of depression. The doctor said to avoid a potential rupture, I could not fly to Washington. He made Cricket map out hospitals on the way down, which we did not need. She did stay the week to watch over me.

The day after the hearing, the *New York Times* had a front-page picture of the four of us (Bernanke, Paulson, Cox, and me) and many articles; but thankfully I was not mentioned in any of the articles. The coverage was not very complimentary of the senators or the TARP proposal. The *Times* editorial on September 24 suggested alternatives such as direct equity investments in banks or taking warrants when the Treasury bought assets.

Another editorial on September 24 complained about a recent Fed rule that "taxpayers are being asked to buy up banks' junkie assets with little expectation of return. At the same time, private equity firms are being invited to make what are likely to be highly profitable investments in the same banks."[130]

The Bush administration was making a full court press on TARP. On the twenty-third, President Bush spoke at the United Nations. *The New York Times*[131] reported that "he sought to reassure world leaders that his administration was taking 'bold steps' to staunch the economic crisis in United States, which he said 'would have a devastating impact on other economies around the world." The *Times* also reported FBI director Robert Mueller was investigating Fannie, Freddie, Lehman, and AIG for fraud.

Obama was saying that "this is not the time for my way or the highway." The *Times* also reported on one of his campaign TV ads: "A broken economy. Failing banks. Unstable markets. Families struggling. To protect us in retirement, Social Security has never been more important. But John McCain has voted three times in favor of privatizing Social Security[,] . . . cutting benefits in half. Risking Social Security on the stock markets."[132]

To their credit, the *Times* called the ad false. The article also mentioned Obama's eventual NEC chair, Jason Furman. In 2017, Furman was asked to be the Democratic nominee for trustee of Social Security and Medicare when I was asked to be the Republican trustee nominee. He said yes, but after a year of never filing his paperwork, he said no.

There were many irate letters to the editor in that edition of the *New York Times*. One that caught my eye was from my Yale friend, former senator Dayton. He wrote, "It's fundamentally wrong to borrow $700 billion or more from our children and grandchildren, without their consent, to bail out grown-up financiers and investors."

There was plenty of pushback from the Republicans as well. *The Wall Street Journal*[133] wrote, "Mr. Gingrich . . . predicted 'a populist reaction of the first order' against a Wall Street rescue and called on the president to dump his economic team and 'try again.'"

While the TARP drama was playing out, there was a lot to do at the FHFA. Conservatorship created a strange relationship with the CEOs. As head of the FHFA, I made the key final decisions. The two CEOs, Allison and Moffett, as experienced executives, sometimes chafed at that.

What we were trying to conserve became an issue. Was it each company's financials, or the housing and mortgage markets, or, even more broadly, saving the US economy after the Lehman failure? To help lessen the confusion, we decided to have separate teams, with one acting as the regulator and the other as conservator.

The House Financial Services Committee had scheduled a hearing on the conservatorships with Paulson, Bernanke, and me on September 25. It morphed into a first panel with me only and a second panel with the two CEOs.

As Representative Michele Bachmann (R-MN) said, "A week ago, it would have been inconceivable that today's hearing, focused as it is on the government bailout of Fannie Mae and Freddie Mac, could take a back seat to anything." Despite the TARP controversy, there was a good turnout of members. The hearing gave them an opportunity to vent.

In my opening I said: "In the absence of access to new capital, the only alternative left to the firms was to cease new business and shed assets in a weak market. That would have been disastrous for the mortgage markets."

Allison, Moffett, and I were asked questions about foreclosure prevention, loan modifications, affordable housing, and the enterprises' charitable deductions. I was asked whether the enterprises were going to fund HERA's Housing Trust Fund. I said it had not been decided yet.

Representative Keith Ellison (D-MN) asked whether HUD's affordable housing goals were to blame for the downfall of Fannie and Freddie. I answered, "As they [the goals] escalated, it became harder and harder for the two companies to meet those goals. Sometimes they had to stretch, and sometimes that stretch meant that they potentially lowered their underwriting standards. Certainly, they got credit for many of the subprime mortgages in those AAA securities." I said that "Freddie's PLS were $20 billion underwater."

There were many questions on the future of Fannie and Freddie. Representative Jeb Hensarling (R-TX) said he was going to introduce legislation later that day to slowly unwind them.

There was a half hour break for votes during my testimony. Congressman Watt (D-NC) came up to me and asked me why I had not responded to his letters. I said I did not think we had received any letters from him. Near the end of my Q&A session, he said he had confused me with HUD secretary Preston and then said, "I want to publicly apologize to Mr. Lockhart." Watt became head of the FHFA in 2014.

During the CEOs' question period, Watt raised a question that he said he had wanted to ask me: "If it's supporting housing for richer people rather than affordable housing, why couldn't that be done through the regular private market without any government subsidy?" The CEOs handled that and other questions well. Watt, disappointingly to me, never tried to answer his question in his five years as director. He did not push for GSE reform, saying it was Congress's responsibility. Early in his FHFA tenure, I did meet with him and offered to help. He never tried to meet again.

Despite the Herculean efforts of the administration, Hank and his team, and the House leadership, on Monday, September 29, the House voted down TARP 228–205. As Paulson wrote in *On the Brink*, "The Dow had posted its largest one-day point decline ever, almost 778 points, or 7 percent, while the S&P 500 suffered an 8.8 percent drop, for its worst day since October 1987 crash."

I was watching the TARP passage closely as we hoped it would help stabilize the prices of the PLS that Fannie, Freddie, and the Federal Home Loan Banks owned. The revised and much expanded legislation created administration and legislative oversight boards. A draft had the Fed chair, SEC chair, HUD secretary, and FDIC chair as members of the administration's Financial Services Oversight Board. I never knew why, but somewhere during the redrafting, the FHFA director was substituted for the FDIC chair.

The Senate passed the revised TARP legislation, the Emergency Economic Stabilization Act (EESA), on Wednesday, October 1. The House bowed to the inevitable on Friday, October 3, by a 263–171 vote. Importantly, the FDIC's insurance for deposit was increased from $100,000 to $250,000. During the Great Recession, over 500 banks were taken over by the FDIC, with all depositors being protected. Another 2,000 were merged, reducing the number of US banks by a third. In almost all cases, it was not the Fannie and Freddie preferred stocks but bad residential and commercial real estate loans that caused the failures and mergers.

Obama's 2013 *President's Budget Submission: Emergency Economic Stabilization Act Programs* stated, "TARP succeeded in helping to stop widespread financial panic and helped prevent what could have been a devastating collapse of our financial system."

On Friday, October 3, we announced the enterprises were

rolling back their planned guarantee fee increases. On the following Monday, the sixth, the *Washington Post* quoted me saying, "Do they have to make up for all those losses from previous years by really inflating the margins on new business?" Lockhart said. "The answer to me is no." The article also said: "Lockhart assigned about 15 liaisons to be paired with each of the senior executives at the companies. . . . The FHFA liaisons attend almost every key meeting, relaying information back to Lockhart, whom Allison and Moffett talk to every day or so."[134]

On October 7 the Financial Services Oversight Board (FSOB or TARP board) had its first meeting at the Treasury. Bernanke was nominated by Cox to be the chair, and I seconded him. As the meeting was about to start, General Petraeus was walking out of Paulson's office. The general said Hank was needed for a "surge" in the economy, referring to Petraeus's successful surge in Iraq.

In a major change, in the FSOB meeting it was agreed that equity injections into banks would be key. One of the proposed requirements for a bank to be eligible was no pending investigations. I was against that, saying that no financial institution could participate as so many had ongoing investigations. Paulson agreed. The strategy discussed was 50 percent investments in troubled banks and 50 percent troubled asset purchases.

It was becoming apparent that the troubled asset purchase program was going to be very complicated. To hire managers and then implement the purchase program would take some time as pricing assets was so difficult in a falling market. Things continued to go downhill for many US banks and European banks.

It was Columbus Day weekend. Cricket and I were invited to the wedding anniversary party in Paris for the American ambassador to France. The ambassador, Craig Stapleton, and his wife, Debbie, are friends and neighbors in Greenwich. Debbie is G. H. W. Bush's cousin. We had visited them in Prague in Stapleton's previous assignment as the ambassador to the Czech

Republic. They knew how to pick assignments with truly elegant, palatial residences. The party was spectacular, including an evening cruise on the River Seine.

I did mix in some business; Ambassador Stapleton had scheduled a meeting for me with members of the French Banking Federation on Friday morning. My task was to reassure them about the creditworthiness of Fannie and Freddie. There were questions concerning why mortgage lending was so loose in the US. One participant said that in France, to get a mortgage a person had to get a physical examination. Before the party I had a call with BlackRock, which gave us an update on the loss projections for Fannie and Freddie. It was not pretty.

Sunday, October 12, we flew to London. Optimistically, we had originally planned to spend a few days there, choosing a hotel near our old mews house in Knightsbridge. I disappointed Cricket again: we flew out Monday evening after I gave a Monday luncheon speech to members of the Centre for the Study of Financial Innovation. I was peppered with questions about Fannie and Freddie, TARP, and the US financial situation. However, they had other things on their minds as well. The UK government had just injected £37 billion into the Royal Bank of Scotland (RBS), HBOS, and Lloyds TSB. The £20 billion invested into RBS effectively nationalized them as the government received 63 percent of the stock. The CEO was fired.

Meanwhile, as we were getting on a plane back to Dulles Airport, Paulson, Bernanke, and the other bank regulators were meeting with the nine major US banks to tell them that they were going to take $125 billion in TARP funds as investments in new preferred stock. The Treasury received a 5 percent dividend, which would rise to 9 percent after five years if not redeemed, as well as warrants in the banks' common stock. Executive compensation was limited.

On October 14, Paulson announced that a total of $250 billion would be allocated to banks in similar deals to the big nine. To be eligible, banks had to be recommended by the regulator. The idea was that by providing capital, TARP would get much more bang for the buck as it could be leveraged over ten to one. On the other hand, selling trouble assets would clean up a bank's balance sheet but run the real risk of a capital hit if the troubled asset were sold at a price less than the carrying value.

Banks were not the only entities knocking on the TARP door. General Electric, AIG again, and the three auto companies were all having problems. On September 30 I had met with Tom Marano, CEO of GMAC's ResCap Mortgage company. It was the first of several meetings. ResCap was a major mortgage originator and servicer having serious liquidity issues, partially reflecting General Motors' problems. When a homeowner does not make a mortgage payment, the servicer must make the payment to the PLS trustee or to Fannie and Freddie for their MBS for a period of months.

The key asset for a servicer is their mortgage servicing rights (MSR), as the servicer generally gets an annual fee of twenty-five basis points, which is much more than the normal servicing costs. If the mortgage goes into default, the cost of servicing goes up and the value of the MSR goes down. As GMAC was losing money and at risk of bankruptcy, Fannie and Freddie had the right to move the servicing to another servicer. That would have forced a ResCap bankruptcy.

I was also starting to hear from the mortgage insurers (MI); there was speculation that they might need TARP assistance. As Fannie and Freddie could only make loans up to 80 percent loan-to-value (LTV), mortgage insurers provide insurance for any loans with higher than the 80 percent LTV. Given that those loans tended to be the riskier loans, the insurance protected the enterprises only if the MI company was solvent. One had already ceased business.

On October 15, Bernanke gave a speech at the Economic Club of New York, which is a favorite venue for major economic speeches. In another attempt to reassure the markets, he said, "The problems now evident in the markets and in the economy are large and complex, but, in my judgment, our government now has the tools it needs to confront and solve them." Summarizing what had happened, he said:

> This financial crisis . . . was sparked by the end of the US housing boom, which revealed the weaknesses and excesses that had occurred in subprime mortgage lending. However, as subsequent events have demonstrated, the problem was much broader than subprime lending. Large inflows of capital into the United States and other countries stimulated a reaching for yield, an underpricing of risk, excessive leverage, and the development of complex and opaque financial instruments that seemed to work well during the credit boom but have been shown to be fragile under stress. The unwinding of these developments, including . . . a tightening of credit[,] . . . has hamstrung economic growth.

He added that the FHFA and Treasury's "actions appear to have stabilized the GSEs, although, like virtually all other firms, they are experiencing effects of the current crisis."

On October 20, I was in San Francisco for the Mortgage Bankers Association's ninety-fifth annual convention. Allison, Moffett, and I spoke at the opening general session panel, but first we had to wind our way through an angry crowd protesting foreclosures. That year there were only 2,500 attendees, less than half of those who attended in 2006. The MBA was predicting $1.8 trillion in mortgage originations in 2008 against $2.6 trillion in 2007 and $3.3 trillion each in the boom years of 2005 and 2006.

Our discussion focused on foreclosure prevention, the financial strategy of Fannie and Freddie, and the government backing. As we talked, a protester and cofounder of the group Code Pink walked up. She said to the CEOs, "Since the public bailed out your companies, the public should have a right to ask a question. We need a moratorium on foreclosures. Will you please call for that, sirs?"[135] She was escorted off the stage. Both CEOs calmly answered that they were working on developing better mortgage modification programs.

A *Marketwatch* article quoted me: "Their aim isn't to save everybody, Lockhart said. 'There are some people who speculated and bought five houses and there's no reason those shouldn't be foreclosed on,' he said. 'But we need a way to keep people who got a bad mortgage or are having tough times, we need to be able to keep them in their houses.'"[136] The article went on, "Lockhart said the government's asset purchase program would make their job easier. 'We need to get some of those troubled assets off balance sheets of financial institutions. We need to rework those loans. It's been very hard to do that in these private-label securities because of all those tranches. I'm hoping in this process we can be much more aggressive.'"

On the future strategy, there was some discussion on pricing and maximizing returns. Allison said that was no longer the goal. Moffett's answer was more enigmatic. As the *San Francisco Chronicle*[137] quoted me, "We're trying to help restore the enterprises to financial health. It's even more important to get them to do their mission. We need them to go out and support the mortgage markets, providing stability, liquidity."

Another negative to the crowd was that mortgage rates had backed up to 6.61 percent. In the *Wall Street Journal*,[138] I was quoted as saying there was an "effective" guarantee and "the US government will be behind them short, medium and long term." I did not have a clue at the time how long was long term.

What type of government guarantee the Treasury was providing became a controversial topic at the Senate Banking

Committee hearing on Thursday, October 23. The large panel included the FDIC's Bair, interim Treasury assistant secretary for TARP Neel Kashkari, the FHA's Brian Montgomery, Fed governor Elizabeth Duke, and me. Given all the failures, rescues, and government guarantee programs, the mortgage markets were confused how the Treasury's preferred stock worked. I did not help dispel the confusion.

My written testimony said, "The conservatorships and the access to credit from the US Treasury provide an *explicit guarantee* to existing and future debt holders of Fannie Mae and Freddie Mac" (emphasis added). The markets reacted positively. I am not sure how "explicit" got into the testimony. Perhaps a typo for "implicit"? The statement was wrong. My written testimony also had another sentence, which I repeated in my oral testimony, saying, "Effectively, it [the Treasury preferred] is a government guarantee of their existing and future debt and MBS."

The markets liked "explicit," and spreads fell. My "effective" correction caused the spread on the enterprises' five-year bonds to Treasury preferred stock to rise to near record levels.

The "explicit" versus "effective" was not the only controversy in the hearing. Mortgage modification became a very hot topic. In *On the Brink*, Paulson wrote, "We at Treasury would later call this the 'ambush hearing.'" Bair testified: "Loan guarantees could be used as an incentive for servicers to modify loans. Specifically, the government could establish standards for loan modifications and provide guarantees for loans meeting those standards. . . . The FDIC is working closely and creatively with Treasury to realize the potential benefits of this authority."

In her view, the loan guarantee would be provided by TARP. The Treasury was working on a competing proposal for loan modifications. In the last week of October, there was a whole series of housing-policy principals' papers and meetings, and Treasury papers. Several of the presentations included a White

House Council of Economic Advisors chart. Of the $11.4 trillion in 59 million mortgages, it predicted $1.4 trillion (6.4 million loans) would be delinquent, 2.7 million ($575 billion) of which would be "unpreventable foreclosures."

There was another housing-policy paper for the principals meeting on Halloween. As of August 31, 2008, Fannie had 1.57 percent delinquencies over ninety days and Freddie 1.11 percent. The core of the paper dealt with the dueling Treasury and FDIC mortgage modification plans, which were both designed to get borrowers down to a 31 percent debt-to-income level and help 2.8 million homeowners. The FDIC proposal's estimated cost was $72 billion, and the Treasury's was less than half at $34 billion.

In *Bull By the Horns* Bair wrote, "This was Washington at its most myopic, concluding against all the evidence to the contrary that the burgeoning number of foreclosed, empty houses had nothing to do with declining home values. We did get some constructive input and support from James Lockhart, the head of Fannie and Freddie's regulator, the Federal Housing Finance Agency. But the rest had already decided that they were going to block us."[139]

Bair was opposed to the Treasury's proposal as she said it did not help prevent re-defaults. In the end, Paulson decided not to do either as it would have meant his having to go back to Congress to ask for the second half of the $350 billion for TARP.

The foreclosure prevention ball was now in the FHFA's court. We had been working with the Treasury, HUD, and Faith Schwartz of Hope Now on a streamlined mortgage modification program, which we announced on November 11 in a press conference with Kashkari, Montgomery, Schwartz, and Mike Heid of Wells Fargo. In my opening remarks I said, "As a Navy veteran, I do not like interfering with your Veterans Day, but as you all know, there is a battle going on in the housing market. Foreclosures hurt families, their neighbors, whole communities and the overall housing market. We need to stop this downward spiral." The program was designed to get ninety-day-plus delinquent borrowers' debt-to-income level down to 38 percent through a mix of reducing the interest rate, extending the life of the loan, and/or principal repayment deferrals.

The plan was designed not only for Fannie and Freddie but also to inspire other mortgage holders so that it would become the "new standard." I noted that Fannie and Freddie held 58 percent of the mortgages in the US but only 20 percent of the serious delinquencies, while PLS held 20 percent of the mortgages but 60 percent of the serious delinquencies.

The speakers acknowledged the help and inspiration of the FDIC in developing this approach. Bair's statement was "This is a step in the right direction but falls short of what is needed to achieve wide-scale modifications of distressed mortgages, particularly those held in private securitization trusts."[140]

She was right about the PLS trusts. Later in the month I sent a letter to servicers, investors, and trustees of PLS, urging them to adopt our streamlined approach, to no avail. On December 23, I had a New York meeting with the four largest trustees of private-label securities and the five most significant nonbank servicers of the subprime and Alt-A loans backing those securities. My message was that if they did not allow mortgage modifications, overall losses in the PLS would be higher. The trustees were afraid to act because they thought they would be sued if a modification led to disproportionate losses to lower tranches.

At a Sunday, November 9, evening TARP oversight meeting, we approved an investment in AIG, which was announced Monday. At the TARP meeting, we discussed not investing in troubled mortgage assets. It surprised the markets when Paulson announced that change in a major speech on November 12.

When discussing the GSEs, he spoke of an *effective* guarantee. He said mitigating mortgage foreclosures was a priority even more now that TARP was not going to purchase troubled mortgages. He praised Bair's efforts. Paulson said that with the streamlined proposal, which we announced the day before in preparation for his speech, "GSEs and large portfolio investors are setting a new industry standard of foreclosure mitigation." He acknowledged more had to be done but worried it would "require substantial government subsidies" and would not be recovered under the TARP program. The next stage in mortgage modifications was passed to Obama.

Fannie Mae reported on November 10 a $29 billion loss for the third quarter, including a $21.4 billion valuation allowance on their deferred tax asset and $9.2 billion in credit losses. The loss wiped out almost all their capital, but just barely; they did not need to draw on the Treasury's preferred. On the fourteenth, Freddie followed up, reporting a $25.3 billion loss comprising $14.3 billion in deferred tax assets, $9.1 billion in OTTI on their PLS, and $9.1 billion of credit losses. We asked the Treasury for a $14 billion preferred injection. Concerns were already being expressed by analysts that the Treasury commitment of $100 billion each was not enough.

The week before Thanksgiving was busy. We had just announced the much-lobbied-for foreclosure moratorium for the holidays, starting November 26 through January 9. It also gave us time to start the implementation of the streamlined mortgage modification program on December 15. The large GSE losses and confusion about Treasury support were keeping mortgage rates and GSE rates high. The Fed's Thanksgiving present to the mortgage market, announced on Tuesday November 25, was a commitment to buy $500 billion of Fannie and Freddie MBS and $100 billion of their debt. Bernanke later wrote that this was the start of "'QE' short for quantitative easing" and the Fed was "a buyer of last resort" for MBS.[141] In an understatement, I called it "a very positive step" as mortgage rates fell forty basis points.

CHAPTER 23

New Captain—Repairs Ongoing, Still Underwater

"What scared me is not doing anything, which would have caused there to be a huge financial meltdown and the conceivable scenario that we'd have been in a depression greater than the Great Depression. . . . I'm a little upset that we didn't get the reforms to Fannie and Freddie. . . . [I]t would've helped a lot. . . . [P]eople will say that this administration tried hard to get a regulator. . . . [I]t didn't happen for pure political reasons."

—President George W. Bush, interview with Charlie Gibson, ABC News, December 1, 2008

"We start 2009 in the midst of a crisis unlike any we have seen in our lifetime, a crisis that is only deepened over the last few weeks. . . . We must also work with the same sense of urgency to stabilize and repair the financial system. . . . It means launching a sweeping effort to address the foreclosure crisis so that we can keep responsible families in their homes."

—President-Elect Barack Obama, speech on the economy at George Mason University, January 8, 2009.

HOUSING PRICES CONTINUED to fall even faster than the rest of the economy. Everyone wanted more mortgage modifications to prevent foreclosures. A big challenge many mortgages shared was that they were underwater. A mortgage is underwater when the mortgage's outstanding principal is higher than the value of the house. Some have suggested the "underwater" phrase came from "drowning in debt." Too many Americans were underwater, not only on their mortgages but also on credit cards, consumer loans, and student loans.

CoreLogic, a data firm, reported that as of September 30, 2008, underwater mortgages were 18 percent of total mortgages but were very concentrated. Nevada was 47.8 percent underwater, Michigan 38.6 percent, Arizona 29.2 percent, Florida 29.2 percent, and California 27.4 percent. At the peak in December 2010, underwater mortgages comprised 25.1 percent of the total. Then, 68.3 percent of Nevada's mortgages were underwater, 50.5 percent in Florida, and 53.1 percent in Arizona. Housing prices had a slow recovery; but six years later the underwater number was 6.2 percent.

As the starting quotes of this chapter say, it took too long to get reform, and it took unprecedented steps to ameliorate the crisis. As the Bush administration was winding down, many articles looked back at the ongoing crisis. A *Washington Post* article of December 8, 2008, subtitled "Fannie, Freddie Tilt from Profit Goals Toward Public Mission to Buoy Market" quoted me as saying, "If housing prices continue to fall, losses will mount at Fannie and Freddie. There's no doubt that the sooner we get stability to the mortgage market, the better off they will be."

A slanted front-page article in the Sunday, December 21, *New York Times* was entitled "White House Philosophy Stoked Mortgage Bonfire." It started with an October 15, 2002, quote from President Bush: "We can put light where there is darkness. . . . And part of it is working together as a nation to encourage folks to own their own home." The very long article admitted that "Mr. Bush did foresee the danger posed by Fannie Mae and Freddie Mac. . . . The regulator Mr. Bush chose to oversee them— an old prep school buddy—pronounced the company sound as they headed to insolvency."

The article said that on my watch "both Freddie and Fannie had plunged into the riskiest part of the market, gobbling up more than $400 billion in subprime and older alternate mortgages." It did not mention that we had capped their portfolios, nor that many of these mortgages were bought to meet affordable housing goals. Nor did it mention that I had warned numerous times of the enterprises' potential problems and the need for legislative reform.

The FCIC preliminary staff report,[142] *Securitization and the Mortgage Crisis*, had a chart of Fannie's subprime (less than 660 FICO) and Alt-A holdings from 2004 to 2008. Subprime mortgages represented 16 percent of their total portfolio in 2004, 15 percent in 2005 through 2007, and then fell to 14 percent in 2008. Alt-A rose from 8 percent in 2004 to 9 percent in 2005, 11 percent in 2006, and 12 percent in 2007, and then fell to 11 percent in 2008. Those percentages represented some overlap and were much lower than the market growth from 2004 to 2008.

The *Times* article reported that according to two sources, Geithner in March 2008 "had been advocating that the administration seize them or take other steps to reassure the market that the government would back their debt." Of course, that would have been impossible without congressional legislation. As late as August, many Democratic leaders were saying they were not in trouble. Republicans would have been adamantly opposed. Geithner's advice was ignored.

The NEC's Thomas was quoted liberally in the *Times* article, including a July 2008 email I had never seen that said I was "pimping for the stock prices for the undercapitalized firms" I was regulating. The article went on, "Mr. Lockhart defended himself, insisting in an interview that he was aware of the companies' vulnerabilities, but did not want to rattle markets. A regulator, he said, 'does not air dirty laundry in public.'"

Andrew Davidson, CEO of a mortgage data and software firm bearing his name, wrote an email to the *Times* that Sunday:

> Generally, a good article today. However, I believe you were overly critical of Lockhart. He imposed numerous controls on the operations of Fannie and Freddie, froze their portfolio growth, and required additional capital. Over the past year he has reduced limits on them, but that was designed to help the housing market. In addition, he is a very capable manager who has greatly strengthened OFHEO, now FHFA. As a result, Fannie and Freddie continue to operate (under conservatorship). Along with Montgomery's FHA loans, the GSEs are just about the only portion of the housing finance system that is still functioning.

When the email was forwarded to me by a staff member, my response was, "Please thank Andrew, although I have to disagree with his first sentence." The FHFA's response the next day was as follows:

> Any review of the Office of Federal Housing Enterprise Oversight's actions and statements over the past two and a half years would reveal countless public warnings and speeches, testimony, news releases and media interviews including some with the *New York Times*. The warnings detail the inadequacies of Fannie Mae and Freddie Mac's capital relative to their risk and identified the systemic risk they pose to the financial system. Director Lockhart

also made repeated calls for Congress to provide the regulator with the authorities needed to ensure safety and soundness. In retrospect, by the time Congress enacted those reforms in July it was already too late.

We concluded, "There is much research to be done, and history to be written, to understand all the causes and consequences of the current housing and financial crisis. It is unfortunate that Sunday's *New York Times* article did not provide a broader, or more accurate, portrayal of what is a matter of public record."

Sunday's White House response was more hard-hitting, accusing the *Times* of "gross negligence" and rebutted the key assertions in the article. It said President Bush called for reform "at least 17 times in 2008."

Obama announced Geithner as Treasury secretary and Summers as NEC head in November. We looked forward to working with them and were developing ideas for the next $350 billion TARP tranche. Mortgage rates were still disturbingly high even as Fannie and Freddie's MBS were selling at rates similar to the fully US-government-guaranteed Ginnie Mae MBS. The Paulson Treasury had floated the idea of subsidized mortgages to get the rates down to 4.5 percent. Housing prices continued to fall. With our new streamlined modification plan, modifications were picking up but still were much too low.

After our first FHFA Oversight Board meeting on October 30, 2008, Cox sent an email that evening saying our presentation was "well-presented" but asked for more information about the reasons for the conservatorship, as he had been less involved. We responded December 11.

Just before Cox "retired," I received another letter from him on January 16, 2009. He asked for much more information and suggested the oversight board should become more active. As the SEC had approved both Fannie and Freddie's financial statements, some of my staff suspected it was defensive. Throughout the letter he kept making a point that "the statutory and publicly stated goal for the conservatorship is to restore these institutions to financial health. Viewing the conservatorships as merely a 'time out' . . . would undercut the Conservator's primary duty." My view continued to be that if we did not help the housing market in the time-out, there was no way the enterprises would be restored to "financial health."

Much later in 2021, the Supreme Court supported my view that supporting the housing market was important. In *Collins vs. Yellen*, they opined that unlike in a typical conservatorship, HERA authorized the FHFA to act "in the best interests of the regulated entity or the *Agency*." Going on, the court stated that "the FHFA chose a path of rehabilitation that was designed to serve public interests by ensuring Fannie Mae's and Freddie Mac's continued support of the secondary mortgage market."

On January 7, Paulson gave his long-anticipated speech[143] on the future of Fannie and Freddie, saying, "For some time, market participants had questioned whether the GSEs were adequately capitalized for the risk that they were taking, and therefore able to withstand losses without triggering a systemic event. Policymakers acknowledged that the GSE regulator did not have the authorities to address these risks. . . . The consequences of either GSE failing would be catastrophic." He cited the need to replace the flawed GSE structure, giving four alternatives:

✦   Expand FHA/Ginnie Mae, or the GSEs become government entities

✦   Partial guarantee

✦   Privatization

✦   Housing utility

He said the latter "could be the best way to resolve the inherent conflict between public purpose and private gain." Over the years I have given scores of speeches on the future of Fannie and Freddie. I have always rejected that first alternative of "nationalization."

On January 16, 2009, just four days before he left office, President Bush invited me for a chat. As I was walking into the Oval Office, the National Security team was leaving. Chief of Staff Josh Bolten said, "Hi, Juice." Bush again jokingly said only he could call me Juice.

It was a far-ranging conversation about what had happened, but we started with an update on the family, no grandchildren yet. He was chomping on a cigar in a very relaxed mood. He started on Social Security reform. I said it was too bad that Commissioner Jo Anne Barnhart was not in favor of reform and personal accounts. I said I thought she had promised before her Senate confirmation not to have the SSA support reform. It was my understanding that her predecessor had also pledged that.

The president asked me if "Pozen" alone would have worked. Pozen's "progressive price indexing" plan was designed to over time slow down the growth of benefits for average earners and especially higher-income earners, but not that of the lower-income earners. Pozen's plan was proposed as personal accounts were losing traction. I said that a 401(k) structure might have worked. He said it was still his administration's fallback.

He then said that the Social Security reform effort was a good start and "not a third rail." He said, "Obama is going to have to come at it." Bush predicted that Obama would probably set up a commission that would just want to raise taxes and do nothing about benefits. "That won't fix it." My response was that I wouldn't want to be on that commission.

The conversation then turned to Fannie and Freddie. His first question, which he already knew the answer to, was whether if he had put me in the FHFA right away, and if we had gotten legislation, would that have helped? My response was "Yes, we could have reduced their portfolios and more importantly increased their capital requirements. By law they could leverage at 100 to 1, although because of their accounting problems, we reduced it 70 to 1. That was still too low."

Bush then said only about 10 percent of the mortgages were problems, and I agreed. I said that Fannie and Freddie's problem mortgages were even lower than that, but with such high leverage, they blew through their capital. He remarked that a handful of states were the biggest problems.

He said, "I think we are hitting bottom and Obama may turn out to be very lucky." I agreed, saying we were bouncing along the bottom, but there could be spikes down. I added that housing was becoming affordable again with mortgage rates below 5 percent and lower house prices. We next discussed the private-label mortgage-backed securities. He asked why even AAA tranches were hit. I said that the rating agencies failed to properly rate them and had conflicts given their consulting fees. POTUS said, "I am mad at Wall Street. They messed up and were too greedy."

Earlier in the conversation, he said Franklin Raines should have been punished more. I was somewhat defensive on that as we had settled with Raines because our fight was costing so much time and effort.

He asked me, "Hank is a tough guy. How do you get along with him?" My response was "Very well. He is very intense. Hank has a lot of energy that was needed."

President Bush had asked his assistant how the Dow Jones was doing as I entered. He caught me by surprise by asking what he should invest in now. I said I was not sure, but then added some premature advice that at some point MBS, troubled real estate, and vulture funds would be good investments.

Lastly, he asked me what was next for me and whether I

was serving at the pleasure of the president. I said I was at the FHFA until replaced and had not had time to look for a job. I said maybe Wall Street. He agreed I would be good there, but with his earlier comment about the Street, I'm not sure that was a compliment. I ended by saying we still had a lot of work to do at the FHFA and on the TARP board.

I spent Inauguration Day at home, unlike the previous two inaugurations. That week, the Obama administration was greeted with a statement from Freddie that it might need a draw from the Treasury for up to $35 billion. A few days later, Fannie said that they would need $16 billion. A January 29, 2009, editorial in the *Wall Street Journal*, "Fan and Fred's Lunch Tab," seemed less enamored with their "honest socialism" as it reported that the CBO was estimating "a $238 billion charge for rescuing Fan and Fred." It ended, "We are now slowly, and painfully, learning the price of Mr. Frank's famous desire to 'roll the dice' with Fan and Fred. Keep that in mind the next time you hear a politician propose a taxpayer guarantee. The only sure thing is that the taxpayer will pay."

I had very frequent discussions with the new CEOs. Tensions were rising as they and their troops pushed to reduce short-term losses. Allison understood the need for modifications and the resulting short-term losses but still had some trouble answering to a boss with absolute power. He suggested we try to develop a refinance program for homeowners with less than 20 percent equity.

Freddie's CEO, Moffett, was having more trouble understanding that Freddie was effectively part of the government's effort to resolve the housing crisis and what was later called the Global Financial Crisis. He was developing forecasts that the $100 billion was not enough. He was not the only one. Peter Wallison "put the chances of the GSEs exhausting their $100 billion backstops at 100%."[144]

Foreign investors were also worried. Governor Hu Xialian of

China's State Administration of Foreign Exchange (SAFE) visited us on February 4. We tried to reassure her about the strength of the effective US government guarantee.

Geithner had his first meeting of the President's Working Group on Thursday, February 5. The next day, the FHFA, Moffett, and his team met at the Treasury on accounting issues. Moffett made it clear that the $100 billion preferred was not enough support from the Treasury. He said that auditors were threatening to say Freddie had a "going concern" issue, implying that the firm would go out of business.

At 5:45 PM that Friday, there was a housing meeting in the White House's Roosevelt Room. Attendees included Bernanke, Geithner, Summers, Bair, Dugan, me, and others. President Obama made a brief appearance but was not as engaged as President Bush had been in the Roosevelt meetings. I had prepared a list of the baker's dozen action items to support the housing market, updating my November list. They ranged from TARP support for PLS, mortgage insurers, and home equity loans to even Social Security buying Ginnie Mae's (GNMA) securities.

Many of these issues were not addressed; the group wanted to focus on mortgage modifications. In the meeting, there was a decision to build upon the FHFA's streamlined mortgage modification program, which became the Home Affordable Modification Program (HAMP).

Summers asked the group what we could do for homeowners with underwater mortgages. I said I didn't know what we could do about the non-Fannie and Freddie mortgages, but for Fannie and Freddie mortgages, we could help underwater homeowners to lower their monthly mortgage payments by refinancing them even if they were underwater. Despite the requirement that the enterprises could only make loans up to the 80 percent loan-to-value (LTV), we believed that we could legally get around that requirement. Summers liked that idea, as did the others. That program became the very effective Home Affordable Refinance Program (HARP).

That weekend I flew to Las Vegas to keynote the American Securitization Forum (ASF). I decided to go even though there were concerns about going to Las Vegas given the economic crisis. Gambling with taxpayer money? The ASF's members were securitizers, originators, servicers, trustees, rating agencies, and investors. Later, at WL Ross, I joined the ASF's board. My speech focused on PLS as ASF members had originated, securitized, serviced, and bought them. I said that PLS held 16 percent of all mortgages but 62 percent of serious delinquencies. "These are extraordinary times and need extraordinary actions." I pushed them hard to do more modifications, saying, "There will be no excuses going forward not to aggressively pursue standardized modifications to prevent foreclosures and lessen their negative impact on communities and the nation's economy."

I mentioned that I hoped TARP II would help mortgage insurers, which were vital for the enterprises' countercyclical role of buying mortgages at above 80 percent loan-to-value. With all the foreclosure losses, the mortgage insurers' (MI) capital levels were shrinking dramatically, and they were pulling back from the market. I said, "The private and mortgage insurers market share versus FHA/VA fell from nearly 80% in the first quarter 2007 to about 30% in the third quarter of 2008."[145]

I had been frustrated with trying to get MI support in the first tranche of TARP as Paulson had turned it down. Geithner's team was also against helping the MIs, but I kept pushing.

We were working with the Treasury on HAMP and HARP but also on how much the PSPA should be increased. Freddie had provided forecasts through 2011 and Fannie through 2010 under three scenarios: base, stress, and severe stress. The forecasted cumulative draws in millions of dollars on the Treasury senior preferred stocks were as follows:

Base Case			
	2009	2010	2011
Fannie Mae	26	31	
Freddie Mac	64	76	82
TOTAL	**90**	**107**	

Stress			
	2009	2010	2011
Fannie Mae	38	60	
Freddie Mac	87	101	108
TOTAL	**125**	**161**	

Severe Stress			
	2009	2010	2011
Fannie Mae	90	125	
Freddie Mac	128	147	157
TOTAL	**218**	**272**	

Despite being a third smaller than Fannie, Freddie's forecasts were much more pessimistic because they were pushing for doubling the PSPA commitment. As it turned out, 2011 was the last significant year of the draws. At that point, Freddie's cumulative draws were $71.3 billion including dividends, which was less than their $82 billion base case and much less than the original $100 billion commitment they pushed so hard to double.

On the other hand, Fannie's prediction was too optimistic, perhaps still reflecting their original September 2008 view that Freddie was the problem. Through 2010 the draws totaled $90.2 billion—triple their base case and 50 percent more than the stress case. Fannie had $116.1 billion in draws through 2011, exceeding the original $100 billion.

Obama was scheduled to unveil his mortgage crisis plan on February 18, the day after he signed the $787 billion American Recovery and Reinvestment Act. Obama chose Mesa, Arizona, to do his speech as the state had one of the largest underwater mortgage percentages and very high delinquencies. Although Fannie and Freddie were the key players in the mortgage market, HAMP, and HARP, I was not invited to attend. I was still a Bushie. HUD secretary Shaun Donovan, Geithner, and, surprisingly (as she was against HAMP), Bair attended.

Bair wrote in her book, "We were horrified by the administrative complexity of the program [HAMP]. . . . We were equally horrified to learn that they were going to put Fannie Mae and Freddie Mac in charge of the program. That was akin to putting the fox in charge of the chicken coop. Fannie and Freddie were the biggest holders of the Triple-A subprime mortgage-backed securities. Every interest rate that was reduced for a distressed borrower could potentially eat into their returns. They were hopelessly conflicted."[146] I disagreed; the enterprises would be helped if the number of foreclosures were reduced. The FHFA oversaw the "fox." In the end, the enterprises had the expertise and did a good job.

Obama's first proposal was to make it possible for four or five million currently ineligible homeowners to refinance their Fannie and Freddie mortgages (HARP). Obama said that this program would help "families who are underwater—are close to being underwater." The second proposal was a mortgage modification for "sub-prime loans at risk of default and foreclosure." (Actually, HAMP applied to a broader range of mortgages.) The government, through TARP, would make up the gap to get mortgage payments to no more than 31 percent of the borrower's income. The key component of the third proposal was to keep mortgage rates low by increasing the PSPA by $200 billion to ensure Fannie and Freddie would continue to support the mortgage market. The fourth was a "wide range of reforms," including bankruptcy reform so that mortgages could be reduced in bankruptcies.

In my statement on February 18, I said, "Resetting these agreements from $100 billion to $200 billion each should remove any possible concerns that debt and mortgage-backed securities investors have about the strong commitment of the US government to support Fannie Mae and Freddie Mac." House Minority Leader John Boehner (R-OH) was unhappy: "Why should we reward Fannie Mae and Freddie Mac with $200 billion in taxpayer dollars without first reforming these housing entities that were at the heart of the economic meltdown?"[147] Of course, Congress was making no effort to reform the enterprises.

Rick Santelli of CNBC, as quoted on February 23's *Meet the Press*, was very strident about the modifications: "How many people want to pay for your neighbor's mortgage that has an extra bathroom and can't pay his bills?"

There were many questions on how Fannie and Freddie could legally refinance a mortgage above 80 percent LTV. Pollard's legal opinion was that as refinances would reduce the risk of losses (which they did), it was within the enterprises' mission of providing stability and safety and soundness. It was the equivalent of a modification. Mortgage insurers enthusiastically agreed as HARP could reduce their potential losses. They also agreed to roll over any existing mortgage insurance into the new loans. Appraisers threatened to sue because we were not requiring a new appraisal. The original HARP plan had a conservative 105 percent LTV, which we increased to 125 percent in July. The limit was later rightly eliminated by DeMarco.

On February 26, Fannie reported their fourth-quarter and full-year 2008 results. Losses for the quarter were $25.2 billion, "driven primarily by $12.3 billion in net fair value losses [primarily derivative losses as interest rates had fallen], credit-related expenses of $12.0 billion and securities impairments of

$4.6 billion." To eliminate the net worth deficit, I requested a $15.2 billion draw from the Treasury. The total loss for 2008 was $58.7 billion.

On March 11, Freddie Mac reported their 2008 results. The fourth-quarter loss of $23.9 billion included a mark-to-market loss of $13.3 billion, $7.2 billion in credit-related losses, $7.5 billion in securities impairments, and $8.3 billion in additional allowance against the deferred tax asset. The requested draw was $30.8 billion. The loss for 2008 was $50.1 billion. The press release had a quote from Moffett saying Freddie was "doing all we can to help stabilize the financial markets and hasten the recovery in the housing market," adding that they had injected "more than $460 billion in mortgage funding in 2008."

It was his last official act; he had resigned with a March 13 effective date. Koskinen graciously agreed to become the interim CEO, and Glauber took his place as interim chairman.

The articles about Moffett's resignation quoted sources saying he was frustrated "over the need to consult with regulators on all major decisions and follow public-policy mandates that he didn't necessarily see as good for the company."[148] Other articles suggested he was frustrated by the pay ($900,000 plus bonus) and the lack of a clear path to an IPO. It was reported from his speech at the University of Oklahoma in December 2009 that "Mr. Moffett said he quit his position at Freddie Mac because of his opposition to HAMP. 'I said . . . it won't work.'"[149]

He had told me that he thought the HAMP program would cost Freddie $30 billion and wanted to disclose that in the 10-K. We did not believe his number and thought it would be detrimental to disclose because mortgage modifications would be a long-term positive for Freddie. Foreclosures were depressing housing prices and neighborhoods.

The controversy was leaked,[150] but a compromise was reached. The language in the March 10-K was "We have made changes to certain business practices that are designed to provide support for the mortgage market in a manner that serves public policy and other non-financial objectives but that may not contribute to profitability." Looking back, as Freddie's losses were well less than they forecasted, the FHFA's approach was the right one.

On March 4, 2009, the Treasury published guidelines for HARP and HAMP. HAMP was for loans originated before 2009 and had a termination date of December 31, 2012, which was later extended. The TARP fund would share the cost of reducing monthly payments from 38 percent debt-to-income to 31 percent DTI. Interest rates could be reduced to 2 percent, the term could be extended to forty years, or, if necessary, the principal could go into forbearance.

Servicers would be paid $1,000 for each modification and $1,000 per year if the loan was still performing. Homeowners would get $1,000 per year for five years to apply against principal reductions if their mortgage payments were timely. Freddie Mac was charged with auditing compliance. Fannie was the overall administrator of HAMP. The enterprises were chosen because they had the expertise to monitor servicers.

As I learned later while a board member of American Home Mortgage, Bair was right: HAMP was a complicated process, subject to errors and re-defaults. It fell short of its goal of 3 to 4 million mortgages: through its extension date of 2016, it helped 1.8 million homeowners. There were many millions of non-HAMP modifications.

HARP applied to mortgages acquired before May 1, 2009, and was eventually extended until December 31, 2018. It came close to its goal of 4 million with 3.5 million refinances. Fannie and Freddie did another 4 million streamlined refinances through that period.

Retention bonuses for enterprise employees became the next big blowup. As I said in my March 18, 2009, announcement of the retention payments, "We started to design a retention plan with a compensation consultant even before the conservatorship because it was critical to retain their most important asset—their employees—who are being asked to play a vital role in the nation's economic recovery. . . . As the previous senior management teams left, it would have been catastrophic to lose the next layers down and other highly experienced employees."

The timing could have been better as AIG, which had received $170 billion in bailouts, had paid out $165 million dollars in bonuses the weekend before. Morgan Stanley was acquiring Smith Barney's financial advisory group from Citigroup and was reported to be paying billions in retention payments.

I had united Democrats and Republicans. The next day, Frank wrote me a letter "to urge strongly that you rescind the retention bonus program . . . and pursue repayment of any already-paid bonuses. I remain very skeptical that retaining and rewarding people who made the mistakes that contributed to the unsatisfactory performance is a good idea." He raised the heat in a CNN interview, saying, "A retention bonus is a nice word, it turns out, for extortion."[151]

I responded in a letter to Frank the next day. I reminded him of the critical role the enterprises play in the mortgage market and the newly announced Making Home Affordable program. I wrote, "We run the risk of these same employees deciding this is the last straw and walking away. The loss of key personnel would be devastating to the companies and to the government's efforts to stabilize the housing system." To counter his argument about who made the mistakes, I wrote, "Since last August . . . the four highest compensated executives at Freddie Mac and seven of the top eight at Fannie Mae left and are not getting these retention payments."

Senator Barbara Boxer (D-CA) wrote me a letter on March 22. I attached my response to her to a March 27 letter to Senator Charles Grassley (R-IA), then ranking member on the Senate

Finance Committee, whom I had dealt with on Social Security. He is a leading supporter of good-government management.

We included a very extensive description of the retention plans, which covered 4,057 Freddie and 3,545 Fannie employees. Total payments over three years for Freddie were scheduled to be $97.6 million, with $112.6 million for Fannie. I wrote that "the retention payments for these three years, 2008–2010, will likely total between 0.01% and 0.02% of this year's Enterprises loan purchases." And "keeping the Enterprises operating at full speed was best for the housing markets and best for the economy, which clearly also made it best for the taxpayer." My conclusion was that "taking risks with the viability of Fannie Mae and Freddie Mac by not providing adequate compensation would be unwise."

It did not assuage Senator Grassley. *Washington Post* quoted him, "It's hard to see any common sense in management decisions that award hundreds of millions in bonuses when their organizations lost more than $100 billion in a year. And it's an insult that the bonuses were made with an infusion of cash from the taxpayers."[152]

I received a handwritten note on a copy of the article sent to me: *YOU ASSHOLES DESTROYED MY STOCK & RETIREMENT—DO I GET A MILLION BAILOUT—YOU ROTTEN F - - KERS*. The House was working on legislation to tax bonuses at 90 percent for managers making over $250,000 if their organizations had received government money. Grassley did get carried away when talking about the AIG bonuses, saying the executives should "follow the Japanese example" and "resign or go commit suicide."[153]

On April 9, I received a fax letter from Secretary Geithner confirming that we had consulted with the Treasury Department on the 2009 retention payments. It read, "You have previously stated that you believe these payments are necessary to prevent the loss of key personnel which would be devastating to these companies and to the government's efforts to stabilize the housing system."

He nicely ended the letter, "Finally, I appreciate the work of FHFA, Fannie Mae and Freddie Mac to stabilize the housing market in order to help millions of Americans."

On April 21, I had a meeting with Barney Frank. He told me he was happy that the retention pay controversy had blown over.

CHAPTER 24

Bumping Along the Bottom

"I think in terms of promptly supplying massive liquidity, nationalizing Fannie Mae and Freddie Mac, they get an A plus. I think a lot of intelligence and vigor has been displayed. When it gets into the regulatory battle, which lies ahead, I would expect the result to be not as good. . . . I would argue that we need wise restraints that dampen enormously the inevitable bubbles."

–Vice Chairman Charlie Munger, Berkshire Hathaway, Bloomberg, May 1, 2009

THE PRESIDENT'S WORKING Group and the TARP oversight board were having regular meetings to develop ideas to lessen the financial crisis. As Fannie and Freddie worked on HAMP and HARP, a big issue was how to modify rather than foreclose on mortgages held in PLS. The enterprises both proposed complicated alternatives using TARP funds.

The enterprises' PLS portfolios, when purchased, were all AAA. By April, 68 percent had been downgraded to junk levels, 16 percent were downgraded but still had investment-grade ratings, and another 11 percent were on watch for downgrade—a total of 95 percent.

The Fannie and Freddie proposals required too much TARP

funding to be approved. The Treasury did, however, create what turned out to be the successful Legacy Securities Public-Private Investment Program (PPIP). The idea was first proposed in a very short February TARP oversight meeting but was fleshed out at an April 2009 meeting. As we had an FHF Oversight Board meeting in our office that day, the TARP meeting was also held in our offices. I had started to talk with some investment and private equity firms, so I stepped out of the meeting when PPIP was discussed. The plan was to have an investment firm raise a fund (minimum of $500 million), and the Treasury would match the fund raised, then provide debt financing for the total amount of equity to buy those formerly AAA PLS and commercial mortgage-backed securities (CMBS) issued before January 1, 2009. The notion went back to the roots of TARP by buying directly troubled assets.

On July 8, Geithner and Bernanke announced the selection of nine managers. They had to be experienced in managing PLS and CMBS and have over $10 billion in assets under management. All nine successfully raised a range of funds for a total of $7.5 billion. With a TARP equity match and debt, the total purchasing power was $30 billion. I hasten to add I was not involved in the selection process; one of those selected managers was Invesco, the parent of WL Ross. I joined WLR in September and helped raise the funds to invest in PLS by meeting with potential investors. Our fund was different than the rest as we had a sister fund that could buy troubled mortgages.

In total, the managers invested almost $25 billion. At the conclusion of the program in September 2013, the Treasury reported a net profit of $3.8 billion on their $18.6 billion of debt and equity. The managers' returns ranged from 26 to 18 percent per annum. The WLR Invesco Mortgage Recovery fund was at the lower end because Wilbur Ross, head of the investment committee on which I served, was wary of PLS. With Invesco's Louisville office, we pushed to expand our risk tolerance, which we did.

PPIP was not the only successful TARP program. In total, $442 billion of the authorized $700 billion was obligated. The TARP investment program produced profits despite the auto companies' (GM and Chrysler) investments, which after their bankruptcies resulted in a $12 billion loss. There was a small profit in the GMAC/ResCap investment, which I had pushed.

As expected, the costly part of the program was HAMP ($23 billion) and the Hardest Hit fund ($9.6 billion), which aided state housing finance agencies. In my opinion, stabilizing the US economy and the $11 trillion mortgage market was well worth the cost. The only criticism that could be raised is that we did not use more of the TARP fund.

Elizabeth Warren, then a Harvard Law professor, was chairing the congressional TARP oversight panel. In April she came to visit me. We had a cordial meeting, but I had problems with her reports. In February she told the Senate Banking Committee, citing her panel's report criticizing Paulson's implementation of TARP, that "Treasury paid $254 billion for [bank] preferred stock and warrants worth approximately $176 billion, a shortfall of $78 billion."[154]

Somewhat weirdly, as bank investments were designed to help stabilize the markets and the economy, the article went on to quote her: "'They did not price for risk, that's what markets do,' Warren said, suggesting the Treasury's lack of consistency had made the government funds a better deal for some." Dodd agreed that the bank preferred stocks were "poor" investments, and Shelby called them "haphazard." The bank program was very successful, producing over $24 billion in gains. In total, 707 banks received investments; only 34 of those banks failed.

As the enterprises were trying to figure out their new role, it was a tough time for their employees, even though we had successfully fought for their retention bonuses. As we were searching for a Freddie CEO again, Allison was being recruited by the Treasury to run TARP. Tom Stanton, a fellow of the National Academy of Public Administration, was quoted as saying, "From the perspective of the White House, you could believe that Jim Lockhart is in charge, and therefore these companies will continue to operate, even with some departures." An anonymous source said, "It wasn't Allison show or Moffett's show. It's Lockhart's show."[155]

That was an overstatement. We had appointed boards with well-qualified directors. However, the FHFA was driving all the major decisions. One such decision was to tap Mike Williams in April 2022 to be Fannie's new CEO. He was COO, a fourteen-year Fannie veteran, and very well respected.

Once I left the FHFA, I had a one-year "cooling off" period, but after that I tried not to talk with the CEOs very often as I was worried about appearances. WL Ross had invested in several companies that did business with Fannie and Freddie. I did have lunch in the Fannie dining room with Williams in December 2010. As I was leaving, he said I was looking good. He said that they have an expression: after someone left Fannie, they got a "Fannie face lift." He then said, "Maybe there is an FHFA facelift."

The year was tough on Fannie, Freddie, and the FHFA teams. Sadly, the acting CFO of Freddie Mac committed suicide on April 22, 2009. He had been under pressure, given the ongoing accounting investigations by the SEC and the FBI, public disclosure issues, and even his retention bonus being made public. Despite these pressures, he had been doing a very good, conscientious job.

On May 5, I had a meeting with Geithner. We discussed the Mike Williams promotion, my surprising conversation with Frank that he was glad the retention payments furor was over, my ongoing push for TARP mortgage insurer support, and the upcoming Fannie and Freddie first-quarter earnings reports. I also asked him to please ensure that the FHFA was involved in any discussions on the future of the enterprises.

Another topic was the FHFA's first report to Congress, which was scheduled to be released mid-May. An assessment by the FHF Oversight Board of which Geithner was a member was a legislative requirement. The last topic in my notes was a cryptic "Me—Ed." I told him that Ed DeMarco would be an excellent replacement. Geithner had worked with DeMarco when both were career employees in the Treasury Department under the Clinton administration.

On May 8, Fannie Mae reported a $23.7 billion loss, which required a $19 billion draw from the Treasury for a total of $34.2 billion. Even prime mortgages were beginning to experience increases in delinquencies as house prices continued to fall and unemployment rose. On May 12, Freddie reported a much smaller loss of $9.9 billion. The draw from the Treasury was $6.1 billion for a total of $50.7 billion. The acting CEO, Koskinen, commented, "All of us at Freddie Mac remain focused on our most important mission—preserving homeownership for American families."

While all this was going on with the mortgage market, we still had a very small (only 398 employees) but critically important agency to run. On May 18 we sent our 2008 report to Congress, detailing extensive information about the fourteen GSEs. As I said in my letter, it was "a time of unprecedented challenges for the GSEs, United States' economy and the housing and financial markets." I added, "The challenges in the financial markets are slowly abating, but the problems in the housing markets continue." My final sentence in the letter to Congress was "We look forward to working with you in developing a countercyclical, post-conservatorship structure for the Enterprises based upon a well-defined mission, sound insurance principles, clear demarcation of private and public sector, and strong regulatory oversight."

We also published a *2009–2011 Strategic Human Capital*

Plan in which I noted, "Successful human resource management is the foundation of any agency's ability to accomplish goals and achieve its mission." The first performance goal was to have "a diverse workforce that is highly skilled, highly motivated, and results-oriented." The report noted that our demographics matched that of the federal government overall with 44 percent female and 33 percent minorities, but our employees were much more highly educated: 81 percent of the staff had at least a bachelor's degree, versus 44 percent of the federal workforce. Advanced degrees were held by 42 percent of the employees.

In addition to the human resource goals, the *2009–2014 FHFA Strategic Plan* had the following three goals: safety and soundness, housing mission, and conservatorship. The latter had four performance goals—"conserve assets," "delegate appropriate authorities to each Enterprise's management," "reducing preventable foreclosures," and "work with the administration and Congress to develop an effective structure for Enterprises to emerge from conservatorship." Somehow, over the years that latter one got lost.

We had published our *Performance and Accountability Report—2008* (PAR) for the then brand-new agency on November 17, 2008, despite all that was going on. The cover had the symbols of the three agencies—the FHFB, OFHEO, and FHFA. After a design firm failed to come up with a good design, I ended up designing the FHFA's symbol. It was inspired by the FHFB's but had three houses—for the FHLBanks, Fannie, and Freddie.

It was announced in May 2009 that the Association of Government Accountants had selected the FHFA's PAR for its Certificate of Excellence in Accountability Reporting (CEAR). We were one of only seventeen agencies. As we said in our news release, "Director Lockhart is in the unique position of having received the CEAR award at three agencies [the SSA, OFHEO and FHFA]."

To be as transparent as possible, we put out other regular reports. The first-quarter foreclosure report stated that roughly 84 percent of the enterprises' 30.4 million loans were classified as prime with 2.5 percent sixty-plus-days delinquencies. The remaining non-prime mortgages were 9.9 percent delinquent for sixty-plus days. Modifications were rising, but so were foreclosures.

Another May report mentioned the new Treasury program to modify the second lien mortgages when the first mortgage was modified. We wrote, "Statistics show that about half of all at risk mortgages have second liens and 15% have more than one mortgage [so-called piggyback mortgages]. This new program removes the stumbling block of the second liens."

Logically, if a homeowner could not afford the first mortgage or it was underwater, the second mortgage had little or no value. Banks, however, were reluctant to write down their second mortgages. One of the very troubled banks that we invested in at WL Ross, saving it from an FDIC takeover, had a large second mortgage portfolio that it had bought from Countrywide. They took massive losses.

A hearing of a House subcommittee was held on June 3. Prior to the hearing, Bloomberg[156] got a leaked copy of Cox's January 16 letter pushing the FHFA to uphold our legal duty to "preserve and conserve." The reporter wrote the letter "underscores the tension between Fannie Mae and Freddie Mac's responsibilities to investors and government demands that they help in the worst housing crisis since the Great Depression." She quoted a University of Michigan law professor saying that I "may be violating the law requiring FHFA as conservator to preserve and protect. . . . It may be illegal, but who can complain?"

In the hearing, Congressman Hensarling (R-TX) asked how we could serve two masters. He was referring to my opening statement when I said:

As the conservator, FHFA's most important goal is to preserve the assets of Fannie Mae and Freddie Mac over the conservatorship period. That is a statutory responsibility. As the regulator, FHFA's mission is to ensure the Enterprises provide liquidity, stability, and affordability to the mortgage market in a safe and sound manner. . . . The Enterprises own or guarantee 56% of the single-family mortgages in this country or $5.4 trillion. Obviously, given that massive exposure, the best way to preserve their assets and fulfill their mission is to stabilize the mortgage market and strengthen their safety and soundness to serve the mortgage market better. Working with Federal Reserve, the Bush and Obama Administrations, and other regulators, that has been our top priority since the conservatorships began. . . . Mortgage modifications and refinancing homeowners into safer mortgages are important elements of stabilization of the housing market and the US economy.

I took heat from several Republicans on the Fannie and Freddie appraisal code, which had been finalized May 1. There were few questions on the future of the enterprises.

In his opening remarks, Chairman Kanjorski—perhaps picking up on Paulson's sporting analogy of a "time-out"—said GSE reform "will be a long-distance relay between Congress not a 100-meter sprint." That did not stop me from firing the starter's gun even though the Obama administration was putting off any proposals until February 2010. I made the point that "very important decisions have to be made about the future of the mortgage market and the appropriate role of the secondary mortgage market, including the roles of government regulations and programs, before we get to the future of Fannie and Freddie themselves."

I then listed five principles to consider in reform:

1. The first principle is that the Enterprises or any successor should have a well-defined and internally consistent mission. . . .

2. The second principle is that there should be a clear demarcation of the respective roles of the federal government and the private sector. . . . [A]ny federal risk-bearing should be explicit and at actual cost. . . .

3. The third principle is to base any organization that provides credit guarantees or mortgage insurance on sound insurance principles: sound management, strong underwriting and capital positions, risk-based pricing. . . .

4. The fourth principle is to create a regulatory governance structure that ensures risk-taking is prudent. . . .

5. The fifth principle is that housing finance should be subject to supervision that seeks to contain both the riskiness of individual institutions and the systemic risk associated with housing finance, [which] would include policies and countercyclical capital regulations that counter the private sector's tendency to generate lending booms and busts.

As this was going to be my last congressional hearing, I closed "with a few thoughts," as follows: "My career has included work with several private-sector insurance companies and several government insurance programs. My observation is that government insurance programs are high-risk and invite the private sector to shift risk to the government. Among other issues, it is often difficult in a political environment to calculate or charge the actuarially fair price, resist pressure to broaden the mission, and prevent inadequately compensated increases in federal risk-bearing."

And then, bringing up my ongoing concern, I said, "Finally, the regulators need to take a more unified and cohesive approach to supervising mortgage products, markets, and institutions."

The FHFA received an invitation to the White House for our principal to attend a June 17 meeting at 11:40 to 12:10 with the president and a follow-up meeting at 12:45 for a major presidential speech. All financial regulators met in the Roosevelt Room. We had place cards. Mine read JOHN LOCKHART, which I saved as a memento. Obama wandered in for a couple of minutes, saying somewhat haltingly that he was going to give a major speech on financial reform. There was limited discussion.

He gave a good speech in the East Room, announcing what would become the Dodd-Frank law. Those two members of Congress were joined by Senator Durbin, Secretaries Donovan and Geithner, Summers, and Bernanke in the first row on the right side. The regulators, including me, were in the front row on the left side. After the speech, Obama shook hands along the line of regulators, which was captured in a *Wall Street Journal* picture. I did say to Obama that reform should be comprehensive and systemic.

The Wall Street Journal's June 18 edition had a picture of Bernanke holding a copy of the spiral-bound *Financial Regulatory Reform: A New Foundation*. One article, "The Task of Taming Highs and Lows," said the word *stability* was used fifty-three times in the proposal. I did not see my favorite word, *countercyclical*, but lessening the procyclical rules and accounting was proposed.

Doing away with the OTS and the SEC's investment banking oversight was proposed. A Financial Services Oversight Council was proposed, composed of the major regulators, including the FHFA director. One of the duties was to coordinate oversight of SIFIs (systemically important financial institutions). A Consumer Financial Protection Agency was introduced. *The Wall*

Street Journal announced that the Obama administration were taking a pass on GSE reform until the president's 2011 budget but mentioned six alternatives, ranging from nationalization to liquidation.

In the same edition, Peter Wallison's opinion piece, "Too Big to Fail, or Succeed," wrote the administration prefers "stability over innovation, competition and change." The special SIFI (systemically important financial institution) treatment "would create what are essentially government-sponsored enterprises like Fannie Mae and Freddie Mac in every sector of the economy." The accompanying cartoon had a happy Uncle Sam pushing a very shaky baby carriage with a giant, crying baby holding GM and Chrysler toy cars with an AIG bib and Fannie Mae diaper.

There were some signs of housing prices starting to stabilize and house sales picking up. The FHFA's House Price Index for May was up 0.9 percent. As I had told President Bush five months earlier, the housing market was still bouncing along the bottom. Bernanke was quoted as saying the "decline in housing activity appears to have moderated."[157]

In July I made a comment that separating the mission and safety and soundness regulatory responsibilities had been a problem for OFHEO and could be a problem for the new consumer agency, the CFPB. That stirred up some controversy.

The key problem with HUD's mission responsibility was that the required housing goals were much too high. That became a controversial subject in the *Financial Crisis Inquiry Commission Report*. I said in my March 9, 2010, testimony that the separation of the mission authority was "troublesome" and the high affordable housing goals was one of the "major reasons why they lowered their underwriting standards." Mudd testified that the "goals were extremely challenging" as they "were set above the origination levels in the marketplace."

Wallison, serving as one of the commissioners, in his dissent blamed HUD's high affordable housing goals as a major cause of the financial crisis, pushing Fannie and Freddie to acquire "large numbers of subprime and other high-risk loans." In what I have always thought was an overstatement, he stated that half the mortgages in the US were of "inferior quality and likely to default when housing prices were no longer rising."

Fannie Mae missed two of the three major affordable housing goals in 2008, and Freddie missed all three. Working with the housing mission team that was transferred from HUD to the FHFA, which was then reporting to DeMarco, we lowered the goals to 2005 levels.

Freddie had been searching for a CEO for well over a year before the conservatorships. Finally, in July, we announced that we had selected Ed Haldeman, the former CEO of Putnam Investment Management. Koskinen, who had served admirably as acting CEO under tough circumstances since March, went back to his chairman role.

July 30 was the first anniversary of HERA and the FHFA. To commemorate the birthday, I gave a speech at the National Press Club. I had a chart that showed that the mortgage origination share of the enterprises was 72.6 percent and the FHFA/VA 21.6 percent. I said: "Over the long term this high GSE and government share is unhealthy."

Another slide showed that the enterprises' multifamily market share grew from 34 percent in 2006 to 84 percent in 2008. A slide I had updated many times over the years showed subprime ARMs at 36.5 percent seriously delinquent (ninety days), all subprime mortgages at 24.9 percent, all mortgages 7.2 percent, prime loans 4.7 percent, Fannie 3.7 percent, and Freddie 2.8 percent.

I again talked about the role of the conservator, saying, "We recognize that FHFA's duties as conservator means just that, conserving the enterprises' assets. This is our top goal. One of the reasons that Fannie Mae and Freddie Mac have so many problems is that they had a short-term profit maximization focus. As conservator, we must avoid that trap and focus on longer-term results. In particular, with $5.4 trillion of mortgage exposure, stabilizing the housing markets is by far the best way to conserve assets. That is why preventing foreclosures that destabilize families and neighborhoods is so important."

I repeated the five principles for reform that I had given in my House testimony, emphasizing countercyclical policies. I said that they would "curb asset bubbles and dampen credit cycles," "improve the odds that an institution would survive a crisis," and "reduce actions on the part of distressed financial institutions that hurt the broader economy and individuals," such as "fire sales" and "credit crunches." I showed a chart of housing prices from 1975 to 2009's first quarter against the trend line in housing prices. In 2001, prices started to exceed trend, reaching over 20 percent above trend at the peak in 2006 but falling back to trend in 2009. The chart's title was "Countercyclical Capital Could Dampen House Price Shocks."

Listing the three major reform structures, I rejected nationalization. However, I added, "I recognize that there are some risks, such as Social Security longevity risk, that are too big for the private sector. Mortgage catastrophic risk may be one such risk. . . . Such a program could also serve as another countercyclical tool if structured properly."

Ending the speech:

> Speaking of anniversaries, I started my government career forty years ago in the Navy, becoming an officer of the deck of a nuclear ballistic submarine. Twenty years later, when I was sworn in by Elizabeth Dole as the head of PBGC, she said that experience would help me navigate the rough seas of underfunded pensions. Well, the experience helped there and at other troubled seas

in my government career—Social Security, OFHEO and now FHFA. Like the mortgage world, I truly know what it is like being "underwater" for a long time. The financial markets escaped "crush depth" last fall. My submarine surfaced every time, and so will the mortgage market.

Although the administration was making little progress at finding a successor for me, with the mortgage market starting to stabilize, two qualified CEOs in place, strong boards at Fannie and Freddie, and very able acting replacements available, it was getting to be time to return home after seven and a half years in Washington. I had arranged with the Treasury to have their photographer take a picture at what I expected to be my last TARP oversight board meeting on July 29, but Geithner cancelled the photographer. We had an FHF Oversight Board meeting on August 4. The next morning at 10 AM, I had a meeting with Geithner at the Treasury.

My long list of topics for the meeting was titled "FHFA Priorities for the Next Six Months." A new item was NYSE listing. I met at the NY Stock Exchange on August 7 to ask them to delist Fannie and Freddie because I did not want "Mom and Pop" investors buying their stocks, which I believed were worthless. The FHLBanks list included enforcement actions, dividend guidance, and the possible joint insurance fund. Also, I covered accounting issues, the need for an inspector general, future enterprise structure, and mortgage insurers.

As I was telling Geithner in the meeting that I was resigning, I wanted him to have the full list of action items. I also wanted to reassure him that DeMarco would do a great job and get his sign-off on DeMarco. Although the HERA legislation was clear that the FHFA's senior deputy would become acting, DeMarco, being an old Washington hand, had asked for his appointment in writing. He got it.

The Treasury was just two blocks from the FHFA's office, but by the time I got back to my office, the news of my resignation was out. I guessed that was a sign that they really wanted me to leave. I sent an email to my staff with regrets that I did not get to tell them first.

A Bloomberg[158] article quoted Mark Calabria saying not to expect many changes as I had "been quite accommodative to Obama. . . . He's fully supported the Obama administration's plan to use Fannie and Freddie for broader efforts beyond safety and soundness." It was my plan to help save the mortgage market before Obama arrived.

In my August 11 resignation letter to President Obama, I wrote we had "a very strong team at FHFA that will continue our mission." Concluding, I wrote, "I realize that there is some unfinished business including restructuring of the GSEs and the reform of Social Security. I would be pleased to advise on either issue in the future." I was never asked. The reforms are still unfinished!

Surprisingly, Freddie reported a second-quarter net income of $0.8 billion, primarily due to derivative hedging gains prior to its $1.1 billion preferred dividend to the Treasury. They did not require a Treasury draw.

Relative to Freddie, Fannie started to show the impact of its bigger size and their higher percentage of serious delinquencies. It reported a loss of $14.8 billion before its $0.4 billion Treasury preferred dividend. Credit-related expenses were $18.8 billion versus $5.2 billion at Freddie. Fannie's loss required a $10.7 billion draw from the Treasury, bringing their total up to $45.9 billion versus Freddie's still higher $51.7 billion. Fannie did an analysis of Freddie's and their own fair value balance sheets on June 30, 2009. It showed common shareholders had a negative $138 billion value for Fannie and $123 billion for Freddie.

Mortgage insurers continued to be a big risk. All eight had

been rated in the AAs in December 2007. By June 2009, one had ceased business, three were rated junk (BB), two rated BBB+, and two A. The risk in force exposure was $113 billion for Fannie and $64 billion for Freddie.

My last day in the office was August 13. The next day I did a CNBC *Squawk Box* interview with Joe Kiernan and Becky Quick. Joe was jocular as usual, saying, "Low pay, [and] all the foreclosures. You're escaping, right?"

Becky pressed me on that "$10.5 billion that Fannie asked for last week." I said that they were "continuing to put up reserves for future losses." The other guest, Ivanka Trump, responded, "But they are the ones almost single-handedly keeping the refinancing efforts alive." After I said their market share in single-family was 70 percent and 80 percent in multifamily, she rightly said, "Which is just staggering." When asked whether they were going to breach their $200 billion preferred stock ceiling, I said, "We've run pretty stressy stress tests and we got close to the $200 billion."

Also, on that day (August 13), the *American Banker* published my op-ed entitled "Counter Systemic Risk Issues Countercyclically." I started, "The term 'systemic risk' has come a long way. Several years ago it was the 'S-word' in Congressional hearings. Today it is *de rigueur*." I went through the various arguments and included the house price chart. My last sentence was "To head off systemic risks, they [referring to regulators and financial institutions], too, need to think countercyclically."

The last *Wall Street Journal* editorial while I was still director, published on August 17, was entitled "Fannie Mae, Enron, the Sequel." They were wrong when they wrote, "The best solution would be to put the two into run-off." However, they did have a very important point, writing, "As government spending soars, the political temptation to use off-balance-sheet vehicles of various sources increases." The article reflected my "trifecta" editorial board meeting three years earlier:

The politicians who created and pampered Fan and Fred like it that way. They know that offering federal "guarantees" looks much cheaper, in the official accounting, than actual outlays. But whether it's Fan and Fred, or the Pension Benefit Guaranty Corporation or the Federal Housing Administration, these deferred promises seem to come due sooner or later. Perhaps the politicians would be less profligate in issuing such guarantees if they had to admit the cost up front.

It's bad enough that the political class has played this dishonest game with the long-term liabilities of Social Security and Medicare, which are also kept off the balance sheet. But at least those IOUs are held by another branch of government and can be legislated away by some future Congress. Debt held by the public can't be repudiated without the US descending into Argentina-ville.

Despite being on vacation, I sent a letter to the GAO on August 19, 2009, commenting on their report[159] analyzing options for Fannie and Freddie Mac's future. An *American Banker* headline summarized the report, "Two Options for GSEs Get Single Bad Grade; GAO: privatization, public utility ideas are unworkable." The GAO worried about the future of the thirty-year, fixed-rate mortgages if the enterprises were privatized. As for the public utility model, they said the mortgage market is not a "natural" monopoly. That left a government corporation or reconstituted GSEs as options.

My letter concluded: "One aspect of this issue that is not directly addressed relates to the Enterprises' fundamental role as insurers of MBS. My own experience at OFHEO, Social Security, the Pension Benefit Guaranty Corporation (PBGC), and now FHFA, has taught me that government insurance comes with significant risks of moral hazard and perverse incentives. In addition, a key advantage of a well-managed insurance program is that money is charged in the form of premiums in good times to offset losses during bad times."

On a bittersweet note, I returned to DC for a great and gracious goodbye party on September 10. By then it been announced that I had joined WL Ross as vice chairman. Cricket came down for the event at the National Press Club, but she regrets that JB and Graci did not attend. In my remarks I started out by thanking the master of ceremonies, DeMarco, for being a "rock" for me over the last five years.

As they were in attendance, I told Chairman Bernanke that his "advice and support had been invaluable." Of Warsh I said: "We began working together on Social Security personal accounts. He twisted my arm to take OFHEO job." Clay Johnson was an "old friend that showed management works in government and results are achievable." I also thanked Bair for her advice. Paulson was not there, but I was deeply in his debt for the support he gave me.

Speaking of my fourteen-year government career, I said, "As you know, it hasn't always been easy. Sometimes it's been pretty messy. We haven't always succeeded, but we made good progress." To Korbey and Blahous I said, "Even Social Security's day will come."

It was a few days after the first anniversary of the "momentous decision" of conservatorship, and so I thanked the team for making it succeed. But my first thank-you was to Cricket for putting up with me and "by her account driving me to the airport about 750 times," and then to Jimmie Brand for picking me up at the other end. My concluding remarks were as follows:

> It has been a great honor and, yes, a pleasure at times to lead such a strong and dedicated FHFA team as we faced many challenges. . . . We made great progress, but still have a long way to go, but I rest assured that FHFA has

a strong team to continue to meet the challenges. As I go into a new venture, hopefully continuing to help troubled financial companies, I do wish you all the best in your continuing adventure and your critical mission. . . . I will miss you all."

CHAPTER 25

Surfaced but Adrift

"I hope that in focusing attention primarily on the future of specific institutions, we don't put the cart before the horse. Our initial attention should be the role of mortgage finance in our society and how we want the institutions and markets that supply it to function and perform."

—James B. Lockhart III's letter to the GAO on August 19, 2009

FANNIE AND FREDDIE are well into their second decade of conservatorship with no end in sight. Maybe I should not complain because one of the major themes of this book is how hard it is to design, or in this case redesign, government insurance programs. Government insurance programs need to lessen moral hazards, properly price the risk, and react more quickly to market changes.

Congress and the Obama, Trump, and Biden administrations have not acted precipitously. They never put the cart before the horse. The cart and horse are still in the barn. And we are in the never-ending time-out.

My father, being a New Englander, always had sayings. One was "You catch more flies with honey than with vinegar." Both he and I had trouble with that sometimes, but I did try with

Congress, interest groups, and the press when pushing reforms for the PBGC, Social Security, and Fannie and Freddie.

Perhaps the most relevant saying after the Global Financial Crisis and COVID-19 is "An ounce of prevention is worth a pound of cure." Today, it could be recast as "One billion dollars of prevention is worth a trillion dollars of cure."

On the topic of prevention, it is probably worth asking whether the conservatorships worked. On many measures yes, but the human toll was horrible. Housing prices declined over 25 percent nationwide from peak to trough and more than double that in some areas. In total, there were eight million foreclosures. The American Dream of homeownership fell from 69 percent to less than 63 percent. Too many Americans, especially those with low income, saw their net worth wiped out.

The causes were a giant housing bubble fed by excessive worldwide liquidity, mis-priced risk, poor underwriting and even fraud, lack of market discipline, greedy bankers and mortgage originators, exotic and predatory mortgages, inexperienced mortgage servicers, regulatory and rating agency laxness, overpromoting homeownership, and congressional inaction.

The phenomenon of housing bubbles was not just American. For instance, the UK, Spain, and Ireland had higher run-ups in housing prices. The latter two had even bigger falls than the United States.

Without the conservatorships being funded by the last-second addition of Paulson's bazooka and the passage of TARP, it would have been much worse. Bernanke wrote, "September and October of 2008 was the worst financial crisis in global history, including the Great Depression." Of the 13 "most important financial institutions in the United States, 12 were at risk of failure within a period of a week or two."[160]

Fannie and Freddie share in the blame. They stretched much too far for profits and market share, albeit with some push from

HUD's affordable housing goals and Congress. At their peak, in the fourth quarter of 2009, their serious delinquencies (SDQ) (in foreclosure or ninety days delinquent) were 4.9 percent versus 5.4 percent for the VA, 9.4 percent for the FHA, and the overall market's 9.7 percent. The overall subprime mortgages SDQ peaked at over 30 percent.

Three of the enterprises' originators were serious problems, according to a first-quarter 2009 report. Countrywide accounted for a massive 33 percent of their serious delinquent loans and 13 percent of Freddie's. The failed IndyMac had 5 percent and 4 percent, respectively, of all their SDQ with SDQ rates of 11.6 percent at Fannie and 23.3 percent at Freddie. Lehman was even worse with SDQ rates of 13.2 percent at Fannie and 27.4 percent at Freddie.

Despite all the challenges, the conservatorships and HARP worked. According to a New York Fed staff report on HARP,[161] "Refinancing into a lower-rate mortgage reduced borrowers' default rates on mortgages and nonmortgage debts by about 40 percent and 25 percent, respectively."

At one point, I had predicted that the government would never get back all the money advanced to Fannie and Freddie by the Treasury and that we would need a bad bank for the bad loans. I was very wrong.

In August 2012, a third amendment to the Treasury preferred agreement was signed, which eliminated the preferred 10 percent dividend going forward and substituted a "net worth" sweep except for $3 billion each. In other words, all their profits above that $3 billion ceiling were paid to the Treasury.

As of year-end 2019, Fannie Mae had drawn $119.8 billion and paid dividends of $181.3 billion. Despite their alarms, Freddie's draws never reached the original $100 billion limit, peaking at $71.6 billion. They paid $119.9 billion in preferred dividends to the Treasury. Therefore, in total over the eleven-year period, the

Treasury had received dividends of $301.2 billion, still owns $191.4 billion in senior preferred stock, and holds common stock warrants for 79.9 percent. Whether that was adequate compensation for bailing the enterprises out and continuing to back their securities, which now exceed $6 trillion, can be debated.

An amendment in September 2019 increased the allowed capital net retention to $25 billion for Fannie and $20 billion for Freddie. Then, in January 2021, those limits were replaced by an agreement to allow both to retain capital up to their required capital levels. But there was a big caveat, as the Treasury has a liquidation preference for the new retained capital.

Despite the investor lawsuits, it is hard to imagine how the outstanding common or even the publicly owned preferred stock have any value, unless the government cancels their senior preferred stocks and the liquidation preferences.

As the enterprises build capital to the new limits, they are paying nothing for the $6 trillion US government "effective" guarantee of their debt and MBS. The cost of that guarantee should reflect the new capital rules and other reforms. Suggested ranges are five basis points to twenty-five basis points or higher. On a $6 trillion MBS book, that is $3 billion to $15 billion per annum.

In an Economic Club of New York speech on September 9, 2013, Paulson said he was "flabbergast[ed] [that] . . . we have no progress on GSE reform." He added, "I believe the single most important step we took to stem the financial crisis was putting Fannie Mae and Freddie Mac in conservatorship and backstopping their debt and mortgage-backed securities.

"The GSEs were . . . the vortex of the crisis. Those institutions together were nine times the size of Lehman Brothers. . . . They were central to our financial system, and their failure would have dealt a devastating blow to our economy. By almost any measure our GSE actions were successful. We staved off an imminent catastrophe."

He then said that the latest Obama budget projections were that the full amount drawn would be repaid plus "dividends of $50 billion or more. That is welcome news, but it comes with a downside. Now any attempt to reform the GSEs will appear to cost the taxpayer, or excuse me, appear to cost the Treasury. Thus, ironically, as the market heals, the government has a disincentive to make changes in the system that brought us to near ruin. . . . It's now time to tackle GSE reform and phase out the agencies that were the center of the crisis."

There have been myriad papers, task forces, reports, at least four major congressional bills, editorials, and speeches about GSE reform and ending the conservatorships. I have done my fair share. In several speeches, I made the statement, having invested at WL Ross in banks in four European countries and investigated investing into banks in at least another handful of countries around the world, that the US has the most socialistic housing finance system that I have seen. *The Wall Street Journal* editorial writers of 2008 got their wish of a "more honest form of socialism."

What should be the goal of housing reform? The Bipartisan Policy Center had a major commission on housing that put out a February 2013 report. Their goal was that "a successful housing finance system should maximize the range of ownership and rental housing choices at all stages of our lives." That requires a stable and sustainable housing system, shrinking the government's role in housing, and ending the conservatorships of Fannie and Freddie.

Even without the enterprises, the US government plays a much heavier role in housing than most other countries. Prior to the crisis, the combined market share of the FHA/VA was 3 to 4 percent but has averaged in recent years in the high teens. These loans are insured by Ginnie Mae (GNMA) with a full US government guarantee. Fannie and Freddie's market share in 2021 was 54.5 percent but jumped to 63 percent in the first quarter of 2022. As their conforming loan limits were increased dramatically, they took market share from banks, whose share dropped from 25 percent to 19 percent. The PLS market share of MBS issuance peaked in 2006 and 2007 at around 55 percent but is now in low single digits. Total "government" mortgages in the second quarter of 2022 were 67 percent of all mortgages. That is double the pre-crisis level but down from 2009's 90 percent.

The FHA's niche is first-time homebuyers, who account for about 84 percent of their loans, compared to around 50 percent at the VA, Fannie, and Freddie. The FHA's first-time buyers have a starkly different profile than the enterprises', with much higher LTVs and debt-to-income levels and lower credit scores.

There has been another notable change in the mortgage market since the crisis: the nonbank mortgage originators share of Fannie, Freddie, and Ginnie's mortgages have risen from 40 percent to over 75 percent. Many banks have been wary of dealing with the FHA and Ginnie because of potential legal liabilities. Another cause may be that we lost more than 30 percent of our banks in the crisis.

Given the major changes in the mortgage market, it is important to define the government's role in any mortgage reform proposals. The government agencies should have prime responsibility for new home purchasers and other mortgages for individuals with low and moderate income, but they need to upgrade their technology, risk management practices, and product design. The FHFA should work with these housing agencies to develop a unified government approach and reporting system for sustainable, affordable housing.

If there is going to be a subsidy for homeownership, and there should be for affordable housing, it should be concentrated in the government's FHA, VA, Rural Housing, and Ginnie Mae. As government insurance programs, those subsidies should be budgeted, countercyclical, and carefully managed to increase sustainable homeownership.

Mortgage originators and servicers must be well regulated and monitored to ensure that these more vulnerable homeowners are getting safe, sustainable mortgages. That is not an easy task as homeowners with low-down-payment mortgages of 3 to 4 percent are effectively underwater the day they close; realtor fees to sell a house are higher than that. Counseling first-time homebuyers and sticking to standard, lower-risk mortgages are critical to achieving sustainable mortgages.

It is important to note that for some people, and most people at some point in their lives, it is better to be a renter than a homeowner. The FHA, Fannie, and Freddie played an important part in the rental market. Fannie and Freddie, with different, shared risk-taking in the multifamily space, successfully weathered the crisis with delinquencies of 0.8 percent for Fannie and 0.4 percent for Freddie. The complex FHA multifamily programs need to be reviewed and modernized.

The housing market recovered slowly but well from the crisis. There are many different house price indexes, including FHFA's less volatile index. Between 2000 and the 2006–07 peak, house prices rose about 75 percent, only to fall more than 25 percent on average. By 2021, house prices had doubled since the peak, juiced in part by the Fed's low interest rate policy. As of the Second quarter of 2022, the single-family housing market value was valued at $43.9 trillion. As mortgage debt of $13.0 trillion has increased by about 30 percent since the crisis, household equity has almost tripled to $30.9 trillion.[162]

As many lower-income individuals were foreclosed upon during the crisis, this home equity increase may have helped exacerbate the wealth divide in the US. Home equity now exceeds private-sector pension funds in the US.

As we noted in our BPC retirement report, home equity can be an important source of funds in retirement. Many people rather "age in place" while also making their homes more handicap accessible. That desire may be increasing after COVID-19.

The FHA has a home equity conversion mortgage (HECM) product that allows the elderly to borrow payment-free in return for giving up some of their home equity when they move or pass away. HECMs were poorly sold and structured pre-crisis. The rules have been updated to create a better and safer product with required counseling. More can be done, especially on educating the elderly, on properly sizing the home equity mortgage and better special servicing for the FHA.

The next part of my quote in the GAO letter at the start of this chapter was "In particular, that includes determining the most appropriate roles for private and public sector entities, competition and competitiveness, risk and risk management, cyclicality, and the appropriate channels and mechanism for targeting the underserved, and protecting consumers."

The best way to introduce competition is to de-socialize the US housing market by downsizing the government's role. One of the key impediments to reducing the government's market share is a product that few other countries have—the American-as-apple-pie thirty-year fixed-rate mortgage, which is freely prepayable.

Trump's March 27, 2019, "Memorandum on Federal Housing Finance Reform" stated, "The Administration will work with the Federal Housing Finance Agency to . . . ultimately, wind down both institutions" and then stated that the Treasury's first objective was "preserving access for qualified homebuyers to 30 year fixed-rate mortgages."

As mentioned, these thirty-year mortgages are very hard to hedge, given that they are frequently prepaid by refinancing if interest rates fall. And if rates rise, they can last for a long time. It is a very volatile product. Only the big banks can afford to put them on their balance sheets. We stopped one of the community banks that WL Ross invested in from making those thirty-year loans.

Thirty-year fixed-rate mortgages are the most popular mortgage by far, with market shares ranging up to 80 percent. Americans love the built-in free prepayment option. The next most popular product is the fifteen-year fixed-rate mortgage. The advantage of a fifteen-year loan is that equity in the home is built up more quickly. Variable-rate mortgages' market share is now in the mid-single digits versus close to 50 percent prior to the crisis.

Given the American love affair with the freely prepayable thirty-year fixed-rate mortgage, it is hard to conceive how we could have a fully privatized mortgage market based on banks and PLS. That is not to say that PLS should not be encouraged, but they must have better standards and disclosure with third-party monitors as suggested by the asset-backed industry association SIFMA (Securities Industry and Financial Markets Association).

The PLS's market share is much too small. In conservatorship, the playing field is heavily tilted to the enterprises with their capital support from the Treasury. Banks should also be looking to expand market share by issuing covered bonds in which they effectively keep the credit risk but not the interest-rate risk.

As I have written, the FHLBanks play an important and countercyclical role in the secondary mortgage market by making advances against well-collateralized mortgage portfolios. They do not lend to that growing segment of the market—nonbank originators and servicers.

Several years ago, a program the FHFA ended allowed the FHLBanks to make secured advances to captive insurance companies of nonbank originators and real estate investment trusts (REIT). The FHLBanks' captive insurance program should be reestablished by the FHFA. The FHLBanks should also be authorized to make advances to whatever succeeds the enterprises after the end of their conservatorships. That expansion might require congressional action.

Turning to the potential structures for the enterprises, I continued to be against nationalization in any form, given all the flaws in government insurance programs. On the other hand, full privatization seems unworkable.

Some proposals wind down Fannie and Freddie over the years. To me, again using an old saying, that would be throwing the baby out with the bathwater. The two have strong expertise, experienced employees, and extensive data and systems capabilities. That is not to say that the "babies" should not go on a diet.

One way to put the twins on a diet, which is often discussed, is to freeze the conforming loan limits, which in 2022 grew by 18 percent and then for 2023 another 10.5 percent to $715,000 and in high-cost areas up to $1,073,000, which is much too high. The AEI, never a Fannie and Freddie fan, has given up hopes of legislative reform and has therefore suggested an even stricter diet. They recommend eliminating mortgages for second homes, rentals, and cash-out refinancings.

The enterprises, with strong pushes from the FHFA, have made significant progress in many areas during the conservatorship that can be built upon. They have jointly funded the construction of a common securitization platform they both can use, but more importantly it could be used by other and new securitizers. The platform could have been an important ingredient to foster competition for Fannie and Freddie, but the Biden team has restricted it to the enterprises.

Since 2013, the enterprises have also been selling off some of their credit risk through credit risk transfers (CRT). The buyers are money managers, hedge funds, reinsurers, and others. The downside to CRT is that they may be procyclical as the CRT market tends to dry up when the mortgage markets are troubled.

I will spare the readers a review of all the GSE reform proposals, which would take many volumes, and instead concentrate on the two I have put forward. The first would require congressional action, and the second could be done by the administration. Proponents of the latter proposal called that "administrative."

A September 2019 Treasury paper, "Housing Reform Plan," laid out a series of reforms. The administrative reforms were a fallback, but in either case the plan calls for a limited government role, saying, "The existing Government support of the secondary market should be explicitly defined, tailored and paid-for, and GSEs' conservatorships should come to an end."

In my many speeches on reform over the last decade-plus, I would often start with the slide of lessons learned from Fannie and Freddie's troubles. My presentation, "Time in for the Decade Long Time Out," at the 2019 American Mortgage Conference on April 30 shared the following lessons learned:

✦ Cannot back mortgages with 1 percent capital.

✦ Need to have clear demarcation of private and public sector.

　◇ Private-sector, not quasi-government, capital needs to take the first loss.
　◇ Government insurance must be risk-based, transparent, and countercyclical.
　◇ Need to reduce politics role in housing.

✦ Subsidies for affordable housing should be explicit and not buried in affordable housing goals.

✦ Portfolios were much too large and complex to manage and hedge.

✦ Risks of subprime, Alt-A, cash-outs, and HELOCs not properly underwritten.

✦ Stronger regulatory and governance structure needed

to ensure prudent risk-taking based on strong insurance principles, market discipline, and strong capital positions.

    ◇ Systemically prudent supervision should incorporate countercyclicality to limit booms and busts.

✦ Multifamily model worked.

As one looks at the future, a question arises about what we should do about the past. The buyers of the enterprises' debt and MBS have relied on the "effective guarantee" provided by the Treasury's senior preferred. It would be totally unacceptable to eliminate that effective guarantee for existing debt and MBS or to "harden" it to a full-faith-and-credit US government guarantee.

The answer should be a "good bank, good bank" structure with existing book protected by the existing PSPA.

Turning to the preferred congressional reform approach, I believe Congress should act to end the conservatorships and repeal the GSE charters. The FHFA should be granted authority to regulate and charter the new shareholder-owned Fannie, Freddie, and new entrants. Encouraging new entrance is critical to create a competitive market. Keeping the 80 percent loan-to-value rule makes sense as it spreads the risk to mortgage insurers. The FHFA rather than the state insurance commissioners should also become the regulator of those mortgage insurers, as the vast majority of the business MIs do is with Fannie and Freddie.

The FHFA should have the authority to define the enterprises capital, including the usage of the deferred tax asset, and to establish leverage and risk-based capital standards for Fannie, Freddie, and new entrants as well as the mortgage insurers.

The FHFA's new 2020 capital standards for Fannie and Freddie were an excellent foundation with a 4 percent leverage ratio, up from the pre-crisis average of about 1 percent. Also, very importantly, the new rule provides for a countercyclical capital requirement when house prices get 5 percent above trend. Unfortunately, the rules are being watered down.

The new mortgage guarantors would take the "first loss" based on strong capital levels backed up by the mortgage insurers, CRTs, down payments, and strong underwriting criteria. Their debt should not be backed by the government in any way, although they should have the option to receive collateralized advances from the FHLBanks.

Fannie's and Freddie's portfolios have shrunk to around $100 billion each from slightly over the $700 billion level that we froze them at in 2006. The portfolios should primarily provide liquidity for mortgage loans pending securitization. That capability allows them to serve smaller lenders, which is referred to as a cash window.

The catastrophic loss should be government insurance. A Senate Banking Committee bill created a Federal Mortgage Insurance Company (FMIC) based upon the FDIC. My preferred alternative would not be to create another government insurance company but rather to use the existing Ginnie Mae guarantee.

The premiums to the government catastrophic insurer should be risk-based and countercyclical, such that if house prices get too far above trend, premiums should increase. Alternatively, to lessen a down cycle, the premiums could be reduced. Their guaranteed MBS should provide the basis to ensure that there is a robust TBA (to be announced) mortgage market, which is very useful for hedging mortgage interest-rate risk.

Presently, the Consumer Financial Protection Bureau has regulatory authority over nonbank mortgage originators and servicers, but it may be more logical to have the FHFA do that. One of the tools Fannie and Freddie has is to "put back" poorly underwritten mortgages to originators. The threat of put-backs gives originators "skin in the game." The FHFA is already trying to ensure that nonbank originators have adequate capital to run their normal business, pay potential put-backs and make advances for missed mortgage payments.

Both the single-family and multifamily programs should be shrunk and set up in separate companies to reduce systemic risk and allow management focus. The strong multifamily underwriting and risk-sharing approaches have worked. Multifamily has been a very important source of funding for affordable housing. Much of the single-family affordable housing mortgages should continue to be provided by the FHA. The Affordable Housing Fund, which HERA required to be funded by the enterprises, should be kept. Affordable housing goals should be rethought.

With the above moves, the "too big to fail" systemic risk of today's Fannie and Freddie should be reduced significantly. With the appropriate countercyclical capital and premiums dampening the boom-and-bust cycles, the risk to the overall US housing system should be reduced. The countercyclical rules need to be explicit. I used to say that they should be "hardwired," meaning that they should not be subject to manipulation for political purposes.

The last question is what to do with the existing common and preferred shareholders. One option is to wipe them out through receiverships of the old Freddie and Fannie. Another option might be to give the preferred, but not the common, a small conversion right into the common of the new Fannie and Freddie.

The best and right solution is for the administration and Congress to work together to reform the housing and mortgage markets, but the never-ending time-out continues. Instead of seriously pushing Congress for GSE reform, the Trump Treasury and FHFA considered the second alternative: an administrative solution. They hoped that would spur Congress to act. Their approach was to let Fannie and Freddie build capital with a new capital rule and other implemented reforms.

The big problem for us taxpayers is that the Treasury would

have to write off the $191 billion senior preferred and the 79.9 percent common stock warrants. On top of that, the enterprises would have to raise/build capital to $240 billion to meet the new capital standards.

That administrative approach risks returning Fannie and Freddie to the old private profits and socialized losses and all the other inherent problems. Even though the Biden administration has not pushed Congress, the administrative approach seems to be off the table.

My recommended administrative approach would be to create new subsidiaries each for single-family and multifamily. The existing debt and MBS, with the PSPA that backs them, would be kept at the parent level, as would the charters and existing preferred and common shareholders. Their MBS would run off over many years as mortgages are prepaid or mature. The Treasury would keep the $191 billion in preferred stock and the warrants for the 79.9 percent of common shares of Fannie and Freddie.

The four new subsidiaries would be capitalized by their parents' contributing a portion of their portfolios. The goal should be at least a 4 percent leverage ratio requirement, a strong risk-based capital rule, and a countercyclical capital requirement. Almost all the employees would be transferred to the new subsidiaries, as would all the systems and data.

The new subsidiaries' MBS would have a back-to-back "keepwell" with the parent supported by the PSPA, paying an actuarially fair price for the support. A countercyclical fee should be added when housing prices greatly exceed trendline. As for the existing MBS, the parent Fannie and Freddie would enter into a master servicing agreement with their subs. The subs should pay to their parents a fee for the Affordable Housing Fund. There should be fees for other services. The net fees should allow the subs to build capital.

The four new subsidiaries' business should be constrained by some or all the diet restrictions I mentioned above. Their newly issued MBS should be priced to be profitable with a market-based return on equity. The goal would be to create profitable businesses that could have successful initial public offerings within a couple of years. Their parents, the original Fannie and Freddie, could sell their subsidiaries' shares and return the proceeds to the Treasury. As their starting assets would be much smaller than the existing $6 trillion, they would have to raise significantly less capital than the $240 billion.

This administrative structure would also allow for an easy transition to a more permanent congressional solution. The solution should replace the parental keepwells with a paid-for government guarantee, as I described above.

Unfortunately, there is a third option—to do nothing and ignore the lessons of the past by undertaking the following:

✦ Promoting procyclical housing policies as housing prices rise rapidly, which may hurt lower-income new homebuyers again,

✦ Keeping Fannie and Freddie in conservatorship, which provides the US government $6.6 trillion in off-balance sheet financing,

✦ Ignoring the need for a comprehensive housing policy,

✦ Watering down enterprise capital rules again.

Although not specifically stated, the third option seems to be the policy of the Biden administration. Resurrecting the Woodrow Wilson quote from my PBGC chapter, "To do things today exactly the way you did yesterday saves thinking."

It is time to think and act. Action is long overdue. Even Congressman Kanjorski's "long- distance relay" should have gotten off the starting blocks and hit the finish line years ago.

CHAPTER 26

Making Independent Agencies More Effective

"Now the Supreme Court should not have ignored the intent of Congress and allowed the President to remove the (@CFPB) director without cause. . . . Even after today's ruling, the (@ CFPB) is still an independent agency. The director still works for the American people. Not Donald Trump. Not Congress. Not the banking industry. Nothing in the Supreme Court ruling changes that."

–Tweet by Senator Elizabeth Warren, referencing the Supreme Court case *Sheila Law Vs. CFPB*, June 29, 2020

INDEPENDENT GOVERNMENT AGENCIES have a patchwork of governance and funding structures. Even the chain of command is questioned. Ultimately, because independent agencies are part of the executive branch, one assumes they should report to the president, but as displayed in Warren's above quote, not everyone agrees. Is there a fourth branch of government?

When I was at Social Security, I was criticized for working on reform, even though one would expect any responsible manager to work on reforms to make their organization better. The commissioner said Social Security must be "nonpolitical." To me, not working for reform is a dereliction of duty.

It is hard to find a consistent definition of an independent government agency. Some agencies are funded by taxes, fees, premiums, penalties, and direct charges to the regulated entities, while others are appropriated by Congress from general revenues, as are most government departments. Congresses and administrations have never tried to create consistent rules and structures. OFHEO was a hybrid funded by Fannie and Freddie but appropriated by Congress. In the early days, that allowed Congress to rein in OFHEO's regulation of Fannie and Freddie by limiting its funding.

The governance structures of independent agencies have been challenged by the courts, including the *Sheila Law vs. CFBP* and *Collins v. Yellen*, which dealt with the FHFA. The issue was whether Congress could create an agency whose head has a fixed-year term and is only removable by the president for cause, i.e., malfeasance or neglect of duty.

I have seen a variety of agency structures as a senior leader of four major agencies, one of which merged with a fifth. Fannie Mae started life as a government agency as well. At WL Ross, I had the experience of being regulated by several other agencies as a board member of banks and mortgage companies.

Some of the agencies I was involved with are as follows:

The PBGC, as an independent agency within the Labor Department, is chaired by the secretary of labor. When I was executive director, the position served at the pleasure of the president. The other members of the board were the secretaries of treasury and commerce. The executive director reported to the board. There is also a presidentially appointed, bipartisan advisory board of pension experts and interest groups. In subsequent legislation, the executive director was given a five-year term but could be replaced earlier by the president.

Social Security commissioner and the principal deputy commissioner (my position) have six-year terms beginning on a specific date in January every six years—not when they were confirmed. The commissioner can only be removed for cause, such as malfeasance. The commissioner has a pay grade of a cabinet secretary but was never included in the cabinet. There is also a presidentially appointed, bipartisan advisory board. Social Security and Medicare have six trustees charged with putting out the seventy-five-year forecast. The six are the secretaries of treasury, HHS, and labor; the SSA commissioner; and two public trustees (Republican and Democrat). As Social Security's administrative expenses are appropriated by Congress, to save short-term money the SSA does not fund some functions that could save much more money longer term. Beneficiary payments, now over $1 trillion, are not appropriated because they come from taxes, interest on the trust fund, and now drawing down on the trust fund. SSI payments are funded by general revenues.

OFHEO was an independent agency in HUD. It had an acting director when I was parachuted into it in 2006 to finish the Fannie Mae accounting investigation. As I had been approved by the Senate for Social Security, I was quickly confirmed by the Senate. I had good relationships with the HUD secretaries and kept them up to date with monthly written reports and an occasional meeting. As stated, OFHEO was appropriated by Congress, which many people argued allowed Congress to limit its ability to regulate Fannie and Freddie.

The Federal Housing Finance Board (FHFB) was also an independent agency. It had four presidentially approved, full-time board members who had seven-year terms, two from each party. A fifth member was the HUD secretary. It was funded by the FHLBanks.

When the FHFA was created in 2008 by merging OFHEO and FHFB, OFHEO director was designated the director until replaced by a Senate-confirmed successor. There was an acting career director for four years after I resigned. The FHFA has a high-powered advisory board composed of the Treasury and HUD secretaries and the chairman of the SEC. Strangely, the board is chaired by the FHFA director. The presidentially appointed Senate-confirmed (PAS) director had a five-year term unless removed by the president for cause. The FHFA is not appropriated by Congress but is still funded by the GSEs it regulates. That has allowed the FHFA to grow the necessary staff, but the downside is that the inspector general (IG) team now numbers over a hundred.

The Consumer Finance Protection Bureau (CFPB) was created by the Dodd-Frank legislation in 2010 as an independent agency within the Federal Reserve, which provides the CFPB's funding. I understand the CFPB spent a fortune renovating our old OFHEO and OTS offices. It has a very broad mandate overseeing most financial institutions' interactions with consumers. Starting up such a big agency from scratch led to issues, like inexperienced staff. The director has a five-year term and could only be removed by the president for cause. Cause was defined as "inefficiency, neglect of duty or malfeasance."

In the June 2020 *Sheila Law vs. CFPB* case, which Senator Warren tweeted about, the Supreme Court ruled in a 5–4 decision that the "for cause" removal structure violated the Constitution's "separation of powers" clause. However, the decision did not overthrow previous CFPB decisions or rules as Chief Justice Roberts wrote, "The agency may therefore continue to operate, but its director, in light of our decision, must be removable by the president at will." The Trump-appointed director was removed by President Biden.

That Supreme Court decision stated that "the CFPB's structure has no foothold in history or tradition." The court cited three other agencies with this structure: "the Office of the Special Counsel, the Administrator (sic) of the Social Security Administration and the Director of the Federal Housing Agency."

However, it stated, "they do not involve regulatory or enforcement authority comparable to that exercised by the CFPB."

The chief justice cited an example that "an unlucky President might get elected on a consumer-protection platform and enter office only to find herself saddled with a holdover Director from a competing political party who is dead set *against* that agenda." And then there was the real-life "unlucky" President Bush, who appointed a Social Security commissioner who was against his reform agenda.

Quickly, after the CFPB ruling, the Supreme Court agreed to hear a challenge of the constitutionality of the FHFA director position. The suit was designed to overthrow the profit sweep of Fannie and Freddie in the third amendment to the PSPA.

The renamed case, *Collins v. Yellen*, was unanimously decided by the Court on June 23, 2021. The director's position was ruled unconstitutional, but the third-amendment profit sweep was not overruled. President Biden immediately fired Director Calabria and appointed one of the FHFA's experienced deputies as the acting director. She was later nominated and confirmed.

Justice Gorsuch in his concurring opinion answered my fourth branch of government question. He wrote: "Few things could be more perilous to liberty than some 'fourth branch' that does not answer even to the one executive official who is accountable to the body politic."

Justice Kagan in her opinion wrote: "The SSA has a single head with for-cause removal protection; so a betting person might wager that the agency's removal position is next on the chopping block."

Two weeks later, President Biden did the chopping. He asked Commissioner Andrew Saul to resign. When Saul refused, he was fired the same day. The president did not have a "for-cause" reason but cited the CFPB and FHFA cases. Saul's major sin was that his important systems and reform efforts to better serve the

American people upset Social Security's union leaders and some congressional Democrats. Biden appointed as acting commissioner a left-wing idealogue with very limited management experience to manage the largest government agency. She was the only member of our politically balanced Bipartisan Policy Center's Retirement Commission who did not approve our final report.

Terms for top independent agency officials are useful as they tend to lessen the normal turnover of PAS government jobs, which averages about two years. Two years is much too short to make meaningful changes and get meaningful "results" as in Bush's President's Management Agenda. In my experience, most career government managers and employees are very dedicated to their agencies' missions and serving the American people. They adapt to new leadership. However, if they think the leader is a short-termer, they can be passively resistant—not "deep state." Continuity is very important in many agencies as most of the work that they do is "nonpolitical" in nature.

Another argument for terms is that some government employee unions, unfortunately, have a bias against change.

With about 1,200 PAS positions, combined with the slow vetting process and heightened political tensions, too many important positions end up with acting heads for many years. Social Security had acting commissioners for six years until 2019 and only two years later has an acting again. Unlike DeMarco at the FHFA, too many acting heads become caretakers or, even worse, implement major policies changes even though they were never vetted by the Senate.

My Navy training taught me to believe in a strict chain of command but also that responsibility must be delegated. The US government is so large and complex that no one person or group of persons can run it. As I mentioned earlier, members of congressional committees often do not know the details of the programs they oversee.

So, how should independence work? The first step is to appoint people who understand the subject and have had successful management experience. Secondly, those people should be trusted to run the agency on a day-to-day basis without interference from those above them in the executive branch. Major policy decisions and regulations are and should be approved by the OMB and the White House.

I do agree with Senator Warren's point about serving the American people. However, if an appointee has a major disagreement with the president on how best to serve the American people and she/he cannot convince the president otherwise, the best course is to resign.

Another issue that arises is whether it is better to run an agency with a single head or full-time boards. Full-time boards are generally split politically, with the president's party having the deciding vote, but that sometimes takes years into an administration to happen. The issue I see is that the "Sunshine Act" requires a noticed, open meeting for the public if more than one or two board members meet. I had a friend who was a member of the FDIC board who was afraid to meet with other board members for any reason because of the Sunshine Act.

Given the political dynamics, consensus can be hard to reach, which gives a mixed message to the career staff and the public. Full-time boards slow down the decision-making process, which in government is not all bad; but in times of crisis, it can exacerbate the problems.

A blended structure comprises a single head and a part-time board, which could be populated by senior government appointees or public experts. The part-time board can be advisory, or in some cases, like the PBGC, they have legal authority. The problem with boards with cabinet-level members is that the cabinet secretaries are so busy it is hard to arrange meetings.

This hodgepodge of governance and funding structures

combined with the massive number of PAS positions limits government effectiveness. I think most Americans believe we need more effective and results-oriented government. Ideas to achieve that goal are as follows:

1. Have a single agency head with a term of five years, starting when confirmed. A high-powered advisory board should help make sure the agency head is plugged into the administration's policy.

2. The annual performance and accountability reports should clearly spell out long-term needed improvements, including legislative reforms.

3. Although the Supreme Court did not require it with the CFPB and FHFA, it would be good to have the president nominate a replacement before removing an agency head with a term.

4. Bipartisan, nongovernmental advisory boards are useful, but it is questionable whether many of them should require Senate confirmation.

5. The PAS confirmation process is very slow and cumbersome. To streamline the confirmation process, in 2011 the Senate passed Resolution 116 that established a new class of PAS, called "privileged." Senator Schumer was a strong supporter. The idea was that for part-time and nonpolitical jobs, such as CFOs, after normal vetting by the White House, FBI, and appropriate committee staff, the candidate's nomination could go straight to the Senate for a vote without a Senate committee confirmation hearing. Yet a single Senator can still object and force a committee hearing. The "privilege" process is not working. It did not work for me when I was twice nominated as one

of the two public trustees of Social Security and Medicare. The positions have been vacant for over seven years. There should be a three-month limit for staff to review a "privileged" nomination before submitting it to the full Senate.

6. Another issue that slows down the process is that any senator can put a hold on a candidate. Then senator Biden ("Amtrak Joe") put a hold on over fifty nominees after 9/11, including me, because he wanted better security on Amtrak trains for his commute from Wilmington to Washington. That hold was for only three months, but many people put their lives on hold for years. For the trusteeship, I dropped out of a European bank board seat. The process eventually causes many talented people to drop out or not even accept a nomination from the White House. Holds on nominees should have a limited time frame.

7. When vetting senior PAS positions, more emphasis should be placed on management experience. So many government departments and agencies are bigger than most corporations, but too often, appointees focus solely on policy, politics, and media rather than better managing their agency to serve the American people. President Bush required the top deputies to serve as chief operating officer.

8. Agencies do drills for emergencies such as hurricanes and pandemics. They should also be required to game out and develop plans about economic distress that might affect an agency and its constituents.

9. Congress should ask the GAO to do a census on the

purpose and multiple structures of agencies. Based on that survey, a bipartisan commission should be established with a two-pronged goal of first recommending either elimination of outdated or duplicate agencies, and then restructuring the agency to make it more efficient.

10. There are too many PAS positions. A similar GAO and bipartisan commission process as mentioned in number 9 above should be undertaken to reduce the number of PAS positions. The biggest agency, Social Security, has only two PAS, but PAS positions go down too deeply in many departments, and non-PAS even deeper.

CHAPTER 27

Government Insurance: Good Intentions, Conflicting Goals

"Unlike private insurance, the [government insurance] activities do not necessarily have a contract or charge premiums or fees for assuming risk. Even when premiums or fees exist, they may not cover all costs, as federal expenditures can be driven by policy goals or agency missions rather than the aim of fiscal solvency."

—GAO report, *Fiscal Exposure, Federal Insurance and Other Activities that Transfer Risk or Losses to the Government*, March 27, 2019

IF WE HOLD to the aphorism of the government as an insurance company with an army, as Bernanke pointed out in my opening quote in my opening chapter, entitlements are a major and the costliest portion. We need to be much smarter about just throwing money at programs. Just like we cannot do away with the military, the US government cannot do away with many of its insurance functions. Both the military and government insurance programs could be better managed and more cost effective. They need clear, nonconflicting goals. As another Nobel prize–winning economist, Milton Friedman, said, "One of the great mistakes is to judge policies and programs by their intentions rather than their results."[163]

Congress needs to be very wary of creating new government insurance companies and entitlement programs. We already have a plethora of insurers—not just retirement and healthcare, as Bernanke mentioned, but also banking, housing, flood, crop support, and many others.

Every government insurance program should be reviewed periodically to ensure that they are based on sound insurance principles to reduce moral hazards, excessive risk-taking, and other perverse incentives—not just when there is a crisis. They should use true and transparent insurance accounting. If a government subsidy is necessary or wanted, it should be calculated and understood and explicit, not just buried in an off-balance-sheet insurance company.

Most importantly, the periodic review should ascertain whether the government insurance program is fulfilling its mission and whether there are more cost-effective ways to fulfill that mission.

The above quoted GAO paper identified 148 federal government insurance risk-transfer programs. They divided them into the following categories:

Category	Number
Federal insurance programs	5
Federal loan guarantee programs	33
Fannie & Freddie senior preferred stock	2
Large federal employee & veteran benefits	13
Property damage, financial loss, & nonfederal employee benefits	95
TOTAL	148

Federal insurance programs include crop insurance, flood insurance, the PBGC, the FDIC, and credit union deposit insurance. The GAO uses the PBGC to differentiate between explicit and implicit government exposures, stating that the explicit exposure is only up to "PBGC's available resources." Above their available resources, the government's exposure is assumed to be only implicit. The government backing can become explicit in a crisis or, as I put it for Fannie and Freddie, an "effective" guarantee. The PBGC's multiemployer program became explicit with the $86 billion bailout in 2021's American Recovery Plan.

The thirty-three loan guarantee programs—which included the FHA, VA, and rural housing, small business, education, and others as of September 30, 2017—guaranteed loans of $1.9 trillion. The Federal Credit Reform Act of 1990, which I pushed on the Hill, requires a present-value estimate of the cost of these loan guarantee programs annually. That was an excellent good-government move but did not go far enough.

I have already written extensively on the Fannie and Freddie senior preferred stock purchase agreements. The GAO noted that the Treasury senior preferred stocks provided $446 billion in capital support to Fannie and Freddie. I am not sure how that number was calculated, but it does support over $6 trillion in liabilities.

The thirteen federal employee and veterans' pensions and other benefit activities are massive: liabilities were approximately $8.4 trillion as of September 30, 2019, and represented about a third of all federal liabilities of $26.9 trillion.

The remaining ninety-five programs are a hodgepodge of some very big programs, such as Medicaid ($442 billion in 2017), Social Security's Supplemental Security Income program ($63 billion), and unemployment insurance ($34 billion). In the list are some big insurance programs: Ginnie Mae, Farmer Mac, the Overseas Private Investment Corporation, and the Securities

Investors Protection Corporation.

There are also many small ones, often targeted at a specific interest group, like disease, health issue, crop, and trade assistance. The 2014 farm bill created the Livestock Forage, Livestock Indemnity, and Tree Assistance Programs. Being in an interest group myself as chair of the Bruce Museum, I note that there is an Art & Artifacts Indemnity program which insures art borrowed from abroad to exhibit in the US. I am sure many of these programs serve a useful purpose, but there should be a regular review process to ensure that the programs still fulfill a need that cannot be provided by the private sector at a reasonable cost.

The GAO report noted, "The government's primarily cash-based budget generally does not record the full cost of commitments incurred until corresponding payments are made in the future." It states that the GAO recommended in 2009 and in 2014 to expand the use of accrual accounting to better reflect the future cost of insurance decisions. As they wrote, "If the full cost of the spending decision is included in the budget when the decision is made, the decision makers can consider the total cost when setting priorities, compare the cost of an activity with its benefits, or assess the cost of one method of reaching a specific goal against another."

Greater adoption of accrual accounting is well overdue for many government insurance programs. Cost-benefit analysis is needed. Too often, Congress and administrations fly by the seat of their pants, which can lead to a crash landing.

The GAO report had an appendix on the big social insurance programs of Social Security, Medicare, Railroad Retirement, and Black Lung, but did not count those four as part of the total. The latter two are immaterial in size compared to the big two. The GAO cited numbers based on the 2017 trustees report. The trustees reports contain a seventy-five-year present-value forecast. They cite Open Group numbers for the combined programs, which includes all present and future participants over the seventy-five-year period. In their 2017 report, the shortfall was a staggering $48.9 trillion.

In the 2022 trustees report,[164] the present-value shortfall is $72.8 trillion. That is a 49 percent increase in only five years. The breakdown of the 2022 present-value numbers in trillions is as follows:

Program	Open Group (in trillions)
Social Security	$ (20.4)
Medicare Part A	$ (4.9)
Medicare Part B & D	$ (47.5)
TOTAL	$ (72.8)

Seventy-five years is a long time, few people understand present value, and the size of these numbers is incomprehensible; but that does not mean we should disregard them. Hopefully, all five of my grandchildren will be enjoying a happy retirement in seventy-five years. But how do we surface to afford these programs and avoid just passing the bill to the next generation?

CONCLUSION

Underwater Is Unsustainable

"The United States' federal budget has been on an unsustainable path for years now. And that just means the debt is growing faster than the economy, so debt-to-GDP is rising."

—Chair Jeremy Powell, semi-annual testimony to Senate Banking, Housing, and Urban Affairs, June 16, 2020

EIGHT YEARS EARLIER Bernanke had a more dire warning in a House Financial Services Committee hearing: "If market participants are not persuaded that the United States is on a sustainable fiscal course, then eventually something will give. And that could be a financial crisis."[165]

Every year since, the US economy has become more unsustainable. The fiscal year (FY) 2020 deficit of $3.1 trillion is unsustainable. That deficit was 15.2 percent of the total gross domestic product (GDP), the highest since 1945—the year before the first baby boomers were born. After trillions more in deficits, the national debt of the US was $30.9 trillion on September 30, 2022. About $6.6 trillion of the debt is owed to government agencies, including Social Security, and will have to paid. To give context, my presentations on the need for GSE reform used charts showing that the housing GSEs' guarantees and debt exceeded the publicly held debt. Now their debt and guarantees are less than one quarter of that debt.

Some people argued that because interest rates were so low, there was no problem with ballooning deficits. Wishful thinking only works until it does not.

America is deeply underwater and sinking. There are many reasons for how we got here—the Great Recession, major tax cuts, the demise of congressional deficit hawks, the necessary COVID-19 response, poorly designed and managed government programs, and the ever-growing cost of entitlements as our nation ages. But as the Committee for a Responsible Federal Budget wrote[166] in 2020, "Once the economy recovers, our debt cannot continue to grow faster than the economy. . . . [We need] plans to save Social Security and Medicare. The deeper we dig this hole, the harder it will be to claw our way out."

Chair Powell said in an answer to a question in that Senate hearing, "Every generation is entitled to spend what it wants to spend on the things it thinks it needs; but it really ought to pay for them, rather than passing the bills onto the kids."[167]

Preventing a massive burden on future generations and surfacing from our growing fiscal crisis will not be easy or pain-free. We need to put into action the quotes from the Social Security and Medicare trustees that have been used for decades on these two programs and the whole American government: "The Trustees recommend that Congress and the Executive Branch work closely together with a sense of urgency to address these challenges. With informed discussion, creative thinking, and timely legislative action, Social Security can continue to protect future generations."[168]

My father's very prescient paper, "Goal for the USA—A Successful Society," which was the basis of my earlier chapter "Setting Goals," is even more right at present than when it was written thirty years ago. Too bad it never was implemented.

We need a national vision for "present and future" generations to be successful by "advancing opportunities while carefully maximizing the resources of the country." His prescription in the 1996 paper I forwarded to Elizabeth Dole was "We need higher growth; lower, fair taxes; higher savings; better utilization of resources; better education; and a smaller, more efficient government through delegislation, privatization, entitlement reform and better management."

The only part of his prescription that was listened to was lower taxes, but I am afraid we have gone too far. Unfortunately, we will need to smartly raise taxes to help lessen the burden on future generations. But even more importantly, we need to make the government more efficient—because smaller is not happening.

Entitlements are a key place to start; Social Security, Medicare, and Medicaid were almost 50 percent of fiscal year expenditures in the pre-COVID-19 era. It will take a consensus and hard decisions. While focusing on helping the most vulnerable individuals, we will have to slow benefit growth, raise taxes, and deliver those services more efficiently.

Importantly, we need to do more to improve education by both teachers and parents and reduce discrimination. An important part of that education must be to increase financial literacy, which will lessen the number of vulnerable Americans.

Throughout this book I have tried to relate my experiences, especially my government underwater experiences, to give my thoughts on how we can help the US government and the American people surface. In addition to the recommendations made in the previous "Independent Agency?" chapter, we need to undertake the following:

✦   Fix the major entitlement programs of Social Security and Medicare. Our Bipartisan Policy Center Report is an excellent blueprint for Social Security reform.

✦ Get Fannie and Freddie out of conservatorships with countercyclical policies.

✦ Reform the PBGC's multiemployer program and regularly review the single-employer plans.

✦ Set long-term goals to reduce the deficit, including a fairer tax system.

✦ Make government accounting more transparent, including adopting accrual accounting for government insurance programs.

✦ Make management a key component of department and agency leadership, as exemplified by Bush's PMA.

✦ Establish a moratorium on new government programs without thorough reviews of long-term costs versus benefits.

✦ Review not only government insurance programs but also other programs to ensure they are still needed and cost-effective.

✦ Establish plans to increase private pension, other savings, and financial literacy.

✦ Prevent the runaway costs of future crises by better planning and countercyclical policies.

We need to change course, as the lighthouse keeper said in my overused story. It will not be easy. Chairs Powell and Bernanke and many others have said we are on an unsustainable course. Government spending is out of control; its deficits and federal debt are growing rapidly. Many states are not any better, with their large deficits and underfunded pension plans. Interest expenses will sink us as they rise.

I would have preferred to end this book on a submarine "up bubble," not a "down bubble," which means a submarine is going deeper. Unlike my scary effort as a diving officer to stabilize the USS *George Washington Carver* at test depth, there is little will to stop sinking.

The debt-to-GDP ratio (including amounts owed to Social Security and other trust funds) rose from 106 percent in FY 2019 to 124 percent in FY 2022. The *US Financial Report* for FY 2021 warned: "The debt-to-GDP ratio . . . is projected to reach 701 percent by 2096. The projected continuous rise of the debt-to-GDP ratio indicates that current policy is unsustainable."

To put that debt-to-GDP number in context, the ratio reached 106 percent at the end of World War II, its highest point ever until recently.

As the *Report* points out, achieving sustainability would require very large tax increases and expenditure reductions. To avoid the massive tax increases, Congress will have to act to reform Social Security, Medicare, and many other programs and avoid creating new costly, flawed programs. That will require presidential administrations to work better with Congress and do a better job of managing government departments and agencies.

A decade ago, Bernanke called sustainability a "top priority," and yet we continue to sink deeper and deeper in red ink. It is time to man and woman the helm to surface.

We must avoid "crush depth."

LTJG Lockhart Surfacing the USS George Washington Carver (SSBN 656), 1971

USS George Washington Carver (SSBN 656) surfaced

Cricket, J.B., and Graci crossing the Atlantic Ocean in October 1981

Labor Secretary Elizabeth Dole at my PBGC swearing-in ceremony with Cricket, J.B., and Graci, July 11, 1989

PBGC Press Conference 1991

To Cricket and Jim Lockhart
With best wishes, *Gy Bush* *Barbara Bush*

Christmas 1991 at the White House with President George H. W. Bush and Barbara Bush

In my Social Security Administration office, 2004

At Camp David on September 11, 2004

Pitching golf balls at Camp David with Andy Card, Rick Powell, President Bush, JBL III, and Clay Johnson, September 11, 2004

Friends and Family White House Christmas dinner with President George W. Bush and
Laura Bush, December 3, 2004

Social Security Trustees Oval Office meeting with Treasury Secretary John Snow, Labor Secretary Elaine Chao, John Palmer, President Bush, Tom Saving, Social Security Commissioner Jo Anne Barnhart, JBL III; December 9, 2004

Senate Special Aging Committee Hearing, "Social Security: Whose Trust Will Be Broken?" with GAO Comptroller General David Walker and JBL III, September 28, 2005

HUD Secretary Alphonso Jackson swearing me in as OFHEO director; July 24, 2006

Oval Office visit with President Bush and my family including J.B.; Biff, Blake and John Zoephel; Cricket; my mother, Mary Ann Lockhart; JBL III; Ann Harris; Jim and Joan Gardner; Graci and Marko Djuranovic; July 24, 2006

A television interview at the front of the OFHEO Offices, 2007

Meeting in White House's Roosevelt Room of Bush's Working Group on Financial
Markets. On the right Bernanke, Bush, Paulson, Cox and JBL III, March 18, 2008

President Bush signing Housing and Economic Recovery Act (HERA) in Oval Office creating FHFA; with FHA Commissioner Montgomery, HUD Secretary Preston. Treasury Assistant Secretary Nason, and Treasury Secretary Paulson; July 30, 2008

POLITICO

VOL. 2 NO. 84   WEDNESDAY, SEPTEMBER 24, 2008 $3.50

Treasury Secretary **Henry Paulson**, Fed Chairman **Ben Bernanke**, SEC Chairman **Christopher Cox** and Federal Housing Finance Agency Director **James B. Lockhart III** testify Tuesday.

Bailout Hits Bipartisan Snags

| Cheney can't stem tide of Republican anger | Democrats: We won't pass it without GOP | INSIDE Winners: The market crisis | Paulson plan falters on cost, culture clash |

Politico (9/24/08); Senate Banking Committe Hearing introducing TARP with Paulson, Bernanke, Cox and JBL III

President Barack Obama, left, shakes hands with Gary Gensler, chairman of the Commodity Futures Trading Commission, after making remarks on a proposed overhaul of financial-industry regulations at the White House. Some Wall Street insiders criticized the proposal as timid.

Wall Street Journal (6/18/09): President Obama in East Room of the White House after announcing financial reform proposals shaking hands with the regulators: CFTC Gensler, OCC Dugan, JBL III, OTS Bowman, FDIC Bair, Fed Vice Chair Kohn and SEC Schapiro, June 17, 2009

Meeting at the Treasury Department with HUD Secretary Donovan and Treasury Secretary Geithner, 2009

FHFA Speech, 2009

Fed Chairman Ben Bernanke at my FHFA going away party, September 10, 2009

Wilbur Ross, Sir Richard Branson, and JBL III on Necker Island for Virgin Money 2012 board meeting

My latest (tree) housing venture for the Grandkids, 2020

Endnotes

Introduction

1   Brookings and Chicago Booth, "Task Force on Financial Stability," June 2021.

2   Elfrink, Tim, "Obama, Bush and Clinton Release Video Praising Peaceful Transfer of Power, as Trump Skips Inauguration," *The Washington Post*, January 21, 2021.

Chapter 1

3   "Compassionate Conservative Fact Sheet," White House, April 30, 2002.

4   Geithner, Timothy F. *Stress Test, Reflections on the Financial Crisis,* (Crown 2015), 171.

5   Bernanke, Ben, "Interview by Tom Keene," *Bloomberg TV*, May 3, 2017.

6   *Securing Our Financial Future; Report of the Commission on Retirement Security and Personal Savings*, June 2016, Bipartisan Policy Center.

Chapter 2

7   Lockhart, J. Bicknell, Jr., *James Bicknell Lockhart Biography,* (1981, revised 1995).

8   Lockhart, J. Bicknell, Jr., *Be Rich, It is Your Choice,* (1993).

Chapter 3

9   Minutaglio, Bill, *First Son: George W. Bush and the Bush Family Destiny*, (Crown 1999), 60.

10   *Decision Points*, George W. Bush (Crown, 2010), 11.

Chapter 4

11   Admiral Hyman Rickover quotes from GoodReads.com and inspiringquote.us.

Chapter 5

12   Lockhart, J. Bicknell, Jr., "Goal for the USA—A Successful Society," (1990).

Chapter 6

13   Gerth, Jeff, "Underfunded Pension Plans Raise Benefits, GAO Says" *The New York Times*, February 5, 1993

14   General Accounting Office letter of June 23, 1982.

15   Editorial, "Incredibly Inauditable," *Pensions and Investments*, December 9,1991.

Chapter 7

16   Anders, George, "Icahn Is Set to Walk Away From TWA Sadder and at Least $111Million Poorer," *The Wall Street Journal,* December 8, 1992.

17   Vise, David A. and Weintraub, Richard M., "Hill Lobbying Helped Spur TWA Accord, Pension Pact Paves Way for New Financing," *The Washington Post*, December 8, 1992.

18   Halkias, Maria, "Federal pension insurer sues LTV," *Dallas Morning News,* August 31, 1991.

19   Clark, Stephen, "Hanging Tough at the PBGC, For the Pension Guaranty Corp.'s James Lockhart, the fight to bolster pension security has just begun," *Institutional Investor*, September 1990.

20   Noble, Barbara Pressley "Will Pensions Follow the S&L's?", *The New York Times*, March 29, 1992.

21   "Campaign'92: Transcript of the Second Presidential Debate, Unraveling the Safety Net," *The Washington Post*, October 16, 1992.

22   Chernoff, Joel, "President Bush draws a blank on PBGC legislation," *Pensions & Investments,* October 26, 1992.

Chapter 8

23   "A message Transmitting a Report of the Social Security Board Recommending Certain Improvements in the Law," January 16, 1939.

24   Gulick, Luther, "Memorandum on Conference with FDR Concerning Social Security Taxation," Summer 1941.

25   Kennedy, John F., "Statement by the President upon Signing the Social Security Amendments of 1961," June 30, 1961.

26   Light, Paul, *Artful Work—The Politics of Social Security Reform*, (Random House, 1985), 3.

Chapter 9

27   Fournier, Ron, "Bush: Democrats Make 'Pathetic' Attacks," *Associated Press*, September 13, 2004.

28   "Fact Sheet: America's Ownership Society: Expanding Opportunities," White House, August 9, 2004.

29   Representatives Charles Rangel, Lloyd Doggett, Earl Pomeroy, Robert Matsui, Benjamin Carden, and Xavier Becerra, "Letter to President George W. Bush," January 23, 2003.

30   Social Security Press Release, January 28, 2005.

31   Social Security Office of Communications memo, April 24, 2001.

32   Senators Lautenberg, Kennedy, Clinton, Durbin, Dayton, Corzine, Levin, and Reed, "Letter to Comptroller General David Walker," January 26, 2005.

Chapter 10

33   "Social Security Local Education Program," Social Security Administration2003.

34   Strope, Leigh, "AARP drops out of Social Security forums, distances from Bush overhaul plans," *Associated Press,* December 15, 2003.

35   Novelli, Bill, *Good Business, The Talk, Fight, Win Way to Change the World*, (Johns Hopkins University Press, 2021), 169-170.

36   AARP Ad, *The New York Times*, February 20, 2005.

37   Editorial Cartoon, *Washington Times*, April 5, 2005.

38   Pyen, Chong W., "Social Security sides heard Congressman Dingell, Schwartz offer viewpoints on privatizing" *Ann Arbor News*, June 19, 2005.

39   Fillmore, Millard, Editorial Cartoon, *Arkansas Democratic Gazette*, February 22, 2005.

40   *Securing our Financial Future; Report of the Commission on Retirement Security and Personal Savings*, (Bipartisan Policy Center, June 2016).

Chapter 11

41   Branom, Mike, "Edwards Vows Not to Touch Retirement Age" *Associated Press,* October 23, 2004.

Chapter 12

42   "OFHEO Strategic Plan, 2006-2011," 4.

43   *Report of the Special Examination of Fannie Mae,* Office of Federal Housing Oversight, May 2006.

44   Paletta, Damian and Hughes Siobhan, "Republicans Launch Fierce Attack on Fannie Officials'" *Dow Jones Newswire*, 15 June 2006.

45   Ibid.

Chapter 13

46   "Rep. Frank: Likes OFHEO Comment on Fannie, Freddie Oversight," referring to my push for legislation, *Dow Jones,* July 10, 2006.

47   *SNA* no.144, July 27, 2006.

48   Rucker, Patrick, "Fannie Mae, Freddie Mac regulator wants reform," *Reuters*, August 2, 2006.

49   Ludwig, Eugene, "Systemic Risk: A regulator's Perspective," (*Fannie Mae Papers*, Volume II, Issue 1) February 2003.

50   Robert Stowe England, *Black Box Casino, How Wall Street's Risky Shadow Banking Crashed Global Finance,* (Praeger, 2011), 164.

51   Paletta, Damian, "How GOP Failed to Secure GSE Bill After 4-Year Majority," *Dow Jones Newswire*, December 15, 2006.

Chapter 14

52   Poole, William, "The GSEs: Where Do We Stand?", speech, January 17, 2007.

53   Bernanke, Ben, Speech to Independent Community Bankers Association, March 6, 2007.

54   Paletta, Damian, "White House Warns Against Amending House GSE Bill," *Dow Jones Newswires*, May 16, 2007.

55   Paletta, Damian, "2nd Update: House OK's Bill Overhauling Fannie, Freddie Regulator," *Dow Jones Newswires,* May 22, 2007.

56   Tyson, James, "Fannie, Freddie Legislation Approved By U.S. House (Update4)," *Bloomberg.Com,* June 22, 2007.

57   "HUD's Housing Goals for Fannie Mae and Freddie Mac for the Years 2005-2008," Department of Housing and Urban Development, November 2, 2004.

58   Ben S. Bernanke, Timothy F. Geithner and Henry M. Paulson, Jr., *Firefighting, The Financial Crisis and Its Lessons* (Penguin Books, 2019), 3.

59   Hilzenrath, David S., "Fannie Mae Ex-Officials are sued for Disputed Pay,' *The Washington Post*, December 19, 2006.

60   Mogenson, Gretchen, A Year to Suspend Disbelief, *The New York Times,* December 31, 2007.

61   Hilzenrath, David S., "Both Sides on Offense," *The Washington Post*, January 22, 2007.

62   Hilzenrath, David S., "OFHEO Director to Stay on Raines Case; Lockhart Won't Withdraw From Regulatory Proceeding to Recover $84.6 Million," *The Washington Post*, May 6, 2007.

63   Tyson, James, "Fannie Overseer Denies Withholding Papers From Raines (Update1)," *Bloomberg.com*, April 26, 2007.

64   Hilzenrath, David S., "Judge Dismisses Raine's Attempt To Subpoena White House Records," *The Washington Post*, December 21, 2007.

Chapter 15

65   Hagerty, James R., "Fannie Mae Settlement Proves Anticlimactic," *The Wall Street Journal*, April 21,2008

66   "Seeking salvation in subprime" *Economist*, July 7, 2007.

67   Paletta, Damian, " US Sen. Dodd blasts White House, OFHEO Handling of GSE Policy," *Dow Jones Newswires,* August 17,2007.

68   Dizard, John, "Fannie and Freddie to the Rescue? Don't Bet on it.'" *FT.com,* August 28, 2007.

69   "Tiny OFHEO stands up to Fannie, Freddie, Dodd, Schumer, Frank," *Market News International*, September 19, 2007.

70   Freifeld, Karen, Tyson, James and Crenson, Sharon L., "Cuomo Subpoenas Fannie, Freddie, Widening Loan Probe (Update5),"*Bloomberg*, November 7, 2007.

71   Scanell, Kara, "Tensions Rise in Lending Probes" *The Wall Street Journal,* January 31, 2008.

72   Bajaj, Vikas, "In Deal with Cuomo, Mortgage Giants Accept Appraisal Standards," *The New York Times,* March 4, 2008.

73   "New York Attorney General Cuomo Announces Agreement with Fannie Mae, Freddie Mac, and OFHEO," Press Release of Office of New York State Attorney General, March 3, 2008.

74   Sloan, Steven and Kaper, Stacy, "Washington People," *American Banker,* June 23, 2008.

75   Ding, Lei and Nakamura, Leonard, "The Impact of the Home Valuation Code of Conduct on Appraisals and Mortgage Outcomes," Federal Reserve Bank of Philadelphia Working Paper, July2015.

76   "Fannie Mae Introduces 'Adverse Market' Loan Fees, Reduces Financing in Areas Hardest Hit by Price Declines" *Housing Wire*, December 6, 2007.

Chapter 16

77   Bush, George, "Text of Bush's Speech on Mortgage Crisis," *Associated Press,* December 6, 2007.

78   "Secretary of Housing and Urban Development Alphonso R. Jackson and Secretary of Treasury Henry M. Paulson, Jr. Hold a News Conference on Mortgages," *CQ Transcriptions*, December 6, 2007.

79   Sloan, Steven, "Setting an OFHEO Plan, But Wishing Otherwise," *American Banker,* December 21, 2007.

80   Sloan, Steven, "Paulson Loses Credibility with GOP on GSE Issue" *American Banker*, February 8, 2008.

81   *Congress Daily p.m.*, February 27, 2008.

82   Hilzenrath, David S., "Fannie Mae and Freddie Mac Seek to Preserve Capital," *The Washington Post,* March 3, 2008.

83   Laing, Jonathan R., "Is Fannie Mae Toast? As the housing crisis worsens, this mortgage giant's shareholders are likely to suffer further losses. A Government bailout ahead?" *Barron's,* March 10, 2008.

84   Gordon, Marcy, "Easing capital restraints on mortgage giants reveals activist role of gov't, credit rot extent" *Associated Press,* March 19, 2008.

85   Paletta, Damian and Haggerty, James R., " US puts Faith in Fannie and Freddie," *The Wall Street Journal*, March 20, 2008.

86   *Inside the GSEs*, April 30, 2008.

87   Summers, Larry, *Financial Times*, as quoted in *GSE Activity Report*, March 31, 2008.

88   "Paulson says markets emerging from crunch," *Reuters*, May7, 2008.

89   Syron, Richard email, April 11, 2008.

90   "Haggling on the Hill, Reining in Fannie Mae and Freddie Mac," *Economist*, May 22, 2008.

Chapter 18

91   Sloan, Steven, "In Focus: GSE Accord Resurrects Risk Issue," *American Banker*, June 2, 2008.

92   Ahmann, Tim, "Rep Frank: Need to restrain financial risk taking," *Reuters*, July 25, 2008.

93   Sloan, Steven, "Fannie CEO on Critiques and Progress," *American Banker*, June 13, 2008.

94   Isidore, Chris, "Feeling Fannie's and Freddie's pain, The tumbling stock prices for Fannie Mae and Freddie Mac Threaten the chances for housing recovery and economic comeback" *CNNMoney.com*, July 8, 2008.

95   McKay, Peter A., "Financials Lead a Late Stock Surge," *Wall Street Journal*, July 8, 2008.

96   Labaton, Stephen and Weisman, Steven R., " US Weighs Takeover of Two Mortgage Giants" *New York Times*, July 11, 2008.

97   Sorkin, Andrew Ross, *Too Big to Fail. The inside story of how Wall Street and Washington fought to save the financial system—and themselves,* (Viking, 2009), 182.

98   Bohan, Caren, "Obama campaign: Fannie, Freddie are 'essential,'" *Reuters*, July 11, 2008.

99   Laboton, Stephen and Weisman, Steven R., "U.S. Weighs Takeover of Mortgage Giants," *The New York Times*, July 11, 2008.

100   Murray, Brendan, "Paulson Backs Fannie, Freddie in Their Current Form," *Bloomberg.com*, July 11, 2008.

101   Benner, Kate, "The $5 trillion mess, Fannie Mae and Freddie Mac were created by Congress to help more Americans buy homes. Now their shaky condition threatens the entire housing market." *Fortune,* July 14, 2008.

102   Paulson, Henry M., Jr., *On The Brink, Inside the Race to Stop the Collapse of the Global Financial System,* (Business Plus, 2010), 147.

103   Editorial Cartoon, *Tribune Media, South Florida Sun-Sentinel,* July 15, 2008.

104   *CNN Money,* July 15, 2008.

105   Kopecki, Dawn and Lanman, Scott, " Fannie, Freddie Nationalization May Be an Option, Bernanke Says," *Bloomberg.com,* July 16, 2008.

Chapter 19

106   Terris, Henry, "2Q Earnings: Fannie: Buying is Day by Day; Quitting Alt-A," *American Banker*, August 11, 2008.

107   Laing, Jonathan R., "The Endgame Nears for Fannie and Freddie, The almost inevitable government recapitalization of Fannie Mae and Freddie Mac will likely wipe out investors—and management," *Barron's,* August 18, 2008.

108   Hagerty, James R., *The Fateful History of Fannie Mae, New Deal Birth to Mortgage Crisis Fall,* (The History Press, 2012), 183.

109   Paulson, Henry M., Jr., *On The Brink, Inside the Race to Stop the Collapse of the Global Financial System,* (Business Plus, 2010), 169.

110   Ben S. Bernanke, Timothy F. Geithner and Henry M. Paulson, Jr., *Firefighting, The Financial Crisis and Its Lessons* (Penguin Books, 2019), 56.

Chapter 20

111   Frame, W. Scott, Fuster, Andreas, Tracy, Joseph and Vickery, James, "The Rescue of Fannie Mae and Freddie Mac," Federal Reserve Bank of New York Staff Report No. 719, March 2015.

112   Hagerty, James R., *The Fateful History of Fannie Mae, New Deal Birth to Mortgage Crisis Fall,* (The History Press, 2012), 188.

113   "Repeat: US Gov't Takes over Fannie/Freddie Operations," *Market News International,* September 8, 2008.

114   Rice, Tara and Rose, Jonathan, "When Good Investments Go Bad: The Contradiction in Community Bank Lending After the 2018 GSE Takeover," Board of Governors of the Federal Reserve System, International Finance Discussion Papers 1045, March 2012.

115   Hagerty, James R., Simon, Ruth, and Paletta, Damian, "U.S. Seizes Mortgage Giants, Government Ousts CEO's of Fannie, Freddie; Promises up to $200 Billion in Capital" *The Wall Street Journal,* September 8, 2008.

116   "Swift action a boon for mortgage bonds, " *Financial Times,* September 8, 2008.

117   Hilzenrath, David S. and Goldfarb, Zackery A., "Mortgage Giants' Mess Falls to Their Regulator," *The Washington Post*, September 11, 2008.

118   Holzer, Jessica, "Investors Say US Govt Officials Misled Them on GSEs," *Dow Jones International News*, September 11, 2008.

119   Frame, W. Scott, Fuster, Andreas, Tracy, Joseph and Vickery, James, "The Rescue of Fannie Mae and Freddie Mac," Federal Reserve Bank of New York Staff Report No. 719, March 2015.

120   Zibel, Alan, "Government regulator faces tough task handling collapsed mortgage titans," *Associated Press,* September 9, 2008.

121   Adler, Joe and Flitter, Emily, "GSEs may be Forced to Deal on Loan Mods," *American Banker*, September 10, 2008.

Chapter 21

122   Chadborn, Margaret, "US GSE Reform? FHLBanks Try to Figure it out, You're Looking at the Possible Demise of the Federal Home Loan Bank System," *Market News International,* July 3, 2007.

123   "Hail Mary Merger," *GSE Activity Report,* August 9, 2007.

124   Sloan, Steven, "FHFA May Try to Force FHLB Capital Build," *American Banker,* September 5, 2008.

125   Hagerty, James R., "Home-Loan Banks Struggle to Maintain Capital," *The Wall Street Journal,* January 21, 2009.

126   Kopecki, Dawn and Sheen, Jody, "Fannie, Freddie, FHLBs Face New Requirements," *Bloomberg.com*, January 23, 2009.

127   Rozens, Aleksandas, "Home Wreckers", *IDD Magazine,* January 26, 2009.

128   Bair, Sheila, "Bull By The Horns, Fighting to Save Main Street from Wall Street and Wall Street From Itself," Free Press, 2012), 85.

129   Bair, Sheila, "Bull By The Horns, Fighting to Save Main Street from Wall Street and Wall Street From Itself," (Free Press, 2012), 278.

Chapter 22

130   Editorial, "An Inadequate Case for the Bailout," *The New York Times,* September 24, 2008.

131   MacFarquhar, Neil, "Upheaval on Wall St. Stirs Anger in the U.N., Leaders Fearful of Harm's Spread," *The New York Times,* September 24, 2008.

132   Bosman, Julie, "Ad Campaign, McCain and Social Security," *The New York Times,* September 24, 2008.

133   Seib, Gerald, "Bailout Pitch Tests Paulson's Political Skills," *The Wall Street Journal,* September 23, 2008.

134   Goldfarb, Zachary A., "Assembling America's Mortgage Team," *The Washington Post,* October 6, 2008.

135   Said, Carolyn, "Grim mortgage bankers assess uncertain future," *San Francisco Chronicle,* October 21, 2008.

136   Coombes, Andrea, " Focus on foreclosures, liquidity; Fannie, Freddie execs say they're active in mortgage market, foreclosure relief," *MarketWatch,* October 20, 2008.

137   Said, Carolyn, "Grim mortgage bankers assess uncertain future," *San Francisco Chronicle,* October 21, 2008.

138   Hagerty, James R., "Fannie and Freddie's Regulator Suggests U.S. Backs Their Debt," *The Wall Street Journal,* October 21, 2008.

139   Bair, Sheila, "Bull By The Horns, Fighting to Save Main Street from Wall Street and Wall Street From Itself," (Free Press, 2012), 135.

140   Goldfarb, Zachary A., Merle, Renae, and Cho, David, "Government Announces New Program for At-Risk Mortgages, "The *Washington Post,* November 11, 2008.

141   Bernanke, Ben S., *21st Century Monetary Policy. The Federal Reserve from the Great Inflation to COVID-19,* (W. W. Norton & Company, 2022), 136.

Chapter 23

142   "Preliminary Staff Report," Financial Crisis Inquiry Commission, April 7, 2010.

143   Paulson, Henry M., Jr., Remarks "On the Role of the GSEs in Supporting the Housing Recovery before the Economic Club of Washington."

144   Terris, Henry, "Backstop's Erosion Met with Calm'" *American Banker*, February 2, 2009.

145   "FHFA: Let TARP Aid Private Insurers"*American Banker, National Mortgage News,* February 11, 2009.

146   Bair, Sheila, "Bull By The Horns, Fighting to Save Main Street from Wall Street and Wall Street From Itself," (Free Press, 2012), 149.

147   Appelbaum, Binyamin, "U.S. Doubles Fannie, Freddie backing to $400 billion," *The Washington Post,* February 19, 2009.

148   Hagerty, James R. and Lublin, Joann S. "Freddie Chief Quits After Six Months," *The Wall Street Journal,* March 3, 2009.

149   Arnold, Kyle, *Tulsa World,* December 4, 2009.

150   Goldfarb, Zachary A., "Freddie Mac's Duel with Regulator: Does It Report Government's Role in ITS Losses?", *The Washington Post,* March 27, 2009.

151   Rucker, Patrick, "US Rep. Frank wants Fannie, Freddie bonuses halted," *Reuters,* March 20, 2009.

152   Goldfarb, Jonathan A., "Fannie, Freddie Budget $210 million on Bonuses, Draw Lawmakers' Fire," *The Washington Post*, April 4, 2009.

153   Rucker, Patrick, "Lawmaker sees Fannie, Freddie bonus 'Insult,'" *Reuters,* April 4, 2009.

Chapter 24

154   Crittenden, Michael R., "TARP Watchdog: Tsy Overpaid for TARP Investments," *Dow Jones Newswire,* February 5, 2009.

155   Editorial Staff, " In Hindsight, Whose Show Is It?", *Investment Dealers' Digest,* April 17, 2009.

156   Kopecki, Dawn," Cox Questioned Fannie, Freddie Oversight while at SEC," *Bloomberg.com,* May 2, 2009.

157   Rappaport, Alan, "Signs of Life in Housing Market," *Financial Times,* July 23, 2009.

158   Kopecki, Dawn, "FHFA's Lockhart Plans to Leave Agency This Month," *Bloomberg.com*, August 5, 2009.

159   *Fannie Mae and Freddie Mac, Analysis of Options for Revising the Housing Enterprises Long-Term Structures*, General Accountability Office, September 10, 2009.

Chapter 25

160   "Bernanke's statement in an August 22, 2014, document filed with the US Court of Federal Claims concerning the AIG bailout," *The Wall Street Journal,* August 26, 2014.

161   Abel, Joshua and Fuster, Andreas, "How do Mortgage Refinances Affect D ebt, Default and Spending? Evidence from HARP," Federal Reserve of New York Staff Report no. 841, February 2018.

162   "Housing Finance at a Glance, A Monthly Chart Book," Urban Institute, October 2022.

Chapter 27

163   Public Broadcasting Service, "The Open Mind" interview, December 1975.

164   Secretaries Yellen, Walsh and Becerra and Acting Social Security Commissioner Kijakazi, *The 2022 Annual Report of the Board of Trustees of the Federal Old-Age and Survivors Insurance and Federal Disability Insurance Trust Funds*, June 2, 2022.

Conclusion

165   "Highlights: Bernanke's Q&A Testimony to House Panel," Testimony to House Financial Services Committee, *Reuters,* February 29, 2012.

166   Committee for a Responsible Federal Budget , October 16, 2020.

167   Henry, Megan, *Fox Business News,* June 16, 2020.

168   Secretaries Yellen, Walsh and Becerra and Acting Social Security Commissioner Kijakazi, *The 2022 Annual Report of the Board of Trustees of the Federal Hospital Insurance and Federal Supplemental Medical Insurance Trust Funds*, June 2, 2022.

INDEX

CPSIA information can be obtained
at www.ICGtesting com
Printed in the USA
BVHW041925200223
658865BV00012B/130/J

9 781646 639083